KAFILA

A Jhangi Family's Partition Memoir

KAFILA

A Jhangi Family's Partition Memoir

SUMANT BATRA

Om Books International

First published in 2025 by

Om Books International

Corporate & Editorial Office
A-12, Sector 64, Noida 201 301
Uttar Pradesh, India
Phone: +91 120 477 4100
Email: editorial@ombooks.com
Website: www.ombooksinternational.com

Sales Office
107, Ansari Road, Darya Ganj,
New Delhi 110 002, India
Phone: +91 11 4000 9000
Email: sales@ombooks.com
Website: www.ombooks.com

ISBN: 978-93-6395-797-8

Printed in India

10 9 8 7 6 5 4 3 2 1

Dedicated to my paternal grandparents, Late Lala Kesar Dass Batra-ji and Late Mataji Bhagwanti Devi, and my father, Late G.L. Batra, who were forced to leave their land, home and cattle behind in what is now Pakistan in the wake of the 1947 Partition, and were eventually rehabilitated in a village near Hisar. Then part of East Punjab, Hisar later fell to the share of Haryana, the new state carved out in November 1966.

In remembrance of my mother, Late Veena Batra

Assi jhang da vaasi lok sajjan,
Saada dil darya, saadi akh sehra

We, the people of Jhang, are friendly
Our hearts resemble rivers, our eyes are deserts

~ Attributed to an unidentified ascetic writer and playwright,
Muhammad Hassan Miraj

Badha lak Arorian, munah koh Lahor
(When an Arora has girded up his loins, it's only three-quarters of a kos to Lahore)

~ A local proverb in Medieval Punjab

Contents

Preface xi

Prologue xxi

1. Flickering Hope 1
2. Seeds of Partition 14
3. The Great Betrayal 33
4. The Mountbatten Plan 46
5. Fortifying the Village 59
6. The Boundary Commission 70
7. The Exodus 78
8. The Batra Khatris 92
9. Freedom at Midnight 101
10. Kafila 110
11. The Greatest Migration in Human History 128
12. A Sigh of Relief 137
13. India, Finally 149
14. An End and a Beginning 157

15. The Struggle for Rehabilitation 169
16. Hisar: An Unfamiliar Terrain 179
17. A New Homeland 190
18. Rebuilding Life 203
19. A Hope Shattered, Decades of Struggle 212
20. A New Era and the Gurukul 225
21. Shifting Sand Dunes 232
22. The Last Days 243
23. An Inheritance of Loss 249
Epilogue 256
Key Characters 262
Bibliography 265
Index 273
Acknowledgements 283

Preface

In August 2024, as I watched, on television, protesters in Dhaka climb atop a large statue of Sheikh Mujibur Rahman and hammer its head with an axe, I was reminded of Antoinette Burton's foreword in the 2015 book, *The Indian Partition in Literature and Films: History, Politics and Aesthetics*. Partition will never be over. It is destined to return again and again not just as memory, but as history, politics and aesthetics as well, it states. The unruly mob vandalised Rahman's statues and destroyed the memorial museum dedicated to him. The father of Bangladesh's liberation, Rahman, referred to as 'Bangabandhu' or Friend of Bengal, played a pivotal role in freeing the people of East Pakistan (now Bangladesh) from West Pakistan's oppression. Who would have thought that the very people whose freedom Mujibur Rahman ensured would destroy his legacy five decades later? Curiously, the month of August also marked the forty-ninth anniversary of the brutal assassination of Mujibur Rahman. It was on 15 August 1975 that he was brutally murdered along with most of his family members in a coup.

Ironically, the protestors sang D.L. Ray's immortal ode to the motherland, Dhana dhanye pushpe bhara / amader ei basundhara / Tahar majhe achhe desh ek sakal desher sera / Se je swapna diye toiri se desh smriti diye ghera (Filled with a wealth of grains and flowers / is this Mother Earth of ours / in the midst of which is a land more splendid than any other / One that is created by dreams and surrounded by memories) – a song written in the early 1900s to inspire the youth against British rule. The protestors recalled a shared past that, at the time, seemed to be under threat. True to Burton's words, the events in Bangladesh are a reminder that the spectre of Partition lurks in the multiple facets of contemporary times, not only metaphorically but also in contemporary geopolitics of the subcontinent.

As ironic as it could get, barely three days later, in the very same subcontinent divided by borders and conflict, the bond of friendship and the power of shared dreams transcended the deepest divides when the mothers of javelin throwers Arshad Nadeem from Pakistan and Neeraj Chopra from India expressed their heartfelt admiration for their boys winning gold and silver medal respectively at the Olympics, despite the strained relations between the two countries. The two mothers sat side by side, united by their hopes and prayers, watching their sons compete not as rivals but as symbols of a shared history and a hopeful future. As competition gave way to camaraderie, I was reminded that our common humanity is stronger than any division.

The horrifying events of August 2024 in Bangladesh revived memories of another fateful August in the history of the subcontinent witnessed by generations before us. The partition of India into Hindu-majority India and Muslim-majority Pakistan took place in August 1947. It remains one of the most tumultuous events in the subcontinent's history. India's long-awaited independence was paradoxically accompanied and followed by chaos as millions of people scrambled to get to the right side of the border. West Punjab witnessed an exodus of Hindus and Sikhs heading eastward, while Muslims from East Punjab moved westward. Amidst the chaos, a deep suffering permeated people's individual and collective lives. They ran for their lives, many barefooted, leaving behind their land, homes, belongings and a piece of their hearts. Bengal met a similar fate as it was divided into East Pakistan (now Bangladesh) and West Bengal. The twinning of Partition with Independence disrupted any celebratory narrative of Independence for millions of displaced Indians.

The mass exodus, one of the greatest migrations ever recorded in human history, unfolded amidst relentless onslaughts of violence, arson and widespread devastation. More than fourteen million people are estimated to have been uprooted from their ancestral homes and three million are stated to have perished due to violence, hunger, suicide, and disease, although the number of dead and displaced remains disputed. The journey of migrants from West Punjab (now in Pakistan) to East Punjab (now in India and split into three separate states – Punjab, Haryana and Himachal Pradesh) stands out for its scale, brutality, and profound impact on the lives of millions. Many witnessed the destruction of their homes and the deaths of loved ones. Forced to leave their lands and homes behind, the displaced people travelled by any means available – on foot, by bullock cart, by train, and even on makeshift boats. Some had to be evacuated by air.

It was a difficult time and the journey was perilous. Trains packed beyond capacity became targets for armed mobs, leading to gruesome massacres. Convoys of refugees, even those protected by the military, faced attacks from violent groups, leaving trails of dead bodies along the routes. Families were torn apart, children orphaned, and women subjected to abductions, rape, sexual violence and forced conversion. Monsoon rain, storms and floods unleashed their own terror, further compounding the suffering. Those moving to Pakistan from East Punjab faced the wrath of an angered majority in East Punjab determined to take revenge and settle scores. These traumatic experiences left deep, lasting scars on those forced to migrate, scars that would remain etched across generations.

The crooked red line drawn by Sir Cyril Radcliffe, a British barrister who had arrived in India on his first visit just days before Partition, slashed through rivers, villages, fields and homes, triggering a violent upheaval. It not only divided the subcontinent but also, nearly overnight, split and scarred its people on religious lines. The reckless, arbitrary manner in which the division was made – at times the line ran through a house, so that the bathroom fell in one country and the kitchen in another – was a brutal affront to millions of Indians. They had to suffer abrupt displacement while still reeling under the sense of betrayal of the political leadership having given away pieces of their motherland to a nation based on religious ideology.

Among these were the Jhangis, the inhabitants of the Jhang district of West Punjab. Their sudden and dramatic switch from being the dominant class to rootless wanderers, unable to call a single place in independent India as their home, was intensely painful.

Government policies and action seemed out of touch with the ground realities at the time Partition was announced. In the face of escalating violence and complete polarisation along ethnic and religious lines, a bilateral military operation to evacuate stranded minorities was initiated. But the damage had already been done. A whole civilization where traditions, languages and cultures cut across religious groupings, was lost in those few months. Punjab's economy was destroyed as trade and industry were severely hit. Partition forged a new social order inflicting a collective wound and an enduring inheritance of grief and suffering. The displaced got branded as *refugees* in India, and as *muhajir* in Pakistan.

Hundreds and thousands of unfortunate Punjabi Khatris perished in the conflagration – unwept, unsung, unhonoured, and many unremembered. The environment of hostility, suspicion, insecurity and violence, in which all this was cradled, opened up an abyss of despair. Partition was not just a political event; it was a human catastrophe.

In East Punjab, makeshift encampments were set up in monuments, schools, shrines, open grounds, mosques and temples to provide temporary shelter. What was meant to be a temporary arrangement, stretched beyond a year, and for some, more than that. The tens of thousands who entered East Punjab had to stay in these teeming makeshift camps. They utilized every possible material they could find to create a semblance of 'normalcy' for themselves either in these camps or elsewhere.

Among the displaced who survived the genocide and ended up in one of the many overcrowded rehabilitation shelters was my grandfather, Kesar Dass – a middle-aged man from Rodu Sultan, an inconspicuous but blissful village in district Jhang, which fell to Pakistan's share. Kesar Dass arrived in East Punjab in 1947 as a part of one of many caravans of refugees, with his wife, four children and many cousins, old and young, battered and bruised by the hate and violence they had witnessed on the way. The possessions of this prosperous family, which owned hundreds of acres of irrigated land in Rodu Sultan, had been reduced to a bare minimum. The youngest in Kesar Dass's family was his son, my father Gobind, then a mere eight years of age. On their arrival, they were all crammed into makeshift camps erected in the vast expanse of an open ground in Kurukshetra. Life in camps was pitiful. Necessities were in short supply. There were long queues for supplies and fights broke out frequently. The self-respecting and robust Punjabi family, which owned hundreds of acres of land, was constrained to stand in a queue, helplessly flashing their ration card to collect some bread to feed the family for an entire day.

Kesar Dass and his cousins were now faced with the enormous task of rebuilding their lives from scratch. Their hearts were broken, but not their spirit. Their priority was to provide dignity and safety to the women in the family and create a future for their children. The families which had migrated from rural areas of West Punjab, like the Batras from Rodu Sultan and adjacent villages, had to go through a greater suffering. Their occupation was mainly agriculture. Over time, many found ways to cope with their trauma and rebuild their lives. Like children of millions of other displaced persons, they also focused on survival and reconstructing their lives. The Punjabis of

West Punjab were enterprising and laborious. They slowly stitched their life together with their unwavering courage. Wherever they went, they left an indelible mark not just on agriculture, trade and industry, but also on social and cultural life. They either set up small businesses, which were to flourish in years to follow, or found small jobs and worked hard, climbed the ranks and ended up holding many key posts in the central or state governments.

My grandparents never spoke much to us about the unimaginable adversity. My questions to them and my father were mostly met with tense silence. Only when pestered would they hesitatingly narrate some anecdotes which were ample to send a chill crawling down the spine. I could hear in their silence echoes of profound pain from having been uprooted from their home and deprived of their land. Perhaps, they preferred to stay quiet because they did not want to offload their baggage of dreadful memories on us. But their silence hung in the air of our house in Kurri (now Aryanagar), then a nondescript village near Hisar in Haryana, where my grandfather was rehabilitated. I grew up in this house for most of my childhood interpreting that silence intuitively. The modest nineteenth-century house and a fraction of the land deserted by a Muslim zamindar who chose to leave for Pakistan, was given in rehabilitation to my grandfather and his siblings by the Indian government in exchange for the grand house and large tracts of land in Jhang snatched away from them. They lived in that house but never belonged to it – always hoping against hope that they would be able to return to their own house in Rodu Sultan someday, till they realised it was too late. Eventually, they resigned to their fate. The only hurt they could not overcome was of being branded as 'refugees' in their own country.

Sadly, my father inherited the refugee tag. Those who were articulate called our family sharnarthi, an equally offensive description, or as displaced people. It hurt him for not being accepted as the son of the soil and even more for the discrimination on this basis on many occasions. Eventually, he accepted that as an aberration of the few ill-informed and ignorant people compared to the vast majority who did not differentiate even if they viewed them as outsiders. He also drew solace from the fact that the state never discriminated against those who had migrated from West Punjab.

My father went on to hold offices in the government including a high constitutional position, a privilege only a few are able to earn. This would not have been possible had there been a systemic discrimination in India against those who had migrated from West Punjab or East Bengal. A true patriot, my father dedicated his life in the service of this great nation. After he superannuated, he devoted significant time to the village – perhaps to be around places that carried memories of his parents. After my grandmother passed away, he felt lonely in that house but continued to frequent it. He harboured no ill will when he died in 2018. The only remorse he often expressed was of not having been able to ever visit the childhood home in Rodu Sultan. Being a government servant, circumstances did not permit him to visit Pakistan, a country with which hostile relations had continued even seven decades after the split. His memories of the years spent in that village perhaps never left him. The sufferings he endured due to Partition and its after-effects may be different from those experienced by his father, but they were in no way trivial in terms of the profound impression they had on his life.

Neither my grandparents nor my parents ever blamed anyone except their fate for their loss and sufferings. '*Bura waqt haee*' (it was a bad time) is all that they would say in their native language. However, there was a constant feeling of deep hurt at the betrayal of the political leadership of the time.

Though nearly eight decades have elapsed since Partition, its spectre continues to loom large over the three countries. The crisis of displaced persons born of this political fissure is yet to be relegated to the pages of history. Even my generation is sometimes dubbed as refugees. So much so that an association of displaced persons from

West Punjab had to submit a representation to Manohar Lal Khattar (then chief minister of Haryana), himself a refugee from Jhang, to pass a law declaring illegal the use of the word refugee or sharnarthi for immigrants from West Punjab. Like a family heirloom, we have carried the pain of Partition generation after generation. The stories of those who survived this ordeal are a part of the collective memory and identity of the Punjabi people. The dramatic partition of the Indian subcontinent continues to influence how the people of these countries envisage their past, present and future.

The journey of my people from West to East Punjab is emblematic of the broader human suffering and resilience during this period. It serves as a stark reminder of the consequences of division and the enduring power of human resilience and hope. It might have changed form over the decades that followed, but the trauma of Partition continues to trouble the next generations who have inherited its distressing legacy. Millions in India opposed to Partition still consider that it was avoidable and are unwilling to forget what they perceive as a betrayal of the majority Hindu population by some leaders.

Based on a true story, *Kafila*, is a biographical account and the impressions of two generations before me. Real names of some family members and other persons featured in the book have been withheld to protect their identities. Most elders have passed away. It would have been improper to disclose their names without their permission. Some family members including my cousins were not very forthcoming about details of their parents' struggles. I could not understand the reason for their reluctance.

However, this book is not the story of Partition. It neither purports to detail the history of Hindu–Muslim strife, nor the tortuous course of Congress–League–British negotiations leading to Independence and Partition. These remain a far more complex subject than one can possibly delve into. Yet, I have incorporated in the book some historical facts and developments surrounding Partition, of the governments' responses to migration, and the policies framed for rehabilitation of displaced persons. Many aspects of inter-community relations and key developments of 1946-47 have been included in the book to provide context to the central story of the book – my ancestors' forced relocation and struggles of two generations as displaced persons. I have added slices of the history of Jhang and Punjabi Khatris, and that of the Batra clan and my family, as also of the region they inhabited or dominated for centuries, their traditions, customs and way of life. I have taken some creative liberties to serve the need of telling this deeply emotional account.

The book also seeks to bring out the dilemma and contradictions faced by two generations who inherited the ambivalent legacy of Partition – a legacy of both loss and hope – the legacies which must be passed on to the next generation, focused not on a divided past but on a shared future so that both Hindu and Muslim communities can work together to make the subcontinent peaceful and prosperous, setting an example for the rest of the world.

London-based author and blogger Frank Jacobs wrote in an opinion piece in the *New York Times* that the Radcliffe Line was a hastily drawn-up border that remains to be an open wound 'even if dressed in the colourful bandage of Wagah's daily flag-lowering ceremony'. Gen Z and Alpha from the subcontinent should educate themselves about the historical events that inflicted this painful wound and the resultant legacy of distress, so that they may attempt closure with full knowledge and awareness rather than ignorance. This book aims to foster a deeper understanding of the lived experiences of Partition – not to divide, but to build bridges across borders. It serves as a reminder that our commonalities are far greater than our differences. I hope this story resonates with those who believe in the power of literature to bring people together and heal wounds of the past.

Prologue

The history of the Jhangis is buried in the ruins of Sanglawala Tibba, a small rocky hill near the border of Gujranwala, now in Pakistan. Xuanzang, the Chinese monk traveller, who came to India during the reign of King Harshavardhan, visited Sakala (modern-day Sialkot) in AD 630 and associated it with the Sagal of Buddhism, the Sangala of Alexander's historians, and the Sakala of the Brahamanas. In his travelogue, he places Sakala to the west of the Ravi. He also recorded that India was divided into 'five Indies': northern India, western India, central India, eastern India, and southern India. These five divisions contained eighty kingdoms.

Northern India comprised the Punjab, including Kashmir and the adjoining hill states with the whole of eastern Afghanistan beyond the Indus, and the present cis-Sutlej states to the west of the Sarasvati. It also included the districts of Kabul, Jalalabad, Peshawar, Ghazni and Bannu, which were all subject to the ruler of Kapisa, a Hindu Kshatriya and whose capital was most probably at Charikar, twenty-seven miles from Kabul. The whole of the plains, including Multan and Shorkot, were dependent on the ruler of Taki or Sangala, near Lahore. The hilly region was ruled from Kashmir.

According to Brahmanical accounts collected from the Mahabharata, Sakala was the capital of the Madra kingdom, also called Jartikas, and Bahikas, situated on the Apaga rivulet to the west of the Iravati or Ravi, which some believe extended from the Beas to the Jhelum, while others mark it only till the Chenab. The Apaga rivulet, likely the Ayak nadi, originated in the Jammu hills to the north-east of Sialkot. Near Asarur (in Gujranwala) the bed of this stream splits into two branches, which, after passing to the east and west of Asarur, rejoined a few miles to the south of Sanglawala Tibba. Alexander's historians Arrian and Curtius describe it as a great city fortified by brick walls and surrounded by a lake.

Shorkot, another prominent place in Jhang, has a deep history of its own. Xuanzang identified it as the capital town of the central district of the Punjab. It is recorded as one of the towns of the Malli, attacked and taken by Alexander. The ancient town of Shorkot stood below what is now a huge mound of ruins, almost rectangular in shape, surrounded with a wall of large-sized bricks, so high as to be seen for a circuit of six or eight miles. The foundation of the city is attributed by some to Raja Shor. Others claim the name of the town to Taj-ul-din Shori, who came to the Punjab in the wake of the Muhammadan invasion as a follower of Pir Ghazi, and held Shorkot. Pir Ghazi's tomb is still revered in Shorkot.

The invasion of India by Muslim hordes from the north-west altered the geography of India. The first Muslim invasion of India was by the Arabs, led by Muhammad bin Qasim. It took place in the eighth century and resulted in the conquest of Sindh. However, it did not result in a permanent occupation of the country because the Caliphate of Baghdad, by whose order and command the invasion had taken place, was obliged by the middle of the ninth century to withdraw its direct control from this distant province. Sindh was later reoccupied by Muhammad Ghori. Soon after this withdrawal, there began a series of terrible invasions by Muhammad of Ghazni in the year 1001. Ghazni died in 1030, but within the short span of thirty years, he invaded India seventeen times. He was followed by Muhammad Ghori who began his career as an invader in 1173; he was killed in 1206. For another thirty years, Muhammad Ghori harried the country in the same way. Then followed the incursions of the Mughal hordes of Genghis Khan. They first came in 1221. But, they only wintered on the border of India for a long time. Twenty years later, they marched on Lahore and sacked it. Among their inroads, the most terrible was the one under Taimur in 1398.

A new invader appeared on the scene in the person of Babur who invaded India in 1526. However, the invasions of India did not stop with that of Babur. Two more invasions lashed India following Babur. In 1738, Nadir Shah swept over the Punjab like a river in spate. He was followed by Ahmad Shah Abdali who invaded India in 1761.

These Muslim invasions were not undertaken merely out of lust for loot or conquest. There was another objective behind them. The expedition against Sindh by Muhammad bin Qasim was of a punitive character and was undertaken to punish Raja Dahir of Sindh who had refused to make restitution for the seizure of an Arab ship at Debul, one of the seaport towns of Sindh. However, there is no doubt that striking a blow at the idolatry and polytheism of Hindus and establishing Islam in India was another aim of this expedition.

The medieval history of Jhang could be stated to be the history of Sials, the Panwar Rajputs. Some believe, the Sials are descendants of Seu, one of the three sons (Seu, Teu, and Gheu) of Rai Shankar, an influential Rajput. Others claim Sial was Rai Shankar's sole child. There is, however, unanimity that after Rai Shankar's death, there was a great deal of family discord, and his son moved to Punjab. Here he met Sufi sage Hazrat Baba Farid Ganj Shukar in Pakpattan and embraced Islam. He married a woman named Sohag, the daughter of Bhai Khan Maken, a distinguished landowner, who lived in Shahpur Sahiwal, and established a settlement here. He was given the name of Rai Sial by the sage. He then started occupying surrounding areas between Mankera in the Thal and the river Jhelum, east and west, as well as Khushab in the north. This area came to be known as Ilaka Garh Maharaja. Before the arrival of the Sial clan, Jhang was ruled by the Nauls, a Rajput clan. The Sials defeated Naul chief Walidad Khan. On the orders of Hazrat Jalal Shah Surkh Bukhari, a new city was founded in 1288, which was named Jhang Sialan, meaning the forest of Sials. The word Jhang is derived from 'jangala', the Sanskrit word for a forested terrain.

During the Mughal era, the Sials maintained a degree of autonomy while acknowledging Mughal authority. Sultan Bahlol Lodhi, who then ruled Delhi, recognised the hereditary rule of the Sial tribe in the region. They played a crucial role in regional politics, and often acted as intermediaries between the Mughal Empire and local tribes. Among Sial rulers, Ghazi Khan was the first Jhang ruler to recruit a regular army with pay. Jalal Khan took control of the Jhang state upon the passing of Ghazi Khan. Following Jalal Khan, the successive rulers were Rasheed Khan, Feroz Khan, Kabir Khan, Jahan Khan, Ghazi Khan, Sultan Mahmood Khan, Lal Khan, Mahram Khan, Walidad Khan, Inayat-Ullah Khan and others. The eighteenth and last ruler of Jhang was Malik Ahmad Khan Sial, who founded the city of Jhang in 1462. Under his leadership, the Sials consolidated their control over the surrounding areas, and established a stronghold that would sustain for centuries. The Sial rulers were known for their administrative skills, fostering economic growth and cultural development in the region. They built forts, mosques, and irrigation systems, which contributed to Jhang's prosperity.

However, their influence began to wane in the eighteenth century with the decline of the Mughal Empire as Sikhs, and later the British, sought to expand their control over Punjab. In those days, Sikh chiefs occupied different states of Punjab. They captured Chiniot. They also divided Lahore, Sirhind, Multan, Jhang, Khushab and the whole of Punjab among themselves. The Sial tribes resisted Sikhs but despite their efforts, the Sikhs eventually overpowered them, leading to the annexation of Jhang and its integration into the Sikh Empire. Ranjit Singh occupied Jhang in 1816.

Today, the Sial tribe remains an influential community in Jhang, with many of its members actively involved in local politics, agriculture, and business. Their legacy is preserved through oral traditions, historical accounts, and the architectural remnants of their rule, which continue to stand as a testament to their enduring impact on the region's history.

After the annexation of Punjab in 1849, Jhang came under British colonial rule. The British Raj changed the geography of Jhang district. At the time of its annexation by the British, Jhang included the Faruka taluka in Chaj Doab, which was transferred to Shahpur in 1854. A considerable strip of country on the right bank of the Ravi was transferred to the Multan district around the same time. Garh Maharaja and Ahmadpur ilakas were brought into Jhang from Muzaffargarh in 1861, and the Kalowal ilaka transferred from Shahpur in the same year. The British divided Jhang into three tehsils by two lines running right across the district parallel to the base. The north-eastern part constituted the tehsil of Chiniot, the small triangle to the south-west that of Shorkot, and the central part comprised Jhang Maghiana tehsil. Shorkot Tehsil was formed in 1861. Later, in 1880, five villages on the banks of the Ravi were transferred from Shorkot to Sarai Siddhu tehsil of Multan in order to give the deputy commissioner of the latter district complete control of Ravi Sailab.

Even in the geographical form curated by the British while carving it out as a district, Jhang carried interesting attributes. Shaped triangular, with its apex to the south-west and base to the north-east, the district's acute angle of the tip was contained between the two then adjoining districts of Muzaffargarh and Dera Ismail Khan, while its base line marched with Shahpur and Gujranwala. Two rivers, the Chenab and the Jhelum traversed the district as the tract between them formed a lesser triangle within the greater boundary of Jhang. Physically, the formation of the district is stated to be that of an old alluvial flat, remains of which can be found in the Sandal Bar situated to the east of the Chenab, the Thal to the west of the Jhelum, and Kirana Bar located between the two rivers, their tracts geologically synchronous with the great plain of the Punjab, made up of the various doabs. Each bar consists of an elevated tract sloping down to the river valleys on either side. The lowland areas alongside the banks of the Ravi, Chenab and Jhelum are called hithar; and the intermediate zone is known as utar.

In the north, the Sandal Bar rises abruptly from the plain below. The vast extent of the country included within this bar was then, with a few trifling exceptions, wasteland owned by the government. There were no villages here and stray cultivation occurred in areas attached to wells which were held under lease from the government. Most parts of the uplands were inhabited by wild pastoral tribes who lived in temporary hamlets of thatched huts, which were occupied and deserted intermittently. Their flocks grazed on the widespread plains. During a year of good rainfall, patches of rain cultivation could be found sparsely scattered here and there.

The strip of the Thal was an inconsiderable area with an exceedingly narrow strip in the north widening out considerably to the south of the Jhelum. The Thal apparently is a higher plateau similar to the bars except that it was then more or less completely covered with hills and dunes of blown sand. The Kirana Bar, a portion of the Chaj Doab, takes its name from the Kirana Hills found here. Just above Chiniot, one of the three important towns of Jhang, the Chenab flowed picturesquely through a couple of gorges in these hills. The lands of the Kirana Bar to the south and east of the hills were of superb quality. After slight showers of rain, the whole country was carpeted with grass. Better crops were grown here than in the Sandal Bar. The Kirana Bar was demarcated from the utar by the same fall or slope as the Sandal Bar. This ledge created the boundary between the villages and the government wasteland. But few possessed lands beyond the high bank, or Nakka, as it was then called.

Trans-Chenab, from the junction of the Chenab and the Jhelum to Ahmadpur (another important town in Jhang), the sailab lands were bounded by a high bank separating them from the Kachhi tract. At Ahmadpur, the level of the country appeared to sink, the bank disappeared, and the floodwaters of the river passed to the west of Ahmadpur, finding its way through depressions and canals, into the Kandiwal jheel (lake) that lay immediately under the high wall of the Thal. The tract between the Thal and the Jhelum is called Kachhi, which is the name of the alluvial lands of the Indus Valley, as distinct from the Thal and Daman.

The Jhelum meandered below the Thal and the higher portion of the Kachhi, beyond the reach of Jhelum and Chenab floods, until it reached Sherowana village.

The Ravi first touched the district at a point only three kos (a unit of measurement in India, between one and three miles) from where it fell into the Chenab, but the length of its singularly tortuous course between these two points was nearly double that distance. The character of the lower Ravi varied considerably from that of the upper. On the Jhang side, sailab lands were separated by a very high bank from the lands of utar. Its course was the most capricious and inconstant of all the rivers of this district.

It is true to a degree that over the recent centuries, Jhang may have been reduced to a dry waterless tract, a region devoid of living brooks and shady groves, with a sparse jungle of bushy trees and the fringes of cultivation on the banks of the rivers Jhelum and Chenab. But once upon a time, a civilisation that was the envy of the West thrived here. Its prosperity varied with change in its geographical tapestry. But irrigation and other reforms carried out during British rule paved the way for restoring the region's prosperity. The British not only reformed the agriculture sector but also improved infrastructure. Construction of a road network, railway line, postal and telegraph system as well as supply of electricity had a positive impact on the social and economic life of Jhang. Although all these developments were made for colonial interests, these benefited the people of Jhang.

Among British reforms, the most important pertained to agriculture and irrigation. These reforms had a deep impact on the future socio-economic and political set-up of Jhang, and also created a feudal system. With land turning fertile, many tribes made Jhang their home over centuries. Jats, Rajput Sials, Sayads of Rajo, Qureshis and Khatris were in majority during British India. Amongst these, Sayads, Khatris and Jats owned a majority of landed properties in Jhang. In Shorkot, Kuraishi or Qureshi were the important families alongside Khatris. The Qureshi here were descendants of Haveli Bahadar Shah and Pir Abdul Rahman, and not recognised as genuine by the true Hashmi Qureshi, the descendants of the celebrated Muhammadan saint Makhdun Baha-ud-din Zakria. Most land here was owned by Khatris.

A lot of Khatri clans held land in proprietorship in Jhang and made agriculture their occupation. Jats owned and cultivated a substantial chunk of land in all the three tehsils, with Sials and Khatris not trailing far behind. In Shorkot tehsil, it was the Khatris who owned and cultivated a substantial chunk of land but the Qureshis too kept respectable acres. Khatris owned over 40,000 acres out of which about 23,000 acres were cultivated. Shorkot was like an oasis in Jhang, with the river water flowing far into the countryside forming islands, belas or bindis as they were called.

It is here in the beautiful village of Rodu Sultan in Jhang of Shorkot that my ancestors made their home. The Batra clan owned and cultivated substantial land in many villages in Shorkot tehsil. Many generations of Batras lived, worked hard and prospered here till Partition uprooted them from their lands, forced them to leave their village, land, home, cattle, and way of life, to be rendered displaced – to become refugees – in their own country.

1
Flickering Hope

On a humid summer evening, about a dozen men, all in their white kurta and dhoti ensemble, settled down on the mooras and manjees arranged circularly in the middle of the vast courtyard of Chaudhary Tulsi Dass's house. Some still wore their pagdi, others had taken it off and placed it on the charpoy. All men were medium to tall in stature with well-proportioned and athletic builds. Their fair skin had tanned to wheatish from tolling hard in the fields under the scorching sun. Yet it was healthy and glowing. All of them, without any exception, were clean-shaven except for the handlebar moustache, their symbol of manhood. They exuded an air of confidence and pride in their appearance, reflecting strong cultural identity and sense of belonging. The Punjabi Khatris exhibited distinct physical characteristics that distinguished them from the rest. They possessed striking facial features, including prominent noses, and expressive eyes that often sparkled with intelligence.

The women of the house sat huddled on the jute cots a little away, wearing subtle-coloured, loose-fitting salwar and kameez, a long loose shirt, knee-length in size. Some of them had a chunni, a long scarf, draped gracefully over the head and shoulders. None of them wore any jewellery except a gold bangle or two. Their hair was long, thick, and black, worn in elaborate braids. Jhangi women were bold, proud and feared no man. Yet, they carried a sense of earthy grace and authority. Punjabi women were included in all decision making. They participated in all main domestic and business decisions and their views were well regarded by men.

Most aired themselves with pankhas, the hand fans made of native Indian grass khus, waiting anxiously for the conversation to begin. They had already placed hot milk in brass tumblers on a centre table for those who wanted a drink. The children had been shooed away to splash water on the roof to cool it and spread the cots for those who preferred to sleep on the rooftop. The villagers in Rodu Sultan, like in other rural populations, preferred to sleep in the open or in the veranda unless it was raining.

Everyone waited silently for the host, one of the clan's scions, to open the conversation. The mood was gloomy. In the last few days, heartbreaking news of ongoing carnage in parts of Punjab had been arriving in Rodu Sultan, carried by those who had heard of the bloodshed. The radio invariably provided censored news and people in distant places like villages of Shorkot never got to learn of the actual facts. The many hearsay and exaggerated accounts only added to the anxiety.

The only good news had come a few weeks back on 20 February 1947, when the British prime minister, Clement Attlee, declared in London the British intention to leave India by June 1948 after transferring power to responsible Indian hands. Hearing the news, Rodu Sultan erupted in jubilation. There was some catch in Attlee's statement as it implied uncertainties surrounding the conditions of transfer of power but the villagers decided that the announcement called for a big celebration. A mood of unbridled celebration built up at once. Villagers poured out of their homes chanting slogans of '*Bharat Mata Ki Jai*' and '*Vande Mataram*'. The village alleys transformed into a sea of joyous faces, as children danced to the rhythm of drums, while elders exchanged sweets and shared stories of the long-awaited freedom. Shops closed in anticipation of the festivities, and homes were decorated with garlands and portraits of Mahatma Gandhi and other national leaders. In the evening, houses were lit up with diyas. It felt as if Diwali had arrived early. The atmosphere was electrifying, filled with a sense of pride, optimism, and liberation. Villagers embraced each other, their differences melting away in a collective surge of unity and patriotism. The anticipation of forthcoming independence was not only going to herald the end of British Raj but also the dawn of a new era of self-determination.

But the celebration was short-lived as communal violence erupted in Lahore, which rapidly spread to other parts of Punjab. The ambiguity in Atlee's announcement fuelled political manoeuvring and heightened communal tensions. The June 1948 deadline created a sense of urgency, but it also left little time for the British, Congress, and Muslim League to negotiate a smooth transition. Now, one of their own, Ram Lal, husband of Tulsi Dass's youngest sister Nirmala, had just returned from Lahore with first-hand account of the developments around freedom, the political tussle, and the fierce fights that had broken out between Hindus and Muslims.

Finally, Tulsi Dass broke the silence. 'Ram Lal returned from Lahore this morning; he has brought some distressing news. I thought all of you should hear about this as we may have to discuss the implication of the news on Rodu Sultan. Perhaps we may also have to make some unpleasant decisions.' He turned to look at his brother-in-law. Taking the cue, Ram Lal, who was sitting next to Tulsi Dass, looking nervous, started speaking.

'As you all know my wife and I had gone to Lahore in February to drop our daughter Santosh at her husband's house after she delivered our first grandchild here in Rodu Sultan. We were reluctant to go to Lahore as we had heard how the city was tense after the ban on the Muslim League National Guard and the Rashtriya Swayamsevak Sangh (RSS) by the Punjab government on 24 January. In retaliation,

Muslim League leadership resorted to direct action in Punjab. Processions were taken out, many Punjab Muslim League leaders courted arrest, leading to strikes in Lahore and other major cities. The government was forced to come to terms by lifting the ban on the processions and meetings. There were ongoing protests by both organisations. Assessing the situation in Lahore, we suggested to our daamad, Rajender, that we all stay in Rodu Sultan till things settled. But he insisted that we were all safe and must stay put there for a few days. Being employed with the postal department of the Punjab government, he felt there was no reason for us to be concerned. But I could sense that Lahore was sitting on a ticking time bomb ready to explode on a minor provocation.'

Ram Lal paused to catch his breath, and then continued. 'But politics took a nasty turn after Atlee announced that before leaving, they will transfer power to responsible Indian hands. The Congress and League started lobbying with the British. Police and demonstrators clashed at many places. In Amritsar and Jullundur, many protestors were injured.' Ram Lal felt a lump in his throat, as he continued. 'Under pressure from the League, Khizar Hayat Tiwana resigned from the premiership of Punjab on 2 March; and the Nawab of Mamdot staked claim to form the ministry. Muslim League wanted control of the Punjab government at this crucial time to be able to influence ongoing negotiations with the British. Protests erupted in Lahore and a few Muslim policemen fired on the protestors. Many peaceful protestors were killed and over a hundred injured in the firing. This culminated in a riot situation on the same evening as tension escalated between Muslims and Hindus. Master Tara Singh appealed for supreme sacrifice by Hindus and Sikhs to save their country, religion and land. Next day, Lahore was up in flames. The communal tension spread like wildfire engulfing places miles away, like Amritsar, Jullundur, Rawalpindi and Sialkot.'

Listening to this agonising account, some women started sobbing. Tulsi Dass gestured them to stay quiet.

Ram Lal picked up the brass tumbler and gulped the milk down. After a moment, he continued, 'Then came news from Rawalpindi of atrocious killings of Sikh brothers and sisters. The killings were so brutal and inhuman that it enraged our Sikh brothers who swore to avenge the Rawalpindi massacre. The military had to be brought in to control the riots as police failed to curb violence. Hospitals were overflowing with the injured coming in huge numbers. Amidst all this hostility, reports of the likelihood of partition of Punjab continued to aggravate the tension and widen the mistrust between the two communities. Curfew was imposed in Lahore.

'We decided to leave as we could not risk Santosh's baby not being able to access medical aid if it became necessary; the child being barely one year old and sick due to jaundice. Trains from Lahore had been cancelled but we somehow managed to sneak out of the city with the help of a police constable who was a friend of our son-in-law. We hitchhiked on a military truck which was on its way to Lyallpur to deal with the emerging tensions. Considering our grandchild's condition, the military men offered us help and let us stay in the Lyallpur barracks. A few days later they put us on a military vehicle going to Mianwali where our sumddhee lived. Barely a week later, someone brought the news that villages on the border of Lyallpur were being attacked by outsiders. Tens of armed men attacked the village at night and looted whatever they could lay their hands on. Even cattle and camels were taken away. There wasn't enough military around to protect every single village. This madness was expected to reach Mianwali sooner than later, so we decided to come here. We pleaded with Rajender's parents to accompany us but they were not willing to leave as they felt safe in Mianwali. We are here now, along with Santosh, Rajender and their child.'

Ram Lal took a deep breath. He somehow mustered strength and continued. 'First blood has been drawn in Lahore, in the land of our own ancestors. I have never witnessed this kind of mindless bloodshed before. Many people from Khatri and Sikh samaj from

Lahore and other places affected by violence have left for safe places in East Punjab and elsewhere. It is a matter of days before this madness reaches here.' Ram Lal struggled to continue; his eyes welled up and voice choked.

There was a long pause again. Everyone was stunned into silence. Hindus and Muslims had been living peacefully for centuries in Punjab. After the death of Aurangzeb in 1707, there had been a gradual improvement in communal harmony between the two communities. Sufi saints, the Muslim mystics who preached a message of love, tolerance, and unity also played an important role in bridging the gap between Hindus and Muslims, and their teachings helped to create a more tolerant and inclusive society. But now, the order and structure seemed to crumble.

'*Haye rabba*,' the cry of one of the women in the huddle broke the silence. The others whimpered too, unable to hold their emotions. Tulsi Dass once again gestured to the women to stay composed. Ram Lal had more details to share but discerning the reaction of the women, he decided against it. The disturbances were spreading fast. Apart from Lahore and Rawalpindi, Amritsar, Multan, and Jullundur cities, even smaller towns such as Ludhiana, Sialkot, Kamoke in the Gujranwala district, Hoshiarpur, and Khushab in the Shahapur district were affected. A procession of non-Muslims shouting '*Quaid-i-Azam Murdabad*' led to a massacre of 150 Hindus in Multan. The rural disturbances were rapidly turning serious. There were reports of brutalities, and looting and arson became common. Trains were attacked and looted in and around Mianwali. In one village, Sasali, a party of Sikhs, who had surrendered to the Muslim attackers on the promise that their lives would be spared, were murdered. Attacks on non-Muslims had been led in some cases by retired army officers, including pensioners with honorary commission rank. The violence was spreading like a fire fuelled by both reports and rumours, and was not far from Jhang.

Realising Ram Lal's dilemma, Tulsi Dass took over and steered the conversation in another direction. 'There is worse news. The riots appear to have pushed the Congress towards partition. After the Rawalpindi massacre, relations between Hindu and Sikh leaders appear to have become irreconcilable. Sikhs are intent on partition of the Punjab. The Shiromani Akali Dal (SAD) has also adopted a resolution to put forward a demand for Punjab's partition into two provinces and demanded a boundary commission should be set up. It has appealed to all panthic organisations and workers to unite and solidly stand behind this demand. The Congress too seems to have given up hope of peace and reconciliation. It has also passed a resolution on 8 March to see Punjab divided into Muslim and non-Muslim provinces. The Congress leadership now believes that giving Pakistan to the League is the only way out of the impasse and to bring the mindless violence to an end,' Tulsi Dass said. 'In retaliation, Jinnah has asked for the entire Punjab to be part of Pakistan. Nehru has suggested to Mountbatten a temporary partition into three areas, one where Muslims are in majority, the other predominantly Hindus and the third a mixed area. *Sab kuch bada jaldi ho gaya* (all these developments have been very rapid).'

'So much for the decades of struggle to get freedom from the angrez. Were years of sacrifices meant to lead to this madness? Will no one even care to ask us?' a woman from the group cursed.

Tulsi Dass continued. '*Inhaan fasaad di darindagi, be-rahmi te sarasar be-aqli ne donaan baradriyan vich na-qabil-e-faramosh karvaahat, dushmani te nafrat paida kar ditti ae* (the ferocity, cruelty and sheer mindlessness of these riots have created unforgettable bitterness, animosity and hatred among the two communities). Ram Lal is convinced that it is dangerous to continue living here in Rodu Sultan. We have gathered to discuss these tragic developments within the family and decide our action plan before we deliberate it with the biradari. We will have to include them in our discussion. But before that let us freely discuss this within the family.'

'Why should we leave? India and Pakistan are a political matter. No one really cares where we Khatris live. Our lives will go on like today whether here in India or in Pakistan. Our home, lands, cattle, friends – everything is here. There are no choices to be made,' said Satish Chand, one of his cousins.

'Satish is right. Rodu Sultan is the home of our ancestors. Their ruh lives in every single corner of this house, the village, and our fields. We cannot abandon them and go away,' asserted Sudarshan, the sixty-year-old widowed stepsister of Tulsi Dass.

'Bebe is right,' concurred another voice with Sudarshan, who was addressed as Bebe by everyone in the village out of respect for her age. After her husband died of cholera when she was only twenty-two, she was married off to her husband's younger brother. But he too died a few years later from some illness. She moved back to Rodu Sultan with her son, Kartar Singh, from her first husband, refusing to remarry. Sudarshan had been married into a Sikh family. Her late husband had adopted Sikhism as was common after an appeal was made to Hindus by Sikh gurus to give one of their sons in the service of the panth. Many Khatri Arora families turned to Sikhism founded in the fifteenth century by Guru Nanak, a Bedi Khatri.

'We have no reason to feel unsafe here, in our homes. We have lived here for decades, and before us, many of our elders. This is our village, our own people. We know each of them by name. Who do we need to feel threatened by? Be it Musalman or us Hindus and Sikhs, we are all Jhangis. Other than our food habits and the God we pray to, there is nothing uncommon,' Tulsi Dass's younger brother, Narain Dass, said in an attempt to reassure everyone. Their self-assurance was not unfounded. Jhang had been a cradle of spiritual richness and communal harmony for centuries.

Jhang's rural landscape is adorned with thousands of Sufi shrines, varying in size from grand edifices to modest structures, each steeped in a tapestry of associated legends. Numerous saints have graced this land with their wisdom and divine presence. The life and teachings of revered Sufi saint Hazrat Sultan Bahoo, also known as Sultan-ul-Arifeen, continue to inspire millions, transcending time and cultural boundaries. Till date, a student of mysticism begins their journey with the much revered *'Aleph Allah chanbay dee booti'* and graduates to *'Dil darya samundroon doonghay'*. Saint Hazrat Sultan lies buried in Garh Maharaja, only a few kos from Shorkot and his shrine is no less than a place of pilgrimage for devotees seeking blessings and spiritual guidance. His urs (annual commemoration) is celebrated with great reverence and attracts thousands of seekers and admirers. Baba Shahana, a Khatri of Sataghara in the Montgomery district, is another revered saint. The shrines of Hazrat Shah Shiekha, Peer Jabbo Shareef, Shah Kabeer and Rodo Sultan, the Sikh Darbar of Guru Nanak Dev and the Hindu temple in Ware Sulaiman tend to the other faithful. The shrine of Rodo Sultan is located in Rodu Sultan. Jhang has also inspired some of the subcontinent's beloved artists, writers and musicians.

'The entire region had been living amiably until the British and some politicians sparked division in the two communities for their own gains. The danger to our lives and threat to our property is not from our Musalman bhai here in Rodu Sultan or even villages around us but from the *bunyad parast* (fundamentalist) Muslim political and religious leaders who are determined to divide Hindus and Muslims. The rogue elements of our society are taking advantage of the situation and indulging in looting and arson. The fire of rage continues to spread. It will not be long before it reaches Jhang and eventually Rodu Sultan,' Ram Lal responded, having got a hold of himself by now.

Some of the young men in the gathering were fuming with rage. 'Anyone who sets an eye on our village will be cut into pieces,' roared Kartar Singh, a trained Sikh warrior.'

Tulsi Dass snapped back at Kartar. *'Thand rakh oye. Aie josh da vaile naa aayee* (stay calm, this is not the time to show your muscle power). We have to think through this calmly.' Turning to the other men, he declared, 'We must watch the developments for a few days. We cannot rush into a decision. There is nothing to be afraid of in our own village. Mukhtyar will protect us. He is like our family, for years now. If the situation worsens, we will send our elders, women and children to a safe place till things settle down.'

Mukhtyar was the head of the Qureshi tribe in Shorkot. The Batra family shared a bond of deep trust with Qureshis across generations.

'Can we trust him? He will side with the League and the Muslims, won't he?' Satish inquired, sounding doubtful.

'Of course, we can. He is like a brother to us … a part of family,' shot back Ram Lal, offended by the insinuation cast on his best friend. 'Mukhtyar will protect us in all circumstances.'

'They are all the same,' Kartar muttered under his breath.

Tulsi Dass looked at him sharply but decided not to confront him; he could not blame the young men for feeling enraged by the bloodshed. The news of the Rawalpindi massacre would have no doubt shaken Kartar. It was not only shameful but also heart-wrenching.

'Where will we go and when do we plan to leave, Bhai-ji?' asked Dharam Pal this time. He was the husband of Ram Lal's sister.

'Kalanor,' answered Raj Rani, Tulsi Dass's wife. 'My brothers will welcome us like their own. Kalanor is also Kesar Dass's sasural. It is near Delhi, so it should be safe. We had built a dharamshala there last year. It has enough room for all of us. If we must leave, we should not wait for long so that we reach Rohtak before the end of the month of Jeth. We don't want to get caught in the monsoon rains on that treacherous journey. Many low-lying plains on the way are notorious for getting flooded in rains. Trains are cancelled, and roads get submerged. We don't want to get stranded.' Turning to Nand Lal, she instructed, 'You go to Jhang town to tell your elder sister, Parvati, and her family to be ready to leave at short notice.'

Nand Lal who stood leaning against the veranda pillar shifted at once to stand upright. He nodded. Nand Lal's sister was married in Jhang town. Her in-laws had a flourishing business across the northern part of the country.

No one argued when Raj Rani spoke. She was a woman of few words but when she spoke, she uttered measured words of wisdom. Turning this time to her son, Kesar Dass, who sat squatting on the floor beside the elderly men, Raj Rani directed, 'You go with your brother. Take a few friends along. It is better to stay in groups from now on if you venture out of the village.'

'You should find out if there are any families from neighbouring villages who are thinking of leaving as we are. If there are any, we should plan to travel together as far as we can. The greater the number, the better the chances of warding off the rogue elements we may encounter during the journey. Send someone to find out about the welfare of Bhandi and Veera.' It was Tulsi Dass's turn to instruct his younger brother.

Affectionally called Bhandi and Veera, Narayani and Bhagwan were daughters of Tulsi Dass and Raj Rani. The two sisters were married to two brothers whose families were big traders of grain based in Multan town. Their eldest daughter Baro lived with her husband and children in Gohana in East Punjab (now in Haryana). The other three daughters – Chando (Mittar Kaur after marriage), Bassi and Kaki, also married, lived in Meham, Kaithal (both in East Punjab, now, in Haryana) and Delhi.

'If we decide to leave, we must invite our village Sikh brothers to come along. They have a family of about twenty. Together all of us men, women and children will be between eighty and hundred,' Ram Lal said, thinking aloud.

Everyone exchanged silent glances but no one spoke. Ram Lal looked at his brother-in-law for guidance. Tulsi Dass stared at the floor below. As his thoughts deepened, his grip on the lathi he carried for support tightened. There was still a flickering hope in him that this madness would not reach Rodu Sultan. Finally, his reverie was broken. Looking at no one in particular, he spoke calmly, 'We need not get alarmed as Partition is still some time away. But we must be prepared with an action plan in case Jhang falls to Pakistan's share when division takes place and decide…' There was a long pause before he continued, this time in a tone that carried an unmistaken hint of disillusionment, '…whether we wish to continue to live here or sell everything and leave for Kalanor.'

Tulsi Dass was lost in deep thought again. Despite the disturbing news raging over the last month, he had remained hopeful that things will turn out well in the end. The foundation of Jhang was too strong to be shaken by these incidents, he believed. Jhang had witnessed many invaders. It had dealt with the brutality of a few Mughal rulers, and experienced British discrimination. They had also faced many natural calamities – floods and earthquakes. Their resolve was made of steel. But after listening to Ram Lal, his hope was starting to flicker. '*Rab bhala kare* (May God be with us),' he uttered as he stood up, signalling that the meeting was over.

Instructing Narain Dass to convene a biradari meeting in Rodu Sultan, he walked slowly to the veranda where his cot had been laid, a hand pankha resting on its side. As he passed his wife, he remarked jestingly, Ask your Lord Rama, to whom you pray two times a day, why he is making us go through this.' Tulsi Dass was a Shaivite, utterly devoted to Shiva. A dedicated devotee of Lord Rama, Raj Rani was not amused. 'Don't blame my Rama for the follies of the ignorant men who know no humanity,' she mumbled.

Everyone left. Only Narain Dass and his family members stayed back. They lived next door but the two brothers had decided to have a common courtyard.

Outside, Ram Lal signalled Kesar Dass to follow him. He walked to the shed where sacks of grains were stored. Slipping his hand behind one of the sacks, Ram Lal pulled out something wrapped in an old cloth and handed it to Kesar Dass carefully. Kesar Dass unwrapped the cloth and found himself holding a British-made pistol. 'We will have to keep vigil at night one by one. We can't take any chances. Your father will never approve it but in this situation, we need to be prepared to meet the challenge if our village is attacked. Other than Mukhtyar and his family we cannot trust other Muslims in the village. They won't harm us but they won't risk their lives to save ours.' Ram Lal went his way, leaving Kesar Dass with the gun.

Kesar Dass sensed that the danger was real. Suddenly, his legs felt weak and he could no longer stand. He sat down on one of the sacks to calm himself and gather his strength, his hope flickering. The next few days were going to be crucial as leaders determine the fate of his family, home, land, animals, and the village itself, he thought. He needed to be stronger and prepare for the worst, he resolved.

Sitting there, his eyes glued to the pistol, he could not fathom how and when a freedom struggle, fought together by Hindus, Sikhs and Musalman as one, turned into a fight for separate homelands. This turn of events was unthinkable a few years ago as there was no blueprint of a future Pakistan until then. And now, all of a sudden, it appeared that Pakistan might become a reality, and India, even Punjab was going to get divided.

He wondered when the seeds of division were planted.

2

Seeds of Partition

The notion of a separate Muslim nation was not exactly new. Its seed was planted when the idea was first put forth by Muhammad Iqbal, an eminent Urdu poet from Sialkot, in his presidential address to the Muslim League at its annual session held at Lucknow in December 1930. The idea did not receive much traction then. It was to, however, catch the imagination of Indian Muslims exactly a decade later.

On 23 March 1940, Hindu India was startled to attention as it had never been before. On that day, the All-India Muslim League (AIML) at its annual general session held under a multicoloured shamiana erected at Iqbal Park, Lahore, passed a resolution demanding a separate homeland for the Muslims to a thunderous applause with slogans of *Allah-hu-Akbar* and *Muhammad Ali Jinnah zindabad*. The League's president, Muhammad Ali Jinnah, wearing a black achkan and fez cap, raised the demand for a separate independent state for Musalmans. This day was to later become a turning point in the history of the subcontinent.

Passed on day two of the three-day session, the resolution emphatically reiterated that the scheme of federation embodied in the Government of India Act, 1935, was totally unsuited to, and unworkable in the peculiar conditions of the country and altogether unacceptable to Muslim India. It further recorded its emphatic view that while the declaration dated 18 October 1939 made by the British government was reassuring insofar it declared that the policy and plan on which the Government of India Act, 1935, was based will be reconsidered in consultation with the various parties, interests and communities in India, Muslim India will not be satisfied unless the whole constitutional plan was reconsidered de novo and that no revised plan would be acceptable to the Muslims, unless it was framed with their approval and consent.

The resolution further stated that it was the considered view of the League that no constitutional plan would be workable in the country or acceptable to the Muslims unless it was designated on the basic principle, viz., that geographically contiguous units be demarcated into regions which should be so constituted with such territorial readjustments as may be necessary that the areas in which the Muslims are numerically in a majority as in the north-western and eastern zones of India should be grouped to constitute 'Independent States' in which the constituent units shall be autonomous and sovereign.

It went on to state that adequate, effective and mandatory safeguards should be specifically provided in the Constitution for minorities in these units and in the regions for the protection of their religious, cultural, economic, political, administrative and other rights, and interests in consultation with them; and in other parts of India where the Musalmans are in a minority, adequate, effective and mandatory safeguards should be specifically provided in the Constitution for them and other minorities for the protection of their religious, cultural, economic, political, administrative and other rights, and interests in consultation with them.

The resolution authorised the working committee to frame a scheme of Constitution in accordance with these basic principles.

In the Lahore meeting, all League leaders shared Jinnah's belief in the two-nation theory. Virtually all the speakers criticised the then Congress president Maulana Abul Kalam Azad for opposing the Muslim homeland, being a Muslim himself. They dubbed Azad as a 'show boy of Hindus'. In his presidential address at the Congress session held earlier, Azad had vehemently criticised the two-nation theory as it suggested religious separatism. He had exhorted Muslims to preserve a united India as both Hindus and Muslims were Indians who shared deep bonds of brotherhood.

The Lahore Resolution, the first formal statement seeking an independent state based on predominantly Muslim population, shook the nation. It discarded the notion of federalism and the proposal of a united India as outlined in the Government of India Act, 1935.

The Muslim League later appointed a committee which prepared the concept of two Muslim states: one in the north-west (Sindh, Balochistan, North-West National Province and Punjab, together with Delhi after amalgamation with Punjab); the other in the north-east (Assam and Bengal, excluding the districts of Bankura and Midnapur together with the district of Purnea from Bihar). The document did not mention Kashmir. It suggested what appeared as a federal structure with a central machinery concerned with external relations, defence, communications, customs, and safeguards for minorities. In 1941, the resolution was made a part of the League's Constitution. This was the time when in Punjab, Muslims comprised some 58 per cent, Hindus 26 per cent and Sikhs 13 per cent of the population.

In his presidential address to the Muslim League in December 1930 at Lucknow, Iqbal, whose vibrant patriotic poems including '*Sare Jahan Se Achha, Hindustan Hamara*' continued to be sung in schools and colleges all over India, referred to autonomous states being formed, obviously not all-Muslim, based on the unity of languages, race, history, religion and identity of common interests. But Iqbal's blueprint did not envisage a separate Muslim state. He merely made a case for provincial autonomy in Punjab, the North-West Frontier Province, Sindh and Balochistan within the body politic of India. His reasoning was similar to that which prompted the Motilal Nehru Committee of August 1928 to recommend the separation of Sindh from Bombay Presidency, and to constitute the North-West Frontier Province into an 'independent' administrative unit. It is ironic that the same person who believed in the idea of India could also articulate a proposal for the division of the same Hindustan and later write: *Muslim hain hum watan hai sara jahan hamara*.

In fact, Iqbal wrote to the Punjab governor that he was not the author of the Pakistan idea, and it had come from Chaudhary Rahmat Ali, a Muslim nationalist living in London, who founded the Pakistan Movement in 1933. Rahmat Ali came up with a pamphlet titled 'Pakistan Declaration', which was presented in the 1933 Round Table Conference organised by the British government. His idea of Pakistan was composed of five Muslim provinces in the north as an independent state: Punjab, NWFP, Kashmir, Sindh and Balochistan. The rest to him was Hindustan. But his proposal was never officially put forth. Rahmat Ali's scheme, nurtured in Cambridge, was an illustration of obscurantist political eccentricity. It caused much political embarrassment back home and was dismissed as chimerical and impracticable.

Iqbal's proposal to the League placed in its Lucknow meeting was not adopted. Instead, projecting himself as a common front between the Muslims and other non-Muslim minorities, Jinnah chose a moderate approach. The resolution passed by the League deprecated the formation of ministries in certain provinces by the Congress in flagrant violation of the letter and the spirit of the Government of India Act, 1935, and the Instrument of Instructions. It condemned the governors for their failure to enforce the special powers entrusted to them for the safeguards of the interest of Musalmans and other important minorities. It resolved that the objective of the League shall be the establishment of full independence in the form of federation of free democratic states in which the rights and interests of Musalmans and other minorities were adequately and effectively safeguarded in the Constitution. Unfortunately, the catholicity and statesmanship reflected in his approach underlying the resolutions passed in Lucknow did not last long; and Jinnah took a somersault by passing the notorious resolution in favour of Pakistan in Lahore.

The Lahore Resolution became widely popular among Muslims, exceeding even Jinnah's own expectations. Muslims who were truly dazzled by the demand for Pakistan were from the Urdu-speaking United Provinces, Bihar, and Delhi, areas which would never be a part of Pakistan if ever it came into being. Their psyche was not difficult to understand. They considered themselves the ones who had ruled India for thousands of years, and could not reconcile themselves to the idea of a post-British dispensation where they would not enjoy superiority in numbers, power, or status. The dream of being rulers blinded them to the reality that in a democratic polity, the majority would be at the helm of affairs.

Jinnah relentlessly kept elucidating his two-nation theory. Ideological forces aided separatist politics and reinforced communitarian identities. A year earlier, in January 1939, Maulana Azad Sobhani, a prominent Muslim leader, made a divisive and provocative speech at Sylhet, alleging that Hindus were determined to establish Ram Rajya in India and marginalise Muslims. He urged Muslims to fight Hindus, as it was Hindus who were their real enemy and not the British. His speech was published in the *Anandabazar Patrika* the following day, escalating tensions between the two communities and creating seeds of fear and hatred which was optimally exploited by Jinnah for political advantage. *Anandabazar Patrika* quoted his speech thus:

> If there is any eminent leader in India who is in favour of driving out the English from this country, I am that leader. In spite of this I want that there should be no fight with the English on behalf of the Muslim League. Our big fight is with the 22 crores of our Hindu enemies, who constitute

> the majority. Only 4½ crores of Englishmen have practically swallowed the whole world by becoming powerful. And if these 22 crores of Hindus who are equally advanced in learning, intelligence and wealth as in numbers, if they become powerful, these Hindus will swallow Muslim India and gradually even Egypt, Turkey, Kabul, Mecca, Medina and other Muslim principalities, like *Yajuj-Majuj* (it is so mentioned in Koran that before the destruction of the world, they will appear on the earth and will devour whatever they will find)…
>
> The English are gradually becoming weak .. they will go away from India in the near future. So if we do not fight the greatest enemies of Islam, the Hindus, from now on and make them weak, then they will not only establish *Ramrajya* in India but also gradually spread all over the world. It depends on the 9 crores of Indian Muslims either to strengthen or to weaken them (the Hindus). So it is the essential duty of every devout Muslim to fight on by joining the Muslim League so that the Hindus may not be established here and a Muslim rule may be established in India as soon as the English depart…
>
> Though the English are the enemies of the Muslims, yet for the present our fight is not with the English. At first we have to come to some understanding with the Hindus through the Muslim League. Then we shall be easily able to drive out the English and establish Muslim rule in India…
>
> Be careful! Don't fall into the trap of Congress Maulvis; because the Muslim World is never safe in the hands of 22 crores of Hindu enemies.

After the Lahore Resolution, speeches became more ferocious. Such remarks created almost unbridgeable differences between the two communities. Punjabi Khatris who had traditionally enjoyed good relations with Muslims were dismayed by Jinnah's proposal. They were convinced that it would destroy the unity and prosperity of their province. The demand for division invoked a hostile reaction among the Sikhs. On 24 March 1940, Kartar Singh and Master Tara Singh led a Sikh procession in Amritsar and condemned the idea of Pakistan. They advised the Sikhs to get ready for sacrifices. The Shiromani Akali Dal called it a declaration of civil war. Master Tara Singh argued that if Indian Muslims feared the Hindu majority, Sikhs too feared Muslim domination in the Punjab. Sikhs stopped responding to the ongoing recruitment drive by the British for the Second World War. They feared that if they went to the front abroad, there would be no one to protect their women, property, lands and villages.

On 20 May 1940, 125 Sikh leaders gathered in Lahore and established Guru Raj Khalsa Darbar. Sir Chhotu Ram, the Punjab Unionist minister, termed the idea of Pakistan as 'an absurd proposition'. It created a new sense of prejudice in the Muslims and increased apprehension of the non-Muslims, who firmly united in opposition to the demand for Pakistan.

The Lahore Resolution also infuriated the Hindu Mahasabha. The All-India Hindu Mahasabha, the first Hindu organisation of the subcontinent, rose in the year 1915 with the All-India Hindu Seminar held at Haridwar. It sprang up in response to British imperialism and concern over the 'profane nationalism' of the Congress. The chief goals of the Mahasabhaites were to promote greater unity and harmony among all sections of the Hindu communities of the country. Their aim was to take positive steps for religious, moral, educational, social and political welfare of the Hindu community.

The name of Hindu Mahasabha was later changed to Akhil Bharat Hindu Mahasabha. It had no political ambitions. Lajpat Rai, its chief from 1925 to 1927, set his promise for an Indian nationalism beyond the frontiers of religious communities. He was against the Mahasabha entering the political field. His concerns included the necessity for Hindu unity, the elimination of untouchability, and the upgrading of the condition of Hindu women. In 1932, a more aggressive stance was adopted by the Hindu Mahasabha under the aegis of B.S. Moonje, who held the presidency from 1927 to1933. The Mahasabha slowly became vocal about the Hindu community, transforming into a force railing for Hindu nationalism and carrying an evident antagonism about the Congress during the presidency of Bhai Parmanand. This set the stage for dominance of Veer Savarkar and his thoughts.

Savarkar announced a new beginning as president in 1939. It was at this time that the movement expanded beyond its original base in the Hindi heartland and embraced Maharashtra and Bengal. Stellar leaders like Syama Prasad Mookerjee entered the Mahasabha at this juncture. This was also the time when the Second World War broke out. While the Congress governments resigned in the provinces to protest against India's forced involvement in the war, the Hindu Mahasabha took a more cautious stance. Savarkar and many other leaders advocated for the enlistment of Hindu young men into the army so that they could gain military training and experience from the war and serve the nation after freedom. In fact, Hindu Mahasabha leaders were prominent in many war committees.

The Mahasabha was already enraged by Muslim League attempts to impose their agenda using their powers under the Act of 1935 in Bengal which became even more explicit after the Lahore Resolution of 23 March 1940. The Huq Ministry, which had been formed after Fazlul Huq joined the Muslim League and merged his Krishak Praja Party into it, passed a series of legislations which the Mahasabha viewed as moving towards the goal of total Muslim dominance. The Fazlul Huq ministry changed the rules about police recruitment to ensure that not less than 50 per cent of the recruits were Muslims. It also passed legislation that stipulated that 60 per cent of all government appointments be reserved for Muslims.

In 1939, the government instructed local bodies not to propose for appointment to local bodies persons who were known to be actively opposed to the policy of the ministry, and slapped administrative controls on nominations to the union boards, which accounted for one-third of their total membership (all of whom were to be

Muslims). And, in 1939, the Calcutta Municipal Amendment Act reserved seats for Muslims in Calcutta Corporation, far in excess of their proportion of the population. However, the unkindest cut of all came in 1940, when his ministry introduced the Secondary Education Bill, taking control of higher education in the province away from Calcutta University and vesting it instead in an education board in which Muslims were to be given a greater say. This threatened the Hindu-endowed schools, both religious and secular, and created apprehensions of imposition of an Islamic educational curriculum.

The Congress leadership adopted erratic attitudes towards the Lahore Resolution. In the beginning, they tried to conceal their real feelings but they could not help voicing their concerns later. Some leaders condemned the idea of Pakistan as a medieval concept, a quasi-tribal point of view, others termed it as a scheme that would be disastrous to the interests of all the communities equally. In a meeting of the Congress Working Committee held in Wardha between 16 and 19 April 1940 some leaders equated the resolution to declaration of civil war. Yet, some leaders believed that the demand was so absurd, even Muslim masses would never back it. The Congress did not make any formal statement or pass any resolution against the Lahore Resolution until April 1942. As a party, the Congress was not clear as to how they could better deal with it. Their confusion continued till the partition decision was taken.

The British views may have been conducive to Muslim rights but they showed no favour for the Pakistan idea. They had no sympathy for the partitioning scheme presented by the League. In their view, it was Jinnah's political manoeuvring and a desperate stance against the Congress.

As tensions flared up after the Lahore Resolution, a series of negotiations were held between the Muslim League and the Hindu Mahasabha during 1940–42 for communal settlement and avoiding ethnic conflicts. The Hindu Mahasabha formed governments in Sindh and Bengal with Muslim leaders in 1941-42 with an aim to work within the system to secure Hindu interests and prevent monopolisation of government patronage and public office by the Muslim League, which the British government had been encouraging privately.

In the meantime, the Muslim League was busy in spreading the idea of Pakistan among the Muslim masses. The League held several meetings at mosques in Lahore, Amritsar, Rohtak, Jullundur, Jhelum, Karnal, Gurdaspur, Lyallpur, Jhang, Rawalpindi and Simla, celebrated 'Pakistan Day' on 19 April and passed pro-Pakistan resolutions. In the Rawalpindi meeting, Dr Muhammad Alam declared that Muslims were ready to sacrifice their lives for their own cause but not for Hindu Raj.

The Lahore Resolution became an avalanche that swept away all other ideas and changed the fortune of both Muslim League and Jinnah. It positioned the League as an influential body among Muslims. Only the Pathans in the NWFP remained uninfluenced by the resolution. They had been grounded in pluralism. Balochistan too remained distant, and opposed the League. A party torn by factionalism and marred by rowdyism was suddenly rejuvenated after the Lahore Resolution. In the early 1930s, the Muslim League had only 500 members. It was perceived as an upper-class body of easy-going knights, Khan Bahadurs and landlords with little influence on the masses. Suddenly, Muslims gravitated towards the League.

Some scholars believe that a particular scenario contributed to the alteration in the tenor of political discourse in India and created, much to Jinnah's relief, the space for his manoeuvrings. Inter-community relations amongst Muslims were not too cordial after the Khilafat movement. Theological differences of religious leaders from Deoband or Nadwat al-ulama, with other schools of thought on Islam had widened. The Barelvis and the Deobandis had little in common. The Ahmadiyas and the Ahl-i-Hadith had a running battle over doctrinal matters. The lines of cleavage in north India were more sharply drawn between the Sunnis and the Shias than between Hindus and Muslims. These differences impeded the unification of the community. Insecurities and apprehensions were at an all-time high. This situation offered Jinnah a constituency he had not managed to secure for so long. He made the best use of the prevailing situation to galvanise the support of Muslims across all sections.

The League's growth was helped by the Unionist Party signing a pact with the League in October 1937 to contest the next elections jointly, a blunder that was to cost them dearly. The Unionist Party had emerged on the political scene of Punjab in 1923 as the most dominant party of British Punjab. Fazl-i-Hussain, Chaudhary Lal Chand and Sir Chhotu Ram had come together to form this non-communal party which represented the agrarian society belonging to all the three main religious communities of Punjab: Hindus, Muslims and Sikhs. The architects of the party had assured the Hindu and Muslim landlords that they would rise above politics to protect the interest of Punjab. Many senior Unionists visited Shorkot and beseeched the influential zamindars for their support. The Khatri and Muslim landlords who wielded great personal sway in their areas due to the strong bonds of the biradari network were reassured that the Unionist was a party with difference, and free of sectarian politics. Many zamindars from all the three religions patronised it.

With the unwavering support of landlords, the Unionist Party soon emerged on the political scene as the most prominent party of the Punjab. It won 99 out of 175 total seats in the provincial elections of 1936-37, while the Congress got only 18 seats. The others bagged 57 seats. In the 1937 elections, the Muslim League won 4.6 per cent of the total Muslim vote. It had no success in the North-West Frontier, a Muslim province with 92 per cent Muslims, and Sindh with 72 per cent Muslims. In Punjab, it retained only one Muslim seat. In Bengal with 54.7 per cent Muslims, it did better by winning 37 out of 119 Muslim seats. The Unionists signed a pact with the League in October 1937 to contest the next elections jointly which turned Hindu members hostile to Sikandar Hayat Khan, who was then Punjab's premier. Hindu and Sikh zamindars also got disenchanted with the party and this accelerated the downfall of the Unionists.

On the other hand, the pact revitalised the League in pan-India politics. Emboldened by the pact, the League went ahead and vocally pronounced the demand for a separate nation in 1940 which became a battle cry for Muslims who fought the struggle for independence in the name of Islam. The Lahore Resolution was in a way an echo of the poet-philosopher Iqbal's formulation of a separate cultural identity based on racial, social and cultural aspirations. Henceforth, the Muslim League became an authoritative and representative body of the Muslims and changed Jinnah's fortunes. A firm and convinced constitutionalist, Jinnah had no political base before the 1937 elections. He was at best a consultative politician, a sectional leader, quick at producing ready-made formulas for the solution of the Hindu–Muslim question. In his early career, a section of Muslims deemed him dangerously Congress-minded while Congressmen were sceptical about his stance. He had no popular base. Such was his initial political standing. But after the Lahore Resolution, Jinnah became an epitome of Muslim destiny, often greeted in the country as the sole spokesman of the Muslims.

These developments brought the League out of the wilderness. It burst on the political scene and became the voice of Muslims which gradually distanced itself from secular nationalism to create a separate Islamic nation-state. A little more than a paper organisation became a powerful political force. An organisation whose session was adjourned for lack of quorum only a decade ago in 1929, and which had a difficult time attracting people to its meetings, suddenly became an arbiter of Muslim destiny. The fragmented and battered leadership bruised by frequent splits caused by factional feuds rallied under Jinnah. A beleaguered wartime government, which had in the past refused to deal with Jinnah, now turned to him for political and moral support and, in the process, legitimised his critique of the Congress claim to represent all the communities of India.

In March 1942, the British Prime Minister Winston Churchill dispatched a senior Cabinet minister, Sir Stafford Cripps, to India. His mission was to offer India power after the end of the war. At the heart of his proposal was the creation of a de jure Cabinet at the Centre, to be called an executive council under the viceroy who would be the de facto boss. The proposal carried seeds for germinating Pakistan because it stated that any province which did not want to accede to the Union could remain outside it as a separate entity. Cripps also sought Indian support for the British in the Second World War. The proposal granted India dominion status after the war but otherwise conceded few changes to the Government of India Act of 1935. The Congress rejected the proposal outright and characterised it as a post-dated cheque drawn on a failing bank. Accepting Cripps's proposals meant participating in a war, which the Congress realised that Britain had almost lost. London was in no position to maintain its hold over India post-war. The failure of the Cripps Mission further estranged the Congress and the British government. Jinnah, known to be a personal friend of Winston Churchill, was equivocal on Cripps's proposal.

Following the failure of the Cripps Mission, the atmosphere in the subcontinent became increasingly murky. The desire for separation had overtaken most of the Muslims. The demand for the partition gradually gained ground among the overwhelming majority of Indian Muslims. They increasingly flocked to the League, which was emerging as the only representative body in the community. Even many Hindus began to feel that the parting of ways was inevitable.

By the end of the Second World War, Britain's place in the world had changed dramatically and the demand for India's independence could no longer be ignored.

The Lahore Resolution ruptured the harmony between Muslims and Hindus. In a matter of a few years, Punjab slipped into chaos. The Hindus' resentment of the League proposal was quite natural. The parts League was staking its claim on, was part of Aryavarta; these areas had always been a part of India and there was no way these could be given away to Muslims.

Despite the events of the 762 years of incessant Muslim invasions, Hindus had accepted Muslims into their fold. Over more than hundred years that followed, racial and linguistic affinity developed between the two communities. Other than the fact that the Hindus drew their inspiration from the Ramayana, the Mahabharata and the Bhagavadgita, while the Musalmans from the Quran and the Hadis, little could be differentiated between the Punjabi Musalman and the Punjabi Hindu, the UP Musalman and the UP Hindu, the Bihar Musalman and the Bihar Hindu, the Bengal Musalman and the Bengal Hindu, the Deccan Musalman and the Deccan Hindu, and the Bombay Musalman and the Bombay Hindu. In Punjab, both Hindus and Muslims spoke Punjabi. In Sindh, both spoke Sindhi, in Bengal, Bengali. In Gujarat, both spoke Gujarati; and in Maharashtra, Marathi. It was only in towns that the Musalmans spoke Urdu and the Hindus the language of the province. But outside, in the mofussil, there was complete linguistic unity between Hindus and Musalmans.

Social and cultural life of the two communities also shared many commonalities. The social life of many Muslim groups was honeycombed with Hindu customs. For instance, the Awans of the Punjab, though nearly all Muslims, retained Hindu names and kept their genealogies in the Brahmanic fashion. Hindu surnames were also found among Muslims. Chaudhari was a Hindu surname but also common among the Musalmans of United Province and northern India. In the matter of marriage, certain groups of Muslims either followed only the Hindu ceremonies or performed the ceremony first by following the Hindu rites and then called the Qazi and had it performed in the Muslim form. Some sections of Muslim law applied the Hindu law in the matter of marriage, guardianship and inheritance. Before the Shariat Act was passed, this was true even in the Punjab and the North-West Frontier Province. In the social sphere, the caste system was alleged to be as much a part of Muslim society as it was of Hindu society. In the religious sphere, many Muslim pirs had Hindu disciples; and similarly some Hindu yogis had Muslim chelas. The tombs of two ascetics, Jamali Sultan and Diyal Bhawan, who lived in close amity during the early part of the nineteenth century, stood close to one another, and were revered by Hindus and Musalmans alike in Girot, Punjab. Bawa Fathu, a Muslim saint, who lived around AD 1700 and whose tomb is at Ranital in the Kangra district, received the title of prophet by the blessing of Guru Gulab Singh. Baba Shahana, a Hindu saint whose cult was observed in the Jhang district, was the chela of a Muslim pir who changed his original name Mihra to Mir Shah.

After the Lahore Resolution, the forgotten past of the two communities reappeared and rapidly took a violent form. Suddenly, it appeared that as in the past, they were just two armed battalions warring against each other. The bitter memories of the methods of the invaders – destruction of temples and forced conversions, with spoliation of property, slaughter, enslavement and abasement of men, women and children – were revived. The things that divided became far more vital than the things which united them. The political and religious antagonisms now divided Hindus and Musalmans far more deeply than the so-called common things which were able to bind them together. The stark dissimilarities in Islamic and the original Aryan culture in this north-west corner of India surfaced strongly. Their past of mutual animosities, both in the political as well as in the religious fields, had become their present.

In the elections of 1945-46, the Congress, Akali Dal and the Unionists were able to contain the League's growing march. The Congress was the second-largest party bagging 51 seats and the Unionist Party got 20 seats. The Akali Sikhs acquired 22 seats and 7 seats were won by independent candidates. But the Muslim League was able to displace the Unionists in Punjab. It emerged as the leading party with 75 out of 86 Muslim seats in the Punjab province. The League won all 11 of the urban seats and 64 out of 75 rural constituencies in the elections. Further, six members of the Unionists left the party, leaving it only with fourteen members.

A coalition ministry was formed by 51 Congress members, 22 Akali Sikhs and 10 Unionists under Khizar Hayat Tiwana. He headed a Muslim-minority Unionist coalition government in a province where a large number of officers and employees were Muslims and openly sympathised with the League. An overwhelming number of officers and men in the police force being Muslims, they were also more loyal to the League than to the government. With the formation of the Congress–Akali–Unionist ministry in a Muslim-majority province, communal differences were sharply accentuated. Muslims observed 7 and 9 March as 'Traitors' Day'. Communal riots erupted in Amritsar on 15 March, gravely threatening to spread to Jullundur and Hisar but were somehow averted. In May 1946, communal riots erupted in Jhansi and Bareilly, killing many people. Communal trouble also spread to a number of other places. A serious communal riot lashed Patna district on 18 May followed by communal trouble in Peshawar and Hazara. The slogan '*Khun Se Lenge Pakistan*' was gathering strength.

Amidst this turmoil, the call for 'Direct Action' given by Jinnah on 29 July 1946 marked a turning point in the country's communal landscape. Announced as a political demonstration, the agitation quickly degenerated into a communal riot of the worst type and led to what came to be known as the 'Great Killing' in the communal riots in Calcutta from 16 to 20 August 1946. Property worth crores of rupees was damaged. Within the short span of three days from 16 to 19 August, the people of Calcutta hacked, battered, burned, stabbed or shot 6,000 of each other to death, and raped and maimed another 20,000. The dreadful slaughter turned Calcutta into a charnel house for seventy hours in August 1946. It wasn't just murder of many innocent people, but also killing of hopes. It changed the shape of India and the course of history. The corpses of men, women and children lay stinking in the gutters of Chowringhee until the vultures picked them clean. With every mouthful, they pecked away at the fabric of a united India, and finally split it in two.

The Bengal carnage had an inevitable fallout in neighbouring Bihar, and its reverberations were felt in several other provinces. There were clashes in Delhi, Benares, Allahabad, Gorakhpur, Etawah and many faraway places. By the end of the year, more than 4,000 people had become victims of communal violence.

In February 1947 many Muslim League leaders were arrested in Lahore. However, soon after, under pressure and protests from the League, Khizar Hayat ordered their release. The government banned Muslim League National Guard and the RSS but they continued their protest despite the ban. The ban on the two organisations was lifted later.

On 20 February 1947, British Prime Minister Atlee announced that the British would exit India in June 1948 and that before leaving, they would transfer power to responsible Indian hands. But the questions of whom and how the power would be transferred remained unclear. This accelerated the struggle for power between the Congress and the Muslim League. It was this confusion that created a situation of uncertainty in India, particularly in the Punjab. It wasn't just a question of minority versus majority. Essentially it represented a struggle for power in the province of the Punjab. Hectic activity started in Punjab to dominate the political landscape. Towards the end of February 1947, some political activist Muslim women succeeded in removing the Union Jack from the Punjab Civil Secretariat, Lahore, and hoisting the Muslim League flag in its place. Unable to withstand the League's pressure Khizar Hayat resigned from the premiership on 2 March.

Nawab Iftikhar Hussain Mamdot, leader of the Muslim League, staked a claim before the governor to form a ministry. Protests erupted in Lahore. A few Muslim policemen fired on the protestors. Many peaceful protestors were killed and over hundred injured in the firing. This culminated in a riot situation on the same evening as tension escalated between Muslims and Hindus. On top of it, an enraged Master Tara Singh appealed for supreme sacrifice by Hindus and Sikhs to save their country, religion and land. Next day Lahore was up in flames. The communal tension spread like wildfire engulfing places miles away like Amritsar, Jullundur, Rawalpindi and Sialkot. The British decided it would not be proper to let the Nawab form the government in this situation. The governor suspended the Constitution and from 5 March 1947, Punjab was to be governed directly by the governor under Section 93 of the Government of India Act.

Lord Louis Mountbatten arrived in India in March 1947 as the last viceroy of India to oversee its decolonisation. At the time of his arrival, the whole country was in an unsettled state. Mountbatten's main aim was to hand over power as early as possible. He wanted to take on board important leaders, parties, and communities, who could be a potential threat to the peaceful transfer of power. It was his opinion that only negotiated settlement among the three parties could guarantee the success of his mission. After his arrival, Mountbatten met a wide range of Indian politicians, as early as April 1947. He concluded that the only solution that could bring the three main communities, Muslims, Hindus and Sikhs, into some acceptable agreement was the partition of India, including the partition of the Punjab and Bengal, on communal lines. For him, the division of the Punjab along communal lines was a logical corollary of Jinnah's two-nation theory.

In the meantime, in March 1947, the Congress passed a resolution and demanded the division of the Punjab irrespective of India's partition. It believed that non-Muslims were under severe threat of local Muslim domination. Sikh leaders unanimously endorsed the Congress demand for the partition of Punjab on a communal, namely, Muslim and non-Muslim, basis. In the aftermath of killings of Sikhs and Hindus that occurred in Rawalpindi, Attock and Multan districts, Sikh leaders and the Congress demanded partition of the province. This was a few days before Mountbatten's arrival in India.

Mountbatten promptly concluded that differences between the Muslim League and the Congress were irreconcilable and that partition was the only expedient option for independence. He went back to London to discuss his plan with his superiors. The stage was set for India's partition.

For many Indian Muslims, who supported the notion of a separate country based on religion, Mountbatten's helplessness was just the impetus needed for fruition of their goals. They were jubilant. For the majority of Hindus, it was a development beyond their comprehension. The nation was going to suffer disintegration and bloodshed, and change the fortunes of millions of peace-loving Hindus, Sikhs and Muslims living in West and East Punjab, who would get engulfed in the fire of violence sparked by short-sighted and sectarian politicians. Millions of innocent people would be forced to flee their homeland of many generations. Among those to suffer this fate were the inhabitants of Rodu Sultan and the Batra family. It was around this time that Ram Lal left Lahore for Rodu Sultan.

3

The Great Betrayal

Kesar Dass lay bare-chested on the charpoy, staring at the night sky. His hands resting under his head to cushion it from the rough jute ropes beneath, unmindful of the cushioned mattress kept unfolded under his feet. The light from the vast expanse of twinkling stars cast a soft glow over the sleeping village below. The cool April night air was a welcome respite from the warm days when the loo made it impossible to step out. The sound of crickets chirping in the distance filled the air. On any other day, all this would lull him into a peaceful slumber. But not today. The conversation of family elders from the evening still echoed in his mind as he wondered how events might unfold in the coming days.

He was not scared for himself but afraid for the safety of his ageing parents, wife, children and others in the family. He turned to look at his wife, Bhagwanti Devi, sound asleep on a cot next to his. Her face was as calm as ever. Like him, she also did not use a pillow under the head. Bhagwanti was his second marriage as was hers to him. His first wife Shanta had passed away soon after giving birth to Gobind, their youngest child. He loved Shanta and did not want to remarry. But his parents prevailed over him. The children were too young, they needed a mother, he was counselled.

Beside Bhagwanti's cot, their two daughters, Dayavanti and Sumitra, slept peacefully on a cot. Seventeen-year-old Dayavanti, fondly called Daya by her parents, was the eldest of all the siblings. She had already been engaged to a boy who worked in Punjab government's irrigation department and was posted in Faridkot. A year younger to Daya, Sumitra was born out of Bhagwanti's first marriage. Kesar loved Sumitra no less than his own daughter Daya. Ram Saran, the elder son, the same age as Sumitra, lay fast asleep on the cot on his left. The youngest of all, Gobind, was sleeping in the courtyard below next to his grandmother. He thought of his six affectionate sisters – Bano, Bhandi, Veera, Chando, Bassi and Kaki – some older, some younger. The family was closely bonded although they did not display their affection much.

'*Hun tera bharosa hae, Bhagwan* (We are now in your care, God),' Kesar prayed.

In that moment, lying on the rooftop of the village house, Kesar felt a compelling connection to the land and the village people. The sense of belonging was palpable, as if the very earth beneath him was cradling him in its embrace. He closed his eyes and muttered a prayer to Lord Shiva.

In the courtyard below, Tulsi Dass too was unable to sleep as the thought of uncertain times ahead haunted him. His instincts warned him that the situation was dire. The thought of the looming uncertainty perturbed him. He kept shuffling in his bed as sleep eluded him. He got up and started strolling from one end of the courtyard to the other. Walking always calmed him besides helping in thinking clearly. His weathered face bore a pensive frown, eyes distant, as he contemplated the impending challenges, the walking stick tapping softly against the ground, echoing his unease.

Like Ram Lal, Tulsi Dass was also convinced that the violence and bloodshed that had erupted between Hindus and Muslims in other parts of Punjab was bound to reach their village soon. Although he trusted his Muslims neighbours, he knew that in the face of a frenzied mob, they too would be rendered helpless. He realised that they were no longer safe, and going to Kalanor was the only option. The very thought of leaving Jhang devastated him. Jhang was his home, his life, his everything. His parents and before that his father's parents, all had lived and died on this land. The land had been passed down through their forefathers, and both Nand Lal and he had worked hard to produce a good quantity of cotton, wheat, gram and even enough vegetables through the year. The notion of leaving it all behind was like a dagger to his heart. He kept shuffling in his bed as sleep eluded him. Eventually, he decided to walk under the open sky.

Rodu Sultan, his fields, and family were his comfort zone. He did not like stepping beyond his village. Barring a trip to Haridwar every three to four years, he had stopped travelling. Whenever Raj Rani expressed a wish to visit her parents in Kalanor, he would prevail over her to invite them to Rodu Sultan. Travelling tired him and his knees hurt when he walked for a long time. Although he did not know his exact age but from what his mother told him, he was born a year or two before or after Queen Victoria became *Malika-e-Hindustan* (Queen of India) in 1877. So he must be in his late sixties, he guessed. At this age, he didn't have the will or strength left to make the long journey in the summer heat. He considered himself fortunate to have lived that long; his father, uncles and before them, their forefathers all had died in their fifties from one epidemic or the other.

Earlier in the evening, Tulsi Dass had put up a bold face in the presence of the entire family so that they did not panic. He had to act wisely as they all trusted him. But within, he was a shaken man. He was consumed with worry and fear for the safety of his family and the future of their ancestral home. The house, a large kothi, no less a haveli, had been passed down three generations. It was bought from one of the Sayyads of Jhang Sialan. Their fourteen cows and buffaloes, about a dozen hens and roosters, two oxen and two camels for the carts were no less than family members. The thought of leaving them behind was unbearable.

His mind was engulfed by a storm of emotions – grief, anger, fear, and helplessness. Their land was not just soil to him; it was his identity, heritage, and the fruit of generations of labour. The idea of abandoning it, even if for a few months, felt like severing a part of his soul. The fields, village, rivers and air around him were intertwined with memories of his ancestors, childhood, and the life he had built. The safety of his loved ones weighed heavily on his conscience, forcing him to prioritise survival over sentiment. Yet, leaving felt like a betrayal of his roots, filling him with guilt and shame. Anger simmered within him – anger at the political forces that tore apart his world, at the violence that made this exodus inevitable, and at the injustice of losing everything he held dear. He felt powerless, caught in a tide of history he couldn't control.

He felt a profound sense of betrayal by the political leaders who had exposed their prosperous province to division, violence and chaos. Punjab had witnessed relatively fewer disturbances among various religious communities as compared to the communal disturbances in other parts of India. Its record was much better when compared to that of other provinces like Bengal, UP, Bihar, and the NWFP where political developments had a profound impact on the communal relations among the major religious communities. Although subtle tensions between Hindus and Muslims, sparked by the League and fanned by the British, had started surfacing in Punjab over the last decade, Multan had remained largely unaffected and peaceful. But the Rawalpindi massacre was a severe blow to mutual camaraderie and intercommunal harmony. This was not something the Sikhs would let go of without a suitable revenge. Jhang would not stay insulated for long, Tulsi Dass's instincts told him.

As a prominent merchant and landowning community in Punjab, the Punjabi Khatris had long played a pivotal role in the region's politics and economy. The Khatris of Jhang and Multan, who had traditionally enjoyed good relations with Muslims, were dismayed by the League's Lahore Resolution. They felt that it would destroy the unity and prosperity of their province. The Unionist Party had also shown no less perfidy. The Khatris also felt disillusioned by the Congress's lacklustre response to the League's demand. As communal tensions escalated and the shadow of Partition loomed, their trust in their leaders started to shatter. The most profound betrayal had now come from the Congress leadership which had, seven years after the Lahore Resolution, agreed to partition Punjab on religious lines to curb the unstoppable communal violence.

How will they partition the province? Tulsi Dass wondered. Partitioning Punjab, for that matter India, on religious lines was an impossible task. In the case of the North-West Frontier Province, Balochistan and Sindh, the Hindus and the Muslims were intermixed. In these provinces a case for territorial separation for the Hindus seemed impossible. The layout of the population of the Hindus and the Muslims in West and East Punjab was totally different from the other three provinces.

Non-Muslims in the Punjab and Bengal did not live in small islands in the midst of and surrounded by a vast Muslim population spread over the entire surface as was the case with the North-West Frontier Province, Balochistan and Sindh. In Bengal and the Punjab, Hindus occupied two different areas, contiguous and severable. In these circumstances, there was no reason to concede what the Muslim League seemed to demand.

Tulsi Dass hoped that the people of Jhang would hold their composure and not get swayed by the events in other parts of Punjab. He could warrant for his own people in Rodu Sultan and adjacent villages but had little control beyond that on Muslims in the seventy-two villages and hamlets where many members of their own biradari lived alongside Muslims, mostly Sayyads and Sials. In Rodu Sultan and adjacent villages, Muslims were mostly Qureshis. Mukhtyar himself was from a prominent Qureshi family of the region. Mukhtyar's ancestors owned large tracts of land in Jhang on both sides of the Chenab and up in the bar. They sold much of it to the Batras over years as they migrated to

Jhang from Sialkot and Gujranwala during the eighteenth century, seeking opportunities in the booming trade and agriculture of the region. They formed guilds that controlled the market for essential commodities such as grain, cotton, etc. Their business acumen and extensive trade networks contributed significantly to the region's economy.

Over time, they acquired large estates and developed irrigation systems, transforming Jhang into a fertile and prosperous region. Mukhtyar's late father, Sarhad Alam, eventually settled in Shorkot and made home in Rodu Sultan. Sarhad and Tulsi became good friends. Sarhad was a few years older in age and considered Tulsi no less than his own younger brother. Sarhad had passed away three years ago. Mukhtyar respected Tulsi like his own father. Their families shared a warm shareeka, celebrating each other's functions and standing by in their sorrows and adversities. Mukhtyar could be trusted.

Tulsi Dass decided that he would go to meet Mukhtyar before the biradari meet and discuss the way forward with him.

Too tired to walk anymore, Tulsi Dass again reclined on the bed and tried to sleep. Finally, sleep started to engulf his senses. He dreamt that he was standing on the mound two kos beyond their fields. This was his favourite spot in the entire Jhang, particularly at dawn. As a young boy, he would climb atop with his cousins and friends to admire the broad expanses of Shorkot, his village Rodu Sultan, and the fields owned by his family. Standing there now, he saw the sea of grass rippling in the breeze as it turned yellow with the first rays of the sun carpeting the earth. In the distance, the blue water in the Wakefield Wah canal turned into a silver ribbon as daylight cast its reflection on it. Towards the river, long stretches of wheat ready for harvest brought a broad smile on his face. Beyond the river, rose dark against the horizon the trees growing around villages. Bands of kikar trees huddled around the wells. Groves of date palms were scattered here and there. The passages leading to wells and hutments were dotted with ber shrubs.

He could see in the distance the remains of an ancient canal. Legend goes that it was the work of a rich banker of Bhera, whose daughter was married to a resident of one of the Jhang Vichanh villages, the lowest part of the triangle between the Jhelum and the Chenab. When the daughter reached her husband's home, she complained to her father of the scanty supply of water. Her father at once cut the canal to put an end to her trouble. Another version by the elders told of the daughter who vowed that she would not marry the man to whom she was betrothed, unless she could get to his house by water without putting foot to the ground; so her father forthwith proceeded to excavate this canal.

As Tulsi Dass stood there, still dreaming, steeped in nostalgia, his thoughts wandered to memories of his childhood spent in the village and many years in Shorkot where he went to study in the secondary school. The images of the small town of Shorkot flashed before him – the fine bazaar with a gate at each end, lined with tenanted shops built on a uniform plan, a garden, the tehsil and police buildings. He recalled how he and his friends would sneak into the canal rest-house on summer afternoons when the chowkidar took his afternoon nap. There was a large garden attached to the guesthouse full of mango trees laden with the juiciest, thickest and the most aromatic mangoes in Jhang. They would pluck a bagful of ripe mangoes and carry them to their favourite spot – the large hollow to the east of the town created by mining of some material that had turned into a fine tiny lake.

The images of the past faded and he saw his parents appear before him. His mother affectionately placed her hand on his head and his father stood there, his eyes blessing him. Raj Rani also appeared, standing behind his parents, her eyes full of love and respect for him. Tulsi Dass tried to stand up to touch his mother's feet but could not move. He felt as if he had been pinned to the cot with hundreds of nails. He wanted to shout for help but his voice didn't comply. He struggled to free himself but could not move an inch. He looked at his parents helplessly. His wife continued to look at him calmly. Suddenly, his father stepped forward and extended his hand inviting Tulsi Dass to hold it. To his relief, this time he could get up from the cot effortlessly. His face lit up. His father whispered something softly and turned to leave. His mother followed his father. Tulsi Dass joined them, one step behind. Raj Rani stood watching from a distance.

It was Raj Rani's wailing in the morning that announced Tulsi Dass had passed away in sleep.

A sombre mood enveloped the air as news spread of the sudden passing of Tulsi Dass. Men, elderly and young, dropped whatever they were doing and left for Kesar Dass's house, their faces etched with grief. The village square, usually bustling with activity and laughter, now stood silent and solemn. Women hurriedly wrapped up chores at home so that they could also leave to be with the women of the Batra family to share their grief. The relatives started preparing lunch comprising rice, daal and roti for the grieving family members, while the women of neighbouring houses made arrangements for tea and chaanch to be served to the visitors through the day knowing that the kitchens in houses of the Batra brothers would stay idle for a few days as a ritual.

Tulsi Dass's body had been placed on the baithak floor with cotton balls and a bunch of tulsi leaves placed in his nostrils and ears. Marigold flowers had been placed on him. An earthen lamp had been lit on a mound of wheat flour kneaded with water next to his head, symbolising the light that would guide the soul. Narain Dass, Ram Lal, Kesar Dass, Nand Lal and a few other men of the family sat cross-legged on a khes spread on the floor, at a short distance from where Tulsi Dass lay lifeless. Fragrance of incense sticks wafted in the room. The sound of gentle weeping of the women and their whispered prayers emanating from the courtyard nearby created a poignant symphony of sorrow and reverence.

After paying their last respects to Tulsi Dass, the elderly men muttered a word or two in condolence to Narain and placed their hand on the boy's head. The young offered help of any kind that may be needed over the mourning period. After sitting in the room for a few minutes as a tradition, they would leave to make room for other visitors and congregate under the shade of the neem tree in the compound where Subhash, Ram Lal's son, and Nand Lal's friends served them water and tea. They sat in a circle, their heads bowed in reflection as they shared memories of the departed soul. Younger men helped Binder, the owner of the only tent house in Rodu Sultan, erect the shamiana to provide shade to the entire compound. Binder had also placed some crockery in the courtyard. No one had to tell him anything. Although he had brought his helpers along, today Binder felt it was his duty to lead from the front. Not only was Kesar Dass his friend, Binder had started his business with financial support from Tulsi Dass and felt eternally indebted to the family.

Inside, in the courtyard, Binder placed mattresses on the floor and covered them with white sheets. Soon, the courtyard was filled with siahpa, the wailing of women. They would start crying as soon as they entered the compound with their heads covered as they passed the men gathered there. Inside, their wailing would get louder for a while as they consoled each other, pausing occasionally to pass on instructions to the young girls about the rituals to be observed. In Punjabi villages, the raw wailing and mourning is a deeply emotional and culturally significant expression of grief. When a death occurs, women gather to mourn collectively, their cries echoing through the village as a poignant testament to loss. Women beat their chests, their bodies swaying in rhythm with their lamentations. The mourning is not just personal but also communal, as women share pain.

Children, usually full of laughter and mischief, played quietly in the courtyard, their innocence a poignant contrast to the solemnity of the occasion.

All men from the village – blacksmiths, carpenters, potters, shoppers, and weavers – gathered for the funeral. Women stayed back as Hindu tradition did not encourage women and children to be present at a cremation. Many of Kesar Dass's friends lent their shoulder to his bier made of two tikti (bamboo) poles with small bamboo pieces serving as arms as the mourning crowd shouted *Ram naam satya hai* all the way to the cremation ground. The bier was placed on logs of wood, and covered by wooden logs. Pure ghee and sandalwood chips were used as auxiliaries. The family purohit performed the puja. Tulsi Dass was cremated on the ghat next to the canal in accordance with Hindu rituals with his only son, Kesar Dass, performing the last rites. Thereafter, Kesar and many other members of the family had their head shaved and put on one long piece of cloth, as a part of mandatory ritual.

After the cremation, the bereaved family thanked everyone with folded hands. From this point, the family entered a period of mourning. Men went to their houses to bathe, only to reassemble in the compound before sunset. This time, their conversation extended to matters of the village besides recalling their friendship or dealings with Tulsi Dass. Some even cursed the politicians for creating the mess that had caused the discourse of division of the country. They however stayed cautious and did not blame any community or name any political leader, mindful of the presence of members of all communities.

In the compound of Kesar's house, the scent of wood smoke from clay stoves where pots of simmering lentils and rice bubbled, permeated the air. It was customary to serve meals to the community which had joined to share the grief of the deceased's family. The langar was considered no less than prasad, the blessing of God. It had been set up by the women with the help of the children while the men were away at the funeral. As dusk descended upon the village, the priest emerged from the ancient temple at the edge of the village square, his voice resonating with solemnity as he offered prasad to the assembled mourners praying for the departed soul. Later, they were served dinner from the langar. Only Muslim men did not eat. No one found that offensive. Being culturally different, the two communities did not eat from each other's kitchen, a practice that had been observed for centuries. By no means was such refusal considered an insult to the deceased.

This moment of collective mourning blurred the boundaries of caste, creed, and gender as the shared grief united the villagers in a bond of compassion and solidarity. Through their tears and prayers, the men and women of the village paid homage to the departed elder, honouring Tulsi Dass's legacy of kindness, wisdom, and community spirit which, they prayed, would continue to guide them in the days ahead.

Throughout the day, no one in the family brought up the issue of partition or plans to leave. It was an unspoken understanding that no one would talk about it in the thirteen-day mourning period.

Over the next few days, relatives and acquaintances from faraway places began to flock to the house, having received information of Tulsi Dass's sudden demise by post.

Bhagwanti's parents and brothers were amongst the first to arrive. The bonds of fraternal solidarity and the advantages of joint living characterised the ideal set up of a Khatri family. The brihat kutumba (the great family) might not have a common shelter and a common chulah (hearth) and the members might be scattered differently in the city and even outside, but the occasions of festivities and mourning demanded participation of one and all. The participation in a marriage ceremony could be ignored, but even a distant cognate could not afford to be absent in funeral functions. This aspect made the kinship fairly strong. Only two of his six sisters, Bhandi and Veera, who lived in Multan could make it for their father's prayer meeting. The others may not even have learnt about the death of their father though telegrams had been sent to all daughters. In these troubled times, delivering telegrams was also not without disruption. Bano was old, and her knees did not support her anymore. They were all probably coping with their own struggle in the uncertainty of the impending partition. Bhandi and Veera informed that their families were winding up their business quickly and relocating to Amritsar. They were planning to move a few days after they returned to Multan.

Kesar went to the cremation ground every day to fill the water in a pitcher especially hung from the branch of a tree. The ashes were collected on the fourth day and immersed in the Chenab after visiting the shrine of Hazrat Sultan Bahoo to seek his blessings. On the tenth day, before sunrise, Bhagwanti's family provided clothes and cash to the widowed Raj Rani at the Kapradalna ceremony, as was the ritual. The mourning ended on the thirteenth day after the offering of the pindas and performance of obsequial rites. Bhagwanti's father tied the turban around the head of his son-in-law. With that, Kesar assumed the status of the head of the family after Tulsi Dass. This ceremony corresponded to the ancient Murdhabhisheka, the consecration of the head of the family. Brahmins and members of the community were fed a simple meal consisting of puri, aloo (potatoes) cooked in onion and tomato curry, with buttermilk. The Brahmins were given a number of items ranging from foodgrain, to bed, clothing and materials that were of interest and taste to the departed soul of Tulsi Dass, for his use in the other world. With these ceremonies, Kesar Dass, who had lit the pyre, became pure.

The Batra clan had a new head in Kesar Dass. The middle-aged Kesar was quite different in temperament from his father. He was a thinker, and an introvert. Unlike his father, he neither spoke much nor believed in long discussions. He worked hard but enjoyed being with his few friends.

He had many disagreements with his father but respected him and honoured his decisions without any argument. In appearance, too, they were different. Kesar Dass was shorter but much well-built. He did not roll up his heavy moustache at the ends, like his father did. Kesar Dass casually wrapped a cloth around his head, never wearing a proper pagdi, while his father preferred to tie the headgear in a traditional way, by carefully forming layers of folding and tucking of the long white cloth before tying the ends of the cloth to secure an elaborate head covering. It had a distinctive shape peculiar to Punjabis from Jhang Sial. The tall pagdi made him look taller than his actual height.

Kesar Dass felt the weight of a world collapsing on his shoulders. The sudden demise of his father wasn't just a personal tragedy; it was a devastating blow to the family's fragile stability amidst the brewing storm of Partition. The looming threat of migration amplified his anxieties. Yet, beneath the many apprehensions, a steely determination began to solidify. He saw the hope, fear, and helplessness reflected in his mother's eyes, and a new-found resolve surged through him. He would navigate this turbulent period, not unscathed, but with every ounce of courage he could muster, for the sake of those who depended on him, and for the sake of his ancestors, he resolved.

Meanwhile, Rodu Sultan anxiously awaited further news from Delhi. All eyes were fixated on Mountbatten's impending return from London.

4
The Mountbatten Plan

It had been over a month since Tulsi Dass's demise. Life in the village was slowly limping back to normal. It was the third day of the month of June. The residents of Rodu Sultan gathered around their radios in the evening. Many assembled in the small courtyard of the panchayat office where a timeworn radio had been placed on a table. The members of Kesar Dass's family also huddled in the courtyard. All-India Radio had been making repeated announcements that Mountbatten would announce the plan for the British exit and handing over of the country. They all waited with anxious hearts for the broadcast to start.

Mountbatten had just returned from London apparently carrying approval for the plan. In his address, he was expected to announce the plan. Nehru, Jinnah and Baldev Singh, leader of the Sikh community, would speak after him, the announcement said.

Mountbatten spoke first, exhorting that if the transfer of power was to be effected in a peaceful and orderly manner, every 'single one of us' must bend all his efforts to the task.

> For more than a hundred years, hundreds of millions of you have lived together, and this country has been administered as

> a single entity, but it has been impossible to obtain agreement on any plan that would preserve the unity of India. But there can be no question of coercing any large areas in which one community has a majority to live, against their will under a government in which another community has a majority. The only alternative to coercion is partition. The whole plan may not be perfect but like all plans its success will depend on the spirit of goodwill in which it is carried out … This is no time for bickering, much less for the continuation in any shape or form of the disorders and lawlessness of the past few months … May your decisions be wisely guided and may they be carried out in the peaceful and friendly spirit of the Gandhi–Jinnah appeal.

His words sounded hollow and unconvincing.

After he had finished, the full plan was read out in detail in Hindi by a translator. It stated that the British government in London had decided to create a new and separate Constituent Assembly in addition to the existing Assembly. The new Assembly would comprise representatives of areas not part of the existing Constituent Assembly and would have twenty-one members in all from Punjab of which sixteen would be Muslim, four Sikh, and nine Hindu. It would determine the authority or authorities to whom power would be transferred on independence. The Imperial Government proposed to introduce legislation for transfer of power much ahead of June 1948 as earlier proposed. The legislative assembly of Punjab would meet in two parts, one representing the Muslim-majority districts and the other, the remaining districts, and pass resolutions and vote separately on whether or not the province should be partitioned. If the decision involved partition, a boundary commission would be set up by the Governor-General which would demarcate the boundaries of the two parts of Punjab on the basis of contiguous majority areas of Muslims and non-Muslims. For the purpose of determining the religion-wise population of a district, the 1941 census figures were to be taken as authoritative. The Muslim-majority districts in the Punjab and Bengal were set out in the appendix to the text of the announcement.

The statement clearly established, in broad terms, the predetermined contours of the two states of India and Pakistan. The demarcation of districts as proposed was only for ascertaining the wishes of the members of the legislative assemblies.

Mountbatten consoled Sikhs by cleverly cushioning the blow with the following announcement:

> We have given very careful consideration to the position of the Sikhs. This valiant community forms about an eighth of the population of Punjab, but they are so distributed that any partition of the province will inevitably divide them. All of us who have the good of the Sikh community at heart are very sorry to think that the partition of Punjab, which they themselves desire, cannot avoid splitting them to a greater or lesser extent ... the exact degree of the split (sic) will be left to the Boundary Commission on which they will of course be represented.

This was intended to keep the Sikhs quiet, knowing full well that the final outcome of the Boundary Commission award was not likely to meet the Sikh demands in any way.

Nehru spoke next, continuing in English and Hindi. The proposals gave him no joy in his heart, he said, but he had no doubt that it was the correct course. 'It may be', he said, tellingly, 'that this way we reach that united India sooner than otherwise.' At his usual poetic self, Nehru stated, 'We are little men serving great causes, but because the cause is great, something of that greatness falls upon us also. There has been shameful, degrading, and revolting violence in various parts of the country. This must end. We are determined to end it. Standing on a watershed of the past and the future, the people of India should forget all bitterness and adhere to the ideals they cherished. The good of the 400,000,000 Indians must be our supreme objective,' he said. 'Let there be moderation in speech and writing,' he stressed.

His address was followed by Jinnah who spoke in English. He declared that although Mountbatten's plan did not meet the Muslim point of view, the Muslims were ready to consider the proposal and share their comments. He paid tribute to Mountbatten and his 'highest sense of fairness and impartiality'. He seemed excited to be addressing the people through the medium of the powerful instrument of radio. It was the first time many Indians were actually hearing his voice. He appealed to every community and particularly to Muslims to maintain peace and order. Everyone should help ensure that independence was delivered in a peaceful and orderly manner, he asserted. His speech wasn't quite a full acceptance but it was taken to be so by everyone listening to the broadcast. Jinnah could not hide his elation and euphoria for having realised his dream and ended the speech with the words 'Pakistan zindabad', which hardly befitted the occasion. It was the first time this term was heard over the radio although it had been mentioned in print media for some years now. The speech was then translated into Urdu.

Baldev Singh spoke last and most prosaically. 'We have closed a dreary chapter,' he said, 'and a new leaf is now turned. It would be untrue to say I am altogether happy. Seldom has a settlement like this been tarnished with so much fear and sorrow.' It did not please the Sikh community, he said, but urged its acceptance.

Attlee made a simultaneous statement in London. As expected, he made it a point to underscore that power was going to be transferred in accordance with the wishes of the Indian people. At the behest of major political parties in India, the intention of the British government was to transfer power to the two dominions as expeditiously as possible, he declared.

The broadcast left everyone stunned into an angry silence. Only one thought crossed their mind: Jinnah had finally succeeded in his design to get a separate country for the Muslims by dividing Bharat.

It was the first time the whole country had heard definitively what Pakistan was to be. They couldn't bring themselves to the terms of a plebiscite in the North-West Frontier Province, and the assemblies in the Punjab and Bengal deciding on partition and future affiliation of their provinces. Bringing forward the date of independence by almost a year from mid-1948 only meant adding further chaos to the already tumultuous situation. What devastated people was the Congress reneging from its pledge to an Akhand Hindustan (undivided Hindustan) made less than a year back during the 1946 election campaign.

Nonetheless, it was a momentous evening for India. Mountbatten had formally announced the plan of handing over power to India. But for Punjabis, the announcement confirmed their worst fears. Not only the country was being partitioned, the provisional plan conferred seventeen districts of Punjab to Pakistan and only twelve to East Punjab. The entire Lahore division with the exception of the district of Amritsar was to be given to West Punjab. Of course, it was said that the division was provisional and if no consensus was reached, a boundary commission would finally decide the line that would demarcate Punjab but that only meant people would be kept on tenterhooks over the next few months. They would not know till the very last day where some of the hotly contested areas would go. Among these areas was the heart of the Punjab, the capital city of Lahore. West Bengal also faced similar injustice although the inclusion of Calcutta in Hindustan gave some satisfaction. Yet Mountbatten's plan left crucial questions unanswered: Where was India and where was Pakistan? Who was an Indian or a Pakistani?

'*Laanat hain*, shame on our leaders,' Narain Dass said grimly. He was the eldest of all present. 'Have they given Jhang to Pakistan?' he inquired.

'No one knows yet. The plan is tentative but yes, it appears that as of now it is slated to go to Pakistan,' Kesar Dass said as if trying to assure himself, contrary to what they had all just heard.

Everyone tried to comprehend the implications of what had just unfolded. They wondered, what next? The abadi of Rodu Sultan comprised largely of Batras. There were also many Qureshis who were descendants of Pir Fatah Khan, but they were in a minority. Muslims formed nearly 83 per cent of Jhang's total population which meant that the district would go to Pakistan's share.

After hours-long deliberation, it was decided to meet again in a few days to assess the developments in Delhi and decide next steps. The appeal for peace made by Jinnah gave them hope that the violence would subside and people from all communities would now await the outcome of decisions taken in the Assembly and the Boundary Commission report. The meeting dispersed and everyone scrambled out in a hurry to get back home to firm up their own little plans in the larger scheme of decisions taken.

Only a day before, in a meeting called by Mountbatten at his house, the Indian political leadership had conveyed their in-principle approval to the proposed plan. Held in the viceroy's study overlooking the fabulous Mughal Gardens (now called Amrit Udyan), Nehru and Patel represented the Congress, along with Congress president, J.B. Kripalani. Jinnah, Liaquat Ali Khan and Sardar Abdur Rab Nishtar, the minister for communications in the provisional government, represented the League while Baldev Singh represented the Sikhs. Mountbatten updated them about his discussions with Attlee in London and provided details of the plan which he stated was not much of a deviation from its original version submitted by V.P. Menon in May.

Mountbatten declared in the meeting that both India and Pakistan would have to become members of the British Commonwealth; both countries would choose a Governor-General; and British officers could continue to serve in both the civilian administration as well the forces. To everyone's dismay, Mountbatten informed that the British exit had been advanced and would now happen in two-and-a-half months' time, on 15 August 1947, a year ahead of June 1948 as earlier announced. The parliamentary session in the Westminster Parliament was to end in late July, and the plan was proposed to be passed as a bill before that, he apprised.

The meeting had ended with Mountbatten asking the political leaders to take copies of the plan and obtain the written consent and agreement of their parties by the end of the day as he intended to broadcast the plan worldwide the following evening. Mountbatten had requested only Nehru and Jinnah to broadcast news after his announcement of the Partition plan. However, Nehru made a suggestion that Sardar Baldev Singh should also broadcast his acceptance. Baldev Singh at first demurred. He felt that he would have nothing to say. But he was persuaded to change his mind and at least to make a call to end the violence.

Jinnah protested. Later in the evening, he went to see Mountbatten and expressed his reluctance to take the plan to the League. Mountbatten reprimanded him and told him he had no choice. The plan and its execution were a fait-accompli. Kripalani, as Congress president, sent Congress's acceptance letter to Mountbatten with some suggestions.

The riots in Punjab in early 1947 pushed the Congress towards Partition and the British towards an abdication of their Indian empire. Frustrated by the experience of governing in coalition with the Muslim League and deadlocked constitutional negotiations, the Congress leadership saw Partition as a way out of the impasse, as a means of bringing an end to violence, as a way to consolidate their power while pushing the League to the margins of the subcontinent, and as an opportunity to undermine the status of the princely states.

Baldev Singh also communicated acceptance of the plan, but with many suggestions for amendments. Jinnah could play for time no longer. This was yet another clever move, for, if Baldev Singh had not extended his support for the plan, the opposition to it by the Sikhs would have been even more pronounced. In another sense, this also meant that, in public perception, Nehru became a representative of Hindus, Jinnah of Muslims, and Baldev Singh of the Sikhs, at least insofar as the acceptance of the partition plan by the three major communities was concerned.

The same party reassembled on Partition announcement day. Mountbatten informed that all three parties had accepted the plan albeit with some proposed amendments which had no chance of being mutually acceptable, so he saw no point in discussing them further. The meeting broke up agreeing that the broadcasts would go ahead that evening.

With the acceptance of the plan by Nehru, Jinnah and Baldev Singh, the die was finally cast for the partition of India.

In Delhi, Lahore and other places, leaders from all political parties went into a huddle to decide their next move after Mountbatten's address and focus on the reality of what Partition actually meant.

Besides Partition and handing over of power by the British, there were other critical matters to be dealt with, the most significant being the thirty-page document titled 'The Administrative Consequences of Partition'. It explained the different components of the Indian government and its bureaucracy that warranted division. It was a daunting list. Starting with the armed forces, it included government staff and their records, railways, post and telegraphs; broadcasting; civil aviation; meteorology; public works; tax; customs and excise; accounts and audit; scientific services; waterways; power; government buildings and installations; the Reserve Bank and currency holdings; jurisdiction and the courts; powers of domicile and diplomatic representation. It recommended a Partition Committee to undertake the management of this immense and complicated portfolio. The Partition Council was set up in Delhi to carry out the vast process of working out the process of dividing assets between the future dominions of India and Pakistan. The Council made a joint statement giving full assurances of protection to minorities in both dominions.

Master Tara Singh was upset with the Mountbatten Plan. He issued a statement expressing dissatisfaction with the proposal. He said Sikhs felt betrayed and cheated as there was a total lack of provision in the Mountbatten Plan to give the Sikhs any power or status anywhere or even for safeguarding their position or interests. The ultimate acceptance or rejection of the Mountbatten Plan by the Sikhs would depend a good deal on the terms of reference given to the Boundary Commission, he declared. He announced that any plan for division would not be agreeable unless the Chenab was to serve as boundary to divide Punjab, in order to maintain Sikh solidarity. The demarcation of line between East and West Punjab remained the main challenge for the Sikhs. Their cultural, linguistic, spiritual affinities, economic well-being, solidarity and integrity were being jeopardised by the proposed division of Punjab. It also posited a structured transfer of Sikh population and mentioned that Sikhs would not be satisfied unless at least 80 per cent of their population was brought into East Punjab.

While the Muslim League wanted Pakistan, they were opposed to the division of Punjab. Its leaders were keen to come to an arrangement with the Akali leaders to keep the whole, or nearly the whole, of the Punjab in Pakistan. An attempt was made to bring about rapprochement between the Sikhs and Muslims but after the wholesale massacre of Sikhs in Rawalpindi division, the latter were not open to cast their lot with Pakistan. Both the Congress and Muslim League, however, remained opposed to a formal exchange of population.

In terms of violence, Jinnah's appeal for peace had little effect as instead of abating violence, it accentuated it. Baldev Singh's speech neither offered any succour to Sikhs nor addressed their most grave concerns.

On the same day, the Hindus and Sikhs of Dera Ismail Khan who had been living peacefully were suddenly attacked; 1,200 houses were burnt down, 1,600 were looted, 2,000 Hindus and Sikhs were forcibly converted to Islam and the loss of property amounted to Rs 210 crores. As many as 1,200 people were killed. The story was repeated in Bahawalpur state. Posters were put on the city walls asking Hindus to leave or they would be murdered and looted. The actual operations for compelling the Hindus to quit were initiated in the first week of June, when complete demoralisation had seeped in their hearts.

The riots spread to the North-West Frontier Province in June. On the day following the momentous announcement, communal tensions flared up. There was unabated violence in several places – Lahore, Gurgaon, Cawnpore, Calcutta, Bombay, Multan, Benares, New Delhi, and Ahmedabad. Civic life in Lahore had been paralysed with a complete breakdown of food supplies; about a hundred houses had been destroyed by fire. There were demands once again for the imposition of martial law. These were not isolated riots; rather well-planned attacks.

However, there was an unseemly effort to downplay the situation by the British. Birth pangs are always unpleasant, especially if the result is twins!

With the announcement now behind, Evan Meredith Jenkins (last governor of Punjab province) was very anxious to get a divisible coalition government in place, consisting of members who could, when the time came, be split into two groups and form the ministries of the two new provinces carved out of Punjab. It was also decided that after 15 August, Major General Thomas Wynford Rees would operationally control the forces of the two new states in this region, and would be responsible through the supreme commander and the joint defence council, to the new governments.

After taking into his confidence the top leadership of the three main communities, Mountbatten took Punjab matters to the interim government's Cabinet meetings in order to reach a consensus concerning official policy towards the disturbances. The meeting of the Cabinet on 25 June turned out to be difficult as Mountbatten was violently attacked by leaders of both parties for the complete failure of the British to maintain law and order. Nehru demanded the sacking of every government official, from the governor downwards, on the same day. Sardar Vallabhbhai Patel also lashed against the British, asking how the British had had no difficulty in keeping law and order when they were clamping down on the Congress and the freedom movement. League leaders also criticised the British policy in Punjab and suggested that if the situation persisted in Lahore, there would soon be no city left for them to inherit.

Mountbatten obtained unanimous agreement that the Punjab governor should be invited to form a security committee composed of the local leaders representing Hindus, Muslims and Sikhs. It was also agreed that this committee should draw up a list of local officials in whom all three parties would have confidence; and that they should become operative as early as possible. He also suggested that the security committee should meet every day and that all leaders, from the high command downwards, should make every effort to call off violence. He asked the Cabinet to support him in uprooting the first signs of communal war with overwhelming force. The proposed policy was greeted with real enthusiasm by Congress and Muslim League members alike.

The Punjab Legislative Assembly adopted a resolution in favour of the partition on 23 June. The partition committee gave way to a more powerful Partition Council and the latter agreed to invite Sir Cyril Radcliffe to become chairman of the Boundary Commission.

On 27 June, Mountbatten proposed the appointment of Radcliffe as chairman of the Boundary Commission, which was accepted unanimously by the Congress and the League. The other four members of the Commission were: Justice Din Mohammad, Justice Muhammad Munir, Justice Mehar Chand Mahajan, and Justice Teja Singh. The Boundary Commission was instructed to demarcate the boundaries of two parts of the Punjab on the basis of ascertaining the contiguous majority areas of Muslims and non-Muslims. The 'notional' division of Punjab was based on the district boundaries, placing seventeen districts in West Punjab and the remaining twelve in East Punjab. However, the central districts were a sort of disputed territory, consisting of the whole or some parts of the districts of Gujranwala, Sheikhupura, and Lyallpur in the Rechna Doab; Gurdaspur, Amritsar, Lahore, and Montgomery in the Bari Doab; Jullundur and Hoshiarpur in the Bist Doab; and Firozpur on the east of the Sutlej. All parties agreed that the Boundary Commission should finish its work by 15 August.

On the call of the Shiromani Akali Dal, Sikhs observed a strike on 8 July and it was a resounding success. It received strong support from the Hindus as well. Markets remained closed in many cities and towns of the Punjab. Resolutions were passed, demanding solidarity with Sikhs, adequate share in canal waters, and protection of Sikh gurudwaras. Sitting on a huge divan in the Golden Temple complex, Master Tara Singh said that he anticipated a big struggle for their rights and exhorted the Sikhs to be prepared to vindicate their honour and make sacrifices if the award went against them. He had refused to sign a peace pledge, he said further, because it was designed to deceive the Sikhs.

Sensing the growing anxiety, Mountbatten ordered greater vigilance and military presence in the tense districts. Nehru, Jinnah and Baldev Singh appealed for peace and communal harmony. When violence began to escalate in July, the first, and ineffectual, step was the establishment of the Punjab Boundary Force. Yet violence could not be tamed by violence: not only was the size of the force inadequate considering the scale of the problem, but certain units of the force itself became implicated in the violence.

This large-scale violence was mostly fuelled by the uncertainty about the exact boundary in case the award of the Boundary Commission did not come through before 15 August. Contrary to the 3 June statement, the India Independence Bill stated that if the boundary had not been so determined by 15 August, the two new provinces shall be established on the basis of what was commonly described as the 'notional' boundary. While the Muslims were quite happy about the 'notional' boundary as it gave them Lahore and the colony districts, Hindus and the Sikhs were unhappy. Significantly, the total number of disputed districts, as pointed out by one side or the other, were as many as fourteen.

By mid-July, the provincial government was both unable and unwilling to control the violence. British officials withdrew, and the government essentially ceased functioning.

People in West Punjab were now left to fend for themselves. Tension quickly spilled over to rural parts of Jhang, which had thus far remained largely insulated from the fire of hatred and communal division tearing through the rural areas of West Punjab. Many villages in Jhang tehsil, home to close-knit communities of Hindus, Muslims and Sikhs, were turning into a microcosm of communal tension. The villages in Shorkot felt increasingly vulnerable as rumours of mob attacks, arson and forced conversions spread. Rodu Sultan was on high alert as Hindus prepared to defend themselves.

On 1 August 1947, the Partition Council set up the Punjab Boundary Force – a special military command in Punjab to check disturbances and maintain law and order. The Force proved to be ineffective.

5
Fortifying the Village

Raj Rani lay in bed, sobbing silently. The flames of the earthen oil lamps placed in the recesses cast flickering shadows on the weathered walls of the veranda. After weeks surrounded by people mourning for Tulsi Dass, she had finally found a solitary moment to grieve for the man she had been married to for nearly five decades.

Her thoughts raced back to the time when she had come to Rodu Sultan as a young bride, merely nineteen years of age. Tall and broad shouldered, she was a perfect match for the six-foot-tall and well-built Tulsi Dass. She was an imposing figure, straight-backed, with a broad forehead. Raj Rani was the only one in the entire village who was always dressed up in a sari which made her stand out elegantly amongst the other women whose customary dress was the salwar-kameez. The Muslim women dressed up no differently. Raj Rani was strong willed and caring. The motherly texture of her voice instantly won the heart of the younger members of the family. Women were in awe of her elegance. Elders, too, soon took a liking to her warm and affectionate demeanour

Hailing from the Arora clan, Raj Rani too became fond of the family in no time and adapted to their ways, which were not much dissimilar from hers back in Kalanor. Their language was also Punjabi but their dialect and accent were a little different from the way Punjabi was spoken in many parts of East Punjab. Jhangis respected their women and treated them as equals at home. When outside, their culture expected women to keep a low profile. She loved the simple life of the village surrounded by a large family consisting of the elderly, the young men and women, and children in plenty living in joint households. Although her husband had no siblings, it was not uncommon for couples to have between eight and twelve children. It was not considered an unusually big number, and raising them was not deemed to be a humongous task. A few Batras had as many as eight siblings.

Raj Rani had also grown up in a large family, and thus got swiftly accustomed to the ways of the Batras. Her social life revolved around the extended family. They shared resources, responsibilities, joys and sorrows, embodying a sense of close-knit community life. Respect for elders and strong family bonds underpinned the value system of her Jhangi in-laws. Daily life intertwined with religious rituals and festivities. The warm ways of a large family grew on her in no time.

Her day began waking up to the crowing of roosters, and the creaking sound of a water wheel as she observed Tulsi Dass pull out water from the well, a ritual he observed for decades. There were many who offered to do that for him but Tulsi Dass insisted on doing it himself. It strengthened his arm muscles, he would say.

Raj Rani would then engage in household chores. Both Tulsi and she would milk the cows and buffaloes. A woman from the village would come to make cow-dung cakes which were plastered on the wall for use as fuel and fertiliser once dried.

She would then bathe and enter the chauka, the area around the chulah, a sacred place of special preserve for the lady of the house. She entered it only after bathing and prepared the morning meal comprising parathas on the tawa or iron plate. Parathas were served with dollops of butter, pickle and sweet lassi, all home-made with the help of women helpers who lived on the village outskirts. Nobody could have his meal, except after the morning bath and a visit to the temple. Elderly men preferred fresh vegetables or leftover daal from dinner with their roti instead of parathas. On any given day, as many as twenty people would have breakfast, including family members, visitors and helpers. Everyone ate to their heart's content – it being the first of the only two meals a day they had, the other being dinner before sunset.

After breakfast, Tulsi Dass and his father would go to the field or settle in the courtyard where tens of villagers would come and sit to discuss the affairs of the village and their problems with him. These gatherings were also occasions for socialising, matchmaking, and trading goods, all strengthening the communal fabric. Throughout the day, the kitchen would be abuzz with making endless tumblers of tea or lassi depending on the time of the year.

Occasionally, Tulsi would accompany his father Chaudhary Matu Ram Batra to the administrative office in Maghiana to meet the concerned officers. But on most occasions, it was the tehsildar and revenue officials who preferred to visit Rodu Sultan for administrative work, out of respect for the stature of the Batra family head. They would have a lavish dinner in the courtyard every time they made the trip. Chaudhary Matu Ram Batra was a nambardar, like his own father, a title and responsibility that had passed on to Tulsi Dass after his father's death. Matu Ram had worked hard to build irrigation systems for their lands from which all landowners benefitted. He commanded a high stature in the village and was a staunch practitioner of social structures. He became the biggest landlord in the village, owning large tracts of lands as he inherited them, being the eldest son of the family. His voice was the word of Rodu Sultan and many adjacent villages. Tulsi Dass, however, was a man who earned respect from the community because of his helpful, kind and generous deeds.

As the day drew to a close, families gathered for evening meals, which often consisted of simple yet nourishing fare such as lentils, flatbreads, and one fresh vegetable from their own fields, served with raw onion. The aroma of freshly cooked food mingled with bhajan sounds emanating from the village square temple, located near the house, and azaan from the only small mosque in the village, creating an ambience of shared spirituality.

Raj Rani had lived in the village for nearly fifty years but had not once visited all of their fields. She tried to comprehend its vastness only when passing by the fields on way to Jhang or to Lyallpur to catch a train to Haridwar or Kalanor. 'It stretches as far as she could see,' she was told. Their fields yielded bountiful crops of wheat, rice, sugarcane, and cotton, year after year.

Despite the happiness that permeated village life, Rodu Sultan had its unique challenges. Natural calamities such as floods or droughts tested the community's resilience. There was no hospital and they had to rely on traditional nusskhe and remedies prescribed by the village elders. Only a few families like theirs could take the sick to the hospital in Jhang city. Travel was a challenge on muddy paths which often got submerged under water during monsoons. Bullock carts could not wade through large potholes and what was left of the muddy roads after water receded. Yet, they faced all adversities with an unyielding spirit and camaraderie. Life in Rodu Sultan exemplified a harmonious blend of simplicity, contentment and community solidarity.

Rodu Sultan had become an inseparable part of their lives. On the evening before the fateful night, when her husband walked past her to go to bed, Raj Rani saw unbearable sadness in his eyes, unlike anything she had seen before. The probability of leaving his home, fields and village had devastated her husband. But she did not expect it to affect him so severely that he would give up on life. The partition had already claimed its first victim from Rodu Sultan, her husband.

As news of the impending partition and and the outbreak of violence reverberated through the small Punjabi villages in the far-flung district of Jhang, a sense of dread and uncertainty washed over the Hindu community. The violence and bloodshed that had erupted between Hindus and Muslims in other parts of Punjab was bound to reach their village soon. Raj Rani feared for the lives of her family. She was not sure if their honour and property were safe now.

Looking at the rapidly deteriorating situation and growing fear about what lay in store ahead, representatives of minorities from West Punjab and Sindh approached their leaders for advice on next steps in case the territories they lived in became a part of an independent state of Pakistan. During this time, a meeting of the securities committee composed of the district leaders of three communities in Jhang district was summoned by the administration. The patwari and nambardar of the main villages from all three tehsils of Jhang were instructed to be present.

Kesar Dass was also invited to attend the meeting as the village nambardar or lambardar. After Tulsi Dass's death, he had inherited the office and a notification to this effect had been promptly issued by the district administration. Lambardar was a designation given to the powerful families of zamindars under the British Raj. In the middle of the nineteenth century, farmers with large tracts of lands under their ownership were powerful and influential. The most influential among them were given the designations of zaildar and lambardar. Other than collecting malia (land revenue), their duties were to assist government officers, maintain cordiality among the locals, and report regarding various social phenomena of the village, among others. He was often perceived as the representative of the government to the people; and simultaneously a representative of the people to the government.

During the meeting of the security committee, local leaders of the three communities, and one junior-level representative from the administration sat on chairs facing the invitees. After the purpose of summoning the meeting had been stated by the administration's representative, Wasim Khan, a local leader of Muslim League, was invited to speak first. He spoke with a sense of arrogance. 'Our leader, Quaid-i-Azam...' he said, with an emphasis on the title Jinnah had recently acquired, 'has pledged to minorities that their rights would be protected in every possible manner. He has promised them full protection and there will be no discrimination whatsoever if they choose to live in Pakistan. This surety has been offered in presence of leaders of Muslim League so that the message of our leader trickles down to the rural areas.' Pausing, he then picked up a bundle of pamphlets and asked a young boy to distribute them. The pamphlet had an Urdu translation of Jinnah's speech printed in an English newspaper a few days earlier. It stated:

> I shall not depart from what I have stated repeatedly with regard to the minorities. Every time I spoke about the minorities, I meant what I said, and I said what I meant. Minorities to whichever community they belong, will be safeguarded. Their religion or their faith or belief will be protected in every way possible. Their life and property will be secure. There will be no interference of any kind with their freedom of worship. They will have their protection with regard to their religion, their faith, their life, their property, their culture. They will be in all respects the citizens of Pakistan without any distinction of caste, colour, religion or creed ... Along with it goes the obligation of citizenship ... As long as the minorities are loyal to the state and owe true allegiance, [and] as long as I have any power they need have no apprehension.

After allowing the gathering some time to read the pamphlet's contents Wasim spoke again. 'There could not have been a more unambiguous and authoritative pronouncement of the policy of the Government of Pakistan when the state was created. I assure you that our Hindu and Sikh brothers and sisters have nothing to fear and can continue to live here in peace today … and forever … even after the division.'

The Congress leader Hans Raj spoke next. There was a hint of disappointment in his voice. 'Even though many of us present here may have differences on the partition issue, this is not the time to discuss the past.' The emphasis on *us* was hard to miss. He continued, 'The immediate problem of minorities is not political but a fundamental one – of security of life and property. Gandhi-ji has been urging in his prayer meetings that good relations can make the partition harmless. He has been fasting to urge people to stop violence. The Muslim League's assurances about the protection of minorities in West Punjab would be valued according to the corresponding deeds of the Muslims.' He tactfully avoided any reference to Jinnah lest it ended up provoking his Muslim colleague on the dais. 'Gandhi-ji believes that no political solution can protect a minority from fanatical mob violence of the majority. The idea of protection by retaliation is unworthy of any civilised government. It is the duty of the majority to see that justice is done to the Hindu minorities in West Punjab.' After a pause, he said with profound reluctance. 'While the situation is no doubt dire, there is no need to panic.'

Satnam Singh, the Sikh leader, was less tactful when his turn came to speak. 'How can minorities feel safe when the villages are being attacked, our properties looted, our women disgraced and we are being coaxed to leave. Those who are calling for peace have no sense of reality on ground. I can assure that we will not be the first ones to provoke or attack but we will not sit back quietly if provoked.'

The obvious tension amongst the leaders belied their words of assurances. All men present could not help but feel a sense of betrayal and anger towards the government and leaders, who had allowed the situation to escalate to such a degree. Why had they not been able to maintain peace and harmony between the two communities? The meeting ended causing more anxiety than offering any comfort.

It had been raining all day. Like every year, the monsoon had shown its fury, submerging fields, roads and often homes in low-lying areas. The journey back home was slow and bumpy as the cart struggled to wade through the water on the roads everywhere. No one spoke a word on the way. It was dinnertime by the time they entered the village. It was still drizzling. They saw from a distance that many men had gathered in the village chaupal, the community space in villages of north India. It was unusual for so many people to be out at that hour in the rain. As they neared the village square, they noticed that nearly all men were carrying spears and swords. One or two also carried a gun.

'A village in our tehsil on the border of Lyallpur was attacked in the middle of last night by a large gang of armed rogues,' informed an anxious man as soon as Ram Lal stepped into hearing range. 'Hindus and Sikhs were caught unawares. The mob took advantage of rain and thunderstorms. They did not have enough time to organise themselves and put up a fight. In any case, they were outnumbered. They were threatened that their lives would be spared only if they agreed to convert to Islam. Some agreed and a mullah who had accompanied them performed a hurried ceremony. Those who resisted were killed brutally. They also looted their belongings and had empty bullock carts ready to carry their loot. Apparently, some young girls were also abducted.'

Mukhtyar and Kartar had also gone with Kesar Dass to attend the meeting.

'How do you know all this?' Mukhtyar inquired

'My brother's wife is from that village. He had gone there this morning to drop her for a few days to take care of her ailing mother. They found both her parents lying dead in the compound, their throats slit. The house had been ransacked and valuables were missing. A few houses were also set on fire. The village was nearly deserted. They learnt of the ghastly attack from a Muslim woman who was still under shock. She said she had never seen anything like that before in her life. Some men and women survived by hiding in the fields. They left the village in the morning with just a bundle of clothes with the help of some Muslim women. Their men had turned beasts and refused to help anyone. My brother managed to cremate his in-laws with the help of a young man who had stayed back. Fortunately, the rain stopped for some time, otherwise cremation in the open would have been impossible.'

'We could be their next target. We must be prepared to fight. I will not spare anyone who eyes our village or our women,' screamed a furious Kartar. '*Bole So Nihal*,' he cried.

'*Sat Sri Akal*,' many young men responded resolutely to the cry.

'Calm down, calm down.' Ram Lal said, mollifying Kartar. He turned to Mukhtyar for guidance.

Mukhtyar stood silent for a moment, thinking, his dark brown eyes narrowing, his thick greying eyebrows adding to his expressive face. Mukhtyar was a tall man about the same age as Ram Lal, both somewhere in their fifties, but Mukhtyar looked younger with flowing long grey hair speckled with black. His strong jawline, slightly softened with age, sharp nose with a slight curve, trimmed moustache resting on thin lips, added youthful glow to his face. He wore his usual outfit of a loose, but well-stitched, white cotton salwar-kameez, with a beige shawl carefully draped on it, a habit driven more by modesty than the need for warmth. Around his neck, he wore a small, intricately designed amulet, a common cultural practice in the region epitomising protection and faith. His overall appearance was one of dignity and a deep connection to his roots befitting the head of the Qureshi clan. His face mostly carried a serious expression, but it could quickly break into a warm and friendly smile. At the moment, his gaze was blank, steeped in deep contemplation. Everyone stood in silence waiting for him to speak.

Suddenly, as if having made up his mind about something, Mukhtyar climbed the chabutra, a cemented platform, and spoke in his usual authoritative tone. '*Mere puttraan te tusaan saare bhaiyan de ru-ba-ru, main Quran di saun chukkda haan ke main twaadi hifazat inj karaan ga jiwein apne ghar waleyan di karda aan. Assi ikatthe aan es vich* (In presence of my sons and all of you, my brothers, I swear on the Quran to protect you like I would my own family. We are in this together),' Mukhtyar vowed. His reassuring words calmed people.

'We are with you, Mukhtyar Chacha,' said one of the three young men carrying guns. Kesar Dass recognised one of them as the butcher's son; the other two were sons of the tailor who ran a shop at the far end of the village.

'Anyone who dares to keep even a foot on our soil will have to face the bullets from this donali,' Mukhtyar's eldest son, Alam, almost the same age as Kesar Dass, thundered, raising his gun. 'Rodu Sultan will set an example of bhaichara, fellowship, solidarity, for the entire Punjab,' he said, stepping forward to hug Kesar Dass. Cheers went around. Everyone felt visibly relieved by Mukhtyar's assurance.

On Mukhtyar's suggestion, representatives from both communities gathered in his house to discuss steps to guard the village and defend people and property. After elaborate discussions, it was agreed that Radhe Shyam, the village postman, would use his contacts in the postal department to gather intelligence about the situation in nearby villages and find out if any attacks were being planned. They decided to establish a joint village guard consisting of young men from both Hindu and Muslim families. Mukhtyar instructed Kartar, and his youngest son, Qadir, to take turns to keep night vigil on the roof of the house near the village periphery, in case anyone attempted to enter through the fields although that was unlikely as monsoon rain had made the fields sludgy. He commanded his other son, Nazir, 'You and Binder will take turns keeping watch on the rooftop of Binder's house. The access road to the village is visible from there and we will be able to spot any cart approaching the village. If they attack, they won't come in small numbers. Whoever spots anything suspicious will alarm the others on the rooftop by shouting.'

'We should erect makeshift barricades, using carts, tree trunks and available materials at the village entrance. We will contribute labour and resources for this,' Kesar Dass proposed. 'This may not create adequate fortification but will slow down any attackers approaching.' Everyone nodded in agreement.

Ram Lal turned to the temple priest. 'Pandit-ji, when you hear the shouts of alarm, ring the temple bell frantically. That will be the signal for all men to assemble in the chaupal with whatever weapons they possess. No one will fire unless Mukhtyar orders.'

A system of alarm was thus set in place. Families were assigned roles to prepare food and serve the guards. A spirit of collective responsibility prevailed, with an understanding that the village's safety depended on the cooperation of all residents, regardless of their religious affiliation. Rodu Sultan, like many other villages, created its own fortification plan to defend itself from potential attacks.

The battle for survival had begun.

Ram Lal felt dejected. So much for the peace talk by the leaders, he reflected acrimoniously. Hindus had been left to fend for themselves. But he was relieved to at least have Mukhtyar on their side. His eyes welled up with pride to see Kesar Dass taking charge effectively, befitting the one who was now the guiding light of the clan.

Over the next few days, they observed the agreed drill. Every other day, news arrived of an attack on one or the other village in Jhang. In fact, one village had been attacked in broad daylight. There were reports of skirmishes between the two communities threatening to blow into full-fledged riots within Jhang town. It was decided that the people in the village needed to stay alert even during daytime, and not just at night. A few days passed without any untoward incident. But trouble knocked at Rodu Sultan's doors soon.

6
The Boundary Commission

As minorities in West Punjab struggled to come to terms with the events threatening their life and property which had uprooted them from their ancestral land, rendered them homeless and without occupation, the frantic developments in London and Delhi compounded their troubles. Suddenly, on 18 July 1947, Britain's Parliament passed the Indian Independence Act and finalised the demarcation of dominions of India and Pakistan by midnight of 14-15 August 1947, intending to exit from India a year ahead of the period earlier announced.

The assets of the world's largest empire were now to be divided within a single month. Only in March 1947, Mountbatten had assured Nehru that he intended to approach the problem with stark realism and would transfer power in such a way as to minimise the risk of future strife and bloodshed. But neither the stark realism nor the resolve to avoid bloodshed was evident in his subsequent actions. Nehru believed that division of India, if decided upon, would not take less than ten years to be carried out. The separation of Burma from India had taken as much time and anything could happen in ten years, he believed. Just a month ahead of the 3 June announcement, Nehru had presented his plan to Mountbatten which he preferred over the plan contained in the draft announcement for the transfer of power. Nehru's proposal envisaged that power should be demitted to the central government in June 1947. The Congress plan had ruled out the immediate creation of Pakistan. In retaliation, Jinnah too had no option but to ask for immediate transfer of power. No one paid attention to the catastrophic consequences of rushed transfer of power for millions of people. The July announcement created panic and sparked further violence.

The Boundary Commission got into action to meet the 14-15 August deadline set by London. After its preliminary meetings, the commission invited submission of memoranda and representations by interested parties. The public sittings of the commission took place in Lahore, from 21 to 31 July 1947, with the exception of 27 July. Arguments were addressed by counsels of the Congress, Muslim League, and Sikh members of the Punjab Legislative Assembly. A number of other interested parties appeared and argued before the commission. After the close of public sittings, the commission adjourned to Simla for discussions. But it had become evident from discussions in the commission that the divergence of opinion between its members was so wide that a common resolution of the boundary problem was not a possibility. At the end of discussions, members assented that in the absence of an agreed solution, Radcliffe would proceed to take the decision.

Sadly, an outsider was assigned to do the impossible task. Racing the deadline and desperate to complete his task, Radcliffe hastily drew an award dividing Punjab and Bengal, cutting through the middle of villages, towns and fields, disrupting roads, communications and vital irrigation systems. He cut in half the large Sikh population in Punjab. East and West Pakistan were separated by over a thousand miles.

His brief award had voluminous annexures, which provided that:

> The boundary between the East and West Punjab shall commence on the north at the point where the west branch

of the Ujh river enters the Punjab Province from the State of Kashmir. The boundary shall follow the line of that river down the western boundary of the Pathankot Tahsil to the point where the Pathankot, Shakargarh and Gurdaspur tahsils meet. The tahsil boundary and not the actual course of the Ujh river shall constitute the boundary between the East and West Punjab.

From the point of meeting of the three tahsils above mentioned, the boundary between the East and West Punjab shall follow the line of the Ujh river to its junction with the river Ravi and thereafter the line of the river Ravi along the boundary between the tahsils of Gurdaspur and Shakargarh, the boundary between the tahsils of Batala and Shakargarh, the boundary between the tahsils of Batala and Narowal, the boundary between the tahsils of Ajnala and Narowal, and the boundary between the tahsils of Ajnala and Shadara, to the point on the river Ravi where the district of Amritsar is divided from the district of Lahore.

From the point on the river Ravi where the district of Amritsar is divided from the district of Lahore, the boundary between the East and West Punjab shall turn southwards following the boundary between the tahsils of Ajnala and Lahore and then the tahsils of Tarn Taran and Lahore, to the point where the tahsils of Kasur, Lahore and Tarn Taran meet. The line will then turn south-westward along the boundary between the tahsils of Lahore and Kasur to the point where that boundary meets the north-east corner of village Theh Jharolian. It will then run along the eastern boundary of that village to its junction with village Chathianwala, turn along the northern boundary of that village, and then run down its eastern boundary to its junction with village Waigal. It will then run along the eastern boundary of village Waigal to its junction with village Kalia, and then along the southern boundary of village Waigal to its junction with village Panhuwan. The line will then run down the eastern boundary of village Panhuwan to its junction with village Gaddoke. The line will then run down the eastern border of village Gaddoke to its junction with village Nurwala. It will then turn along the southern boundary of village Gaddoke to its junction with village Katluni Kalan. The line will then run down the eastern boundary of village Katluni Kalan to its junction with villages Kals and Mastgarh. It will then run along the southern boundary of village Katluni Kalan to the north-west corner of village Kals. It will then run along the western boundary of village Kals to its junction with village Khem Karan. The line will then run along the western and southern boundaries of village Khem Karan to its junction with village Maewala. It will then run down the western and southern boundaries of village Maewala, proceeding eastward along the boundaries between village Mahaidepur on the north and villages Sheikhupura Kuhna, Kamalpuran, Fatehwala and Mahewala. The line will then turn northward along the western boundary of village Sahjra to its junction with villages Mahaidepur and Machhike. It will then turn north-eastward along the boundaries between villages Machhike and Sahjra and then proceed along the boundary between villages Rattoke and Sahjra to the junction between villages Rattoke, Sahjra and Mabbuke. The line will then run north-east between the villages Rattoke and Mabbuke to the junction of villages Rattoke, Mabbuke, and Gajjal. From that point the line will run along the boundary between villages Mabbuke and Gajjal, and then turn south along the eastern boundary of village Mabbuke to its junction with village Nagar Aimanpur. It will then turn along the north-eastern boundary of village Nagar Aimanpur, and run along its eastern boundary to its junction with village Masteke. From there it will run along the eastern boundary of village Masteke to where it meets the boundary between the tahsils

> of Kasur and Ferozepore. For the purpose of identifying the villages referred to in this paragraph, I attach a map of the Kasur tahsil authorized by the then Settlement Officer, Lahore District, which was supplied to the Commission by the Provincial Government.
>
> The line will then run in a south-westerly direction down the Sutlej River on the boundary between the Districts of Lahore and Ferozepore to the point where the districts of Ferozepore, Lahore and Montgomery meet. It will continue along the boundary between the districts of Ferozepore and Montgomery to the point where this boundary meets the border of Bahawalpur State. The district boundaries, and not the actual course of the Sutlej River, shall in each case constitute the boundary between the East and West Punjab.
>
> The canal headworks at Sulemanke will fall within the territorial jurisdiction of the West Punjab. If the existing delimitation of the boundaries of Montgomery District does not ensure this, I award to the West Punjab so much of the territory concerned as covers the headworks, and the boundary shall be adjusted accordingly.
>
> So much of the Punjab Province as lies to the west of the line so demarcated shall be the territory of the West Punjab. So much of the territory of the Punjab Province as lies to the east of that line shall be the territory of the East Punjab.

The states of Bikaner and Bahawalpur were interested in canals whose headworks were situated in the Punjab province. Both made representations to the Boundary Commission. Radcliffe decided that any agreements that either of those states had made with the provincial government on sharing of water from these canals or otherwise would be respected by whatever government hereafter assumes jurisdiction over the headworks concerned. He made it clear that no decision had been made by the commission intended to affect whatever territorial claim the state of Bahawalpur may have in respect of a number of villages lying between Sulemanke Weir and Gurka Ferry.

Radcliffe noted in his award, 'The task of delimiting a boundary in the Punjab is a difficult one. The claims of the respective parties ranged over a wide field of territory, but in my judgement the truly debatable ground in the end proved to lie in and around the area between the Beas and Sutlej rivers on the one hand, and the river Ravi on the other.'

The fixing of a boundary in this area was further complicated by the existence of canal systems, so vital to the life of the people of the Punjab but developed only under the conception of a single administration, and of systems of road and rail communication, which had been planned in the same way. There was also the stubborn geographical fact of the respective situations of Lahore and Amritsar, and the claims to each or both of these cities which each side vigorously maintained.

Radcliffe observed:

> I have hesitated long over those not inconsiderable areas east of the Sutlej River and in the angle of the Beas and Sutlej Rivers in which Muslim majorities are found. But on the whole I have come to the conclusion that it would be in the true interests of neither State to extend the territories of the West Punjab to a strip on the far side of the Sutlej and that there are factors such as the disruption of railway communications and water systems that ought in this instance to displace the primary claims of contiguous majorities. But I must call attention to the fact that the Dipalpur Canal, which serves areas in the West Punjab, takes off from the Ferozepore headworks and I find it difficult to envisage a satisfactory demarcation of boundary at this point that is not accompanied by some arrangement for joint control of the intake of the different canals dependent on these headworks.

Radcliffe conceded that he had not found it possible to preserve undivided the irrigation system of the Upper Bari Doab Canal, which extends from Madhopur in the Pathankot tehsil to the western border of the district of Lahore, although he made small adjustments of the Lahore–Amritsar district boundary (to mitigate some of the consequences of this severance). He further wrote that he could not find any means of preserving under one territorial jurisdiction the Mandi Hydroelectric Scheme which supplied power in the districts of Kangra, Gurdaspur, Amritsar, Lahore, Jullundur, Ludhiana, Ferozepore, Sheikhupura, and Lyallpur. 'Where the drawing of a boundary line cannot avoid disrupting such unitary services as canal irrigation, railways, and electric power transmission, a solution may be found by agreement between the two States for some joint control of what has hitherto been a valuable common service.'

He admitted that the award was unlikely to satisfy sentiments and aspirations deeply held on either side. If means are to be found to gratify to the full those sentiments and aspirations, they must be found in political arrangements which was not his concern, and not in the decision of a boundary line drawn under the terms of reference of the commission, he suggested.

Partition was no longer a demand or a talk or a discussion; it had become a reality. From the date of his arrival in India, Mountbatten took only seven weeks to obtain the approval of the British government for the transfer of power, only three weeks more to announce it, and he had kept only eleven more weeks to hand over the reins to the two new dominions.

Though Mountbatten's award was ready on 9 August 1947, the government withheld it to avoid repercussions and perhaps, responsibility. The contents of the award were however unofficially out. Hindus, Sikhs and Muslims without exceptions were outraged with the way the division of Punjab had been proposed. Communal violence erupted on an unprecedented scale triggering migration of millions from West and East Punjab, creating one of the largest humanitarian crises in history. The ensuing violence and displacement were to reshape the subcontinent's socio-political landscape, leaving a lasting scar on the three communities.

The Batra family, too, was to be thrust into the deluge of exodus.

7
The Exodus

Binder was on the vigil atop his house when he spotted a jeep approaching the village around noon. It had been raining incessantly for the last three days. There had been no movement on the road all day; it was flooded. No one had left the village in the last two days, and no visitors had arrived. The jeep looked like an official vehicle; it had a large loudspeaker affixed to the top, apparently for broadcasting. It made its way slowly through the bumpy road. Whoever was in the jeep knew the road well. A stranger would have long ago run the vehicle down the crater-sized potholes.

Not wanting to take any chances, Binder rushed down to wake up Nazir, who was taking a nap after having been up all night keeping watch. After alerting Nazir, he ran to inform Kesar Dass. A cousin of his also came running from the other side of the village. 'I just saw a jeep with four people approaching Mukhtyar Chacha's house. If I am not mistaken, one of them is the block development officer … I forget his name … and there are three armed men in some kind of uniform,' said one of them.

Hearing the commotion outside their house, Ram Lal stepped out. Binder apprised him of the visitors. *What is Abdul Qadir doing in the village?* he wondered. 'He should be out there controlling the madness,' he mumbled, thinking aloud. Abdul Qadir was the block development officer, a fairly senior official. He was a family friend and frequently visited their house. He found it very unusual that Abdul would go to Mukhtyar's house and not come to see him. All kinds of thoughts crossed his mind.

Ram Lal felt apprehensive. Over the last two months, the riots had taken a serious turn. Hindus and Sikhs had been living on edge. Abdul was well known to them but he was not sure if anyone could be trusted in this atmosphere inflamed with passions. The ongoing massacres were different from those in other provinces where tension revolved mainly around religious issues – cow slaughter, the playing of music before mosques, the performance of aarti or namaz, and the defiling of religious symbols and institutions. This violence was different from anything he had seen or heard of in the past. The scale, magnitude and brutality of the violence were hard to fathom.

The situation had turned grave in most villages of Jhang district in the month of July. The administrative machinery had rapidly fallen to pieces. Attacks on Hindus and Sikhs in rural areas had intensified. Relatives of residents of Rodu Sultan, who lived peacefully in far-flung villages where Hindu and Sikhs were in minority, had started fleeing their homes and arriving in Rodu Sultan in search of safety. There had been at least two attempts by a band of Muslims in the last ten days to attack Rodu Sultan. Each time Mukhtyar, his sons and other Muslims from the village had confronted them and made them retreat. On one such occasion, Mukhtyar had to even fire in the air to scare them.

The sound of the approaching jeep interrupted his thoughts. Both Mukhtyar and Abdul Qadir got down. Like always, Abdul Qadir and Ram Lal embraced each other in greeting. 'Abdul Sahab has brought some bad news, Ram Lal Bhai,' Mukhtyar said as he held Ram Lal's arm affectionately and walked into the courtyard signalling the others to follow. Inside, they settled on the cots.

Abdul was a Pathan, about the same age as Kesar Dass, perhaps a tad older. He was a tall and handsome man with a striking and rugged appearance. His suntanned skin bore the marks of a life spent under the harsh sun. His deep-set, piercing eyes were a striking shade of brown, exuding intensity and wisdom. His thick but well-groomed beard framed his strong jawline. He wore a pakol (a headgear worn by men in the North-West Frontier Province), symbolising his cultural heritage, paired with a salwar-kameez. He exuded an air of quiet strength and resilience.

Many other village elders had joined them by now. Kesar Dass sat down on the cot facing the guests. Ram Lal rushed inside to pass on instructions to make tea for the visitors.

Abdul got up and sat next to Kesar Dass, placing his arm around his shoulder. He spoke with a heavy heart and a grave demeanour, choosing his words carefully. 'I feel ashamed telling you this but I have definite information that about a hundred armed men will attack Rodu Sultan tonight. Those whose earlier attempts were thwarted by Mukhtyar have been going around from village to village to mobilise support. Most of those who plan to attack tonight are from villages far away. They are heavily armed and intent on killing and looting. I have come to alert you, my brother. You can't imagine how ashamed I feel telling you this.'

No one said a word, waiting for him to continue. Abdul emphasised their long-standing friendship and mutual respect, and highlighted the absurdity of the communal tension. He expressed his personal shame and disgust at the actions of these individuals, asserting that their behaviour did not represent the entire Muslim community or their faith.

'Surely the administration cannot be that helpless, they must be able to do something to stop this?' inquired Satish, his voice betraying the fear that had gripped him.

'The British administration has shunned all responsibility; they seem to have decided that it is better to leave the matter to the new governments to be formed after Independence. Their officials have simply withdrawn. Punjab Border Force is as good as disbanded. I have no police force at my command. The troops are insufficient and their neutrality is affected by the tension around. I am afraid but the police have become unreliable, they cannot be trusted. Hindu policemen have abandoned their duties, the Musalman have stopped taking any instructions from anyone; in fact, many end up joining the mob rather than stopping them. The entire administrative machinery has broken down. The provincial government has ceased functioning, causing a complete breakdown in society. There is a huge political and administrative vacuum with no one at the helm of affairs. I am not getting any instructions from my superiors. The news from Delhi has made things worse.'

'Which news?' inquired Ram Lal.

Abdul took a deep breath. 'The members of the Boundary Commission were unable to reach a consensus and have left it to that gora, Radcliffe, to decide on how to partition Punjab. He has left for Simla to write his award in the solace of mountains, leaving nearly the entire Punjab up in flames. Life has been completely paralysed. There are rioting mobs everywhere. In this part of Punjab, Hindus and Sikhs are being targeted, their women are being abducted or raped. Even children are not being spared. Half of Lahore's Hindu population is believed to have already left the city for safety. Similar news of Muslims leaving the villages for safety is coming from the other side of Punjab. I have heard of riots in Aligarh district and in Gurgaon. Emergency has been proclaimed in Bombay. There is sheer madness everywhere.'

Again, there was stunned silence as everyone tried to comprehend what they had just heard.

Abdul continued, 'Appeals for peace are falling on deaf ears. Gandhi-ji passed through Amritsar and Lahore on his way to Kashmir to persuade the Maharaja of Kashmir to accede to the Indian dominion. An attempt was made near Phillaur to blow up the Frontier Mail in which Mahatma Gandhi was travelling. Thankfully, he escaped. I can't even begin to imagine what would have happened if he was hurt. Undaunted, he resumed his journey. But no one is paying heed to even his advice anymore, it is too late I guess.'

Raj Rani brought the tea for guests herself. Both Abdul and Mukhtyar stood up and greeted her with folded hands.

'What do you suggest we do, son?' she asked Abdul, handing over the tumbler with tea.

'Mataji, Lala Tulsi Dass-ji was like a father to me, and Ram Lal is a dear friend. That is why I am here to offer whatever help I can. For the past ten days, villages in Jhang have been subjected to raids by *buniyad parast* Muslims and bandits. While the military conducted a flag march in Jhang town yesterday to maintain peace, the violence continues in the back lanes. We have two options, Mataji. I have four trusted gunmen. We can stay and fight the mob alongside you all, but we know while we may put up a good fight, it will be no match for hundreds determined to kill, rape and loot. Alternatively, we can leave immediately for a safer location. I can escort you to Toba Tek Singh, where you can stay at my sister's house until things normalise here. *Tuhada hukam sar ankhan te* (your wish is my command), Mataji. You are as dear to me as my mother. As soon as I learned of the looming threat, I rushed here. I first went to Mukhtyar to seek his counsel. We both agreed that we would stand by whatever decision you make.'

Raj Rani spoke instantaneously, moved by Abdul's words, 'We don't want any bloodshed. Some Musalmans may be angry, some of our Hindu and Sikh brothers have also been misguided. Consumed by their rage, they do not know what they are doing. We are grateful to you and Mukhtyar Bhai for standing with us in this time of deep crisis. *Rab dona te meher rakhe!* (May God bless you both),' she blessed both men.

Raj Rani continued, 'Personally, I prefer we leave as suggested by you, Abdul. But if we leave, all my family members must come along. I can't leave any of my family behind. Will your sister accommodate us all? Will the Musalmans in your village not question her?'

Abdul thought for a moment. 'I understand, Mataji. My sister's heart is large enough to take an ocean but her house does not have enough space for so many people. The stable sheds can take about fifty people if you all wouldn't mind staying there. They are regularly cleaned, but still carry an inevitable stench.' Abdul's family bred horses and supplied them to the British army and provincial police.

'That should not be a problem,' answered Ram Lal. 'We men have no problem staying in the stable, women can stay in the house. Please give us family members a few minutes to discuss this. We will be back in a few minutes.'

In the baithak, about twenty family members stood aghast. Raj Rani and Ram Lal were the only ones who appeared to be calm and in control.

'As your elder, I will announce my decision outside on behalf of all of you. You are under no obligation to abide by it. If you wish that we stay back and fight, I will stand alongside. But we know it will be futile. We might win today out of sheer courage and because we have the support of Abdul and Mukhtyar but what about tomorrow? They will keep coming till we surrender or die. Think of your women, your sisters, daughters …what they might have to go through,' Raj Rani's voice, otherwise firm like any mother who only had the interest of her children at heart in all her decisions, choked for a moment, '… Think of your children who have yet to see and experience life ahead. Tell me what you have to say.'

'I agree, Bharjai-ji,' responded Ram Lal, seconding his sister-in-law's decision.

'Mother is right,' Kesar Dass too voiced his support. One by one, all of them agreed with the decision to leave.

'Please go and bring your families at once. Pack only a pair of clothes and a utensil or two and take the bare minimum utilities. Those who have a bullock cart can load a cot and a bag of rice and potatoes. And please don't carry any valuables. That would be like inviting trouble. Hide your jewellery and silverware; bury it somewhere within your house or wherever you feel it would be safe. We can retrieve it after we return.'

She now turned to Ram Lal. 'Our tabbar (the family unit) of Batras will stay with Abdul's sister but we cannot abandon other Hindus in the village. You should go meet the other elderly and tell them of our decision. They can come with us till Toba Tek Singh but we cannot expect Abdul's sister to accommodate all of them, perhaps women and children can stay with us, others will need to find their own way.'

Ram Lal and the others hurriedly left to comply with the instructions.

Raj Rani returned to the courtyard with Kesar Dass. 'We will be ready to leave soon, we just need some time to collect things to carry with us,' she announced. Turning to Mukhtyar, she spoke with folded hands, 'We are leaving everything behind in your hands, Mukhtyar – our house, land, cows, our memories and our village, our Rodu Sultan, my husband's Rodu Sultan. Please hold it in trust till we return.' She could no longer hold back her tears.

Seeing his mother cry, Kesar Dass was also moved to tears. Mukhtyar too started sobbing, unable to hold back his emotions. 'Please forgive me ... I feel so helpless,' he kept muttering.

Abdul walked over to Kesar Dass to console him. 'You have to stay strong, Kesar Dass Bhai. Toba Tek Singh is over sixteen kos from here. We must leave soon so that we can reach before dark. With women and children with us, it won't be safe to travel at night.'

Back inside, Raj Rani issued further directions to everyone. She instructed Nand Lal, 'Load a few cots and bags of grains on both carts. Also, a few logs of dry wood for the fire. We will need to cook our own food. I will get some utensils from the kitchen. We cannot eat from the kitchen of Abdul's sister. She will understand, I am sure.'

in time, trying to come to terms with the reality of their exodus. They had had only a few minutes to grab a small number of things and commence their journey into uncertainty, not knowing what dangers lay ahead or what fate had in store for them. They did not have time to grieve over their loss, not of material things but of belongingness, of having been displaced from their own homes. The thick dark clouds hung above, adding to the air of despair.

Raj Rani sat in Abdul's jeep, weeping silently. Her intuition had warned her of this day but she did not expect it to be so abrupt. She felt sad about leaving the cows behind, concerned if they would be looked after well. All cows were deeply attached to Tulsi Dass and her. After Tulsi Dass's death, their eyes kept searching for him. They were part of the family and could have been brought along but being sacred to Hindus, they would have become the first target of attackers.

Ram Lal walked in silence alongside the cart that carried Nirmala, his daughters and grandchildren. His son, sons-in-law, and the only daughter-in-law and her husband walked a little ahead while keeping an eye on their children in the cart. His other relatives were somewhere behind, with their own families. His eyes were filled with emptiness.

Kesar was going through a similar trauma. He walked at the end of the kafila with a few young men carrying swords walking alongside to deal with any eventuality of attack. Bebe's tragic death had hurt him deeply. Her body lay on one of the carts ahead. What was tormenting him deep inside was his helplessness and inability to give his grandaunt a decent funeral. Bebe had lived with them most of her life. She had always treated him like her own child. She did not deserve to go away like this. Tears started to roll down his unshaven face. He quickly wiped them with the cloth that hung over his shoulder.

As they left the village behind, he turned to see his native place one last time. He thought of his late father and ancestors who had lived and died on this land. The thought of leaving his family land behind, now a grim reality, was like a dagger to his heart. The prospect of not returning soon or ever was too much to bear. He felt as if he was leaving a piece of himself behind. He stood there for long, looking at the place where he was born, had grown up into a young man and aged. He wanted to capture as many visuals of the place as he could so that he could carry them with him as infinite memories.

After a few minutes they reached their farmland. Kesar Dass gazed over the family fields on both sides of the dirt track. Looking at the acres of farmland with rice and sugarcane had a calming effect on his troubled mind. As they passed the dhani where he often ended up spending many nights to feast on drink and eat meat, a wave of nostalgia surged in him. Although the Batras were not strict vegetarians, they preferred not to cook or eat meat at home. Nor did they drink at home. Once in a while when men felt like drinking or eating meat, they would go to the fields and cook chicken or lamb on wood fire. When Kesar Dass was young, he would find an excuse to stay overnight in the dhani every few days where his friends would join them. They had a good supply of rum bottles from one of their relatives in the army. The bottles were hidden on the rooftop. There were no steps to the roof, so there was hardly any risk of any elder detecting it. They would sit in the small clearing behind the dhani where a fire would be lit to cook some good raw meat Alam would bring from one of the butchers in Rodu Sultan. Alam would even cook meat using onion and tomatoes from the farm. He was a great cook.

Ahead of Kesar Dass, Dhani Ram, called Dhania fondly by all, talked to the two bulls to prepare them for a long journey ahead. Dhania had come to their house as a boy. His father died of cholera when Dhani Ram was only ten years of age. His mother worked at the small flour mill in the village. She was barely able to manage their two meals with what the owner of the mill paid. She pleaded with Raj Rani to take the boy in, for tending the cows. Raj Rani took pity and agreed that he could run errands around the house. She also sent him to school with Kesar and Nand Lal. But soon Dhania got bored of studying. He took a liking to driving cart and looking after bulls and cows. Slowly, it became his main occupation. Dhania never married. He lived in a small room next to the warehouse. Although he had his own little kitchen, he ate mostly with the Batra family on the insistence of Raj Rani. Later, as Dhania's mother grew older, she too moved in with him. He took good care of his mother. A few years ago, she passed away.

Kesar Dass bent and picked up a fistful of wet soil from his farmland and knotted it evenly on both ends of the cloth hung on his shoulder. The road ahead was uncertain, and he could not help but worry about what the future had in store for his family.

As they approached a specific point near the dhani, Kesar Dass instructed Dhania to stop. He ran swiftly to bury the family jewellery near the tree, as instructed by his mother. In the rush, he slipped into an unexpected pothole and twisted his ankle. The foot swelled up immediately. Somehow, he managed to limp back and settled down on the last cart to keep an eye on the rear of the caravan.

As the rain had stopped, Kesar requested the tarpaulin cover on the cart to be removed. He sat facing the retreating village with Gobind by his side. Gobind had insisted on sitting with his father while his sisters sat in Mukhtyar's jeep with their mother. Ram Saran was walking alongside Ram Lal up ahead. Kesar Dass respected Ram Lal as his own father. He was worried about his uncle who looked defeated and broken particularly after he saw Bebe's body being pulled out of the well, lifeless. Kesar Dass had instructed his son to stay by the side of his uncle who insisted on walking.

Looking at the fading village Kesar Dass was filled with memories of the time spent there. It was Gobind who broke his stream of thought. 'Pitaji, was Lalaji born in Rodu Sultan?' Gobind inquired. Kesar Dass's children addressed their grandfather as Lalaji like their own father did.

Kesar Dass smiled. 'Yes, we were all born here. So was my grandfather Chaudhary Matu Ram, and his father Ram Dass,' Kesar Dass responded. 'But before your Lalaji arrived, his parents had migrated here from somewhere not too far. The soil here was good but there was no planned irrigation system and only land next to the rivers was agricultural. In many other parts of the province, even big zamindars like ours were dependent on the monsoons for cultivation. In a year of good rainfall, we cultivated patches of land here and there sparsely but the land was mostly bar, a complete wasteland. Much after the British started ruling the country, they decided to irrigate such vast uncultivated land. They did it for their own selfish benefit as more agricultural land meant more lagaan could be collected from owners of land. Lagaan required peasants to pay a fixed portion of their produce or its monetary equivalent as revenue, regardless of crop yield or economic conditions. They also wanted an increase in production of wheat and rice to feed the ever-expanding police and army personnel. So, they started making a series of canals in the western parts of the province so that water could reach the vast stretches of barren land. While this rigid system often led to widespread debt as farmers struggled to meet demands during droughts or poor harvests and lagaan became a symbol of colonial oppression, fuelling resentment and contributing to the growing resistance against British rule in India, over years, the canals transformed millions of acres of bars in Lyallpur, Sorgodha, Shahpur, Montgomery, Multan, Jhang, Gujranwala, Sheikhupura, Gujrat and Sialkot into highly productive land. The land also became perfect ground to raise mares, mules, studs and camels for the imperial forces.'

Kesar Dass paused and looked at Gobind who appeared to be in deep thought. 'What are you thinking?' he asked his son.

'Was all of our farmland bar land in those times?' he asked.

'Most of it here, yes,' replied Kesar. 'We still own a large bar land up somewhere. But we also had cultivable land near Jhelum, I am told. However, after the canals reached here over the years, our ancestors moved in because land and villages next to the river got flooded in the monsoons. Gradually, they sold their land and bought hundreds of acres here. Most of their family relocated and other villagers followed over time. Soon, water became available in plenty. Wheat, gram, cotton, rice and fodder started growing where stray camels once roamed. But millions of acres of bar land in Jhang which is located on a little higher altitude remained unirrigated as canals could not take water upstream. But our ancestors were very hard-working people…'

Dhania patted Kesar Dass's shoulder, pointing to Gobind who had dozed off by now, his head resting against his father, his face still thoughtful. Kesar Dass placed his hand on his son's head affectionately. As their kafila passed through the maze of fields and small villages, his thoughts drifted to his ancestors, the rich legacy of his clan of Khatri Punjabis.

8
The Batra Khatris

It is difficult to trace the history of the Punjabi Khatri community to which the Batra clan belongs, or that of the Batras for that matter, with great accuracy. It is, however, largely accepted that they represent the ancient Kshatriyas of the Aryan stock – the word 'Khatri' is a Prakritised form of the Sanskrit word Kshatriya. Philologically, Kshatriya appears to be connected with the Sanskrit word *kshatra* meaning 'country' although some claim that 'Khatri' is a Punjabi word meaning 'warrior'. According to the *Vishnu Purana*, Bharadwaja, son of Brihaspati by Mamata, given to King Bharata as blessing in return for his prayers, had four grandsons, of whom two became Brahmans while two remained Khatris.

Some scholars argue that Khatris are of the Chandravanshi (lunar) descent, others say they are Suryavanshi, the solar race, and many consider them from Agni-kula. Some historians authoritatively argue that the Bedi sub-caste of the Khatris derives its lineage from Kush, the son of Rama; the descendants of Kush learned the Vedas at Benares and were thus called Bedis (Vedis). Other scholars argue that Kshatriyas are of Aryan stock. Most historians incline towards accepting the claim of Khatris being descendants of the original military class, taking, of course, Khatri as a contraction of Kshatriya.

Whichever version one may rely on, the history of the Khatris is clearly a saga of the Aryan race in India. With a long span of more than three thousand years, the Khatris continue to represent traits of Aryan spirit. As true Kshatriyas, they have displayed their martial character not only in ancient and medieval times but even in the modern era.

The Punjabi Khatris are a diverse and widespread clan. There are four important divisions among the Khatris. The Bahris consist of twelve sub-castes; four of these call themselves dhai-gharey (two-and-a-half). The second group is that of bavanjai or bunjahi from the number (fifty-two); their sub-castes numbered approximately five hundred. Among these, fifty-two were distinguished from the rest. The third group, of the Khakkars, had six sub-castes in the beginning but the number increased with time. The fourth group, of the Sarins, has a hundred sub-castes. Among the Sarins, there were twelve important sub-castes. The Sarasvata Brahmins, the purohits, were the alter ego of the Khatris. As distinguished from the Gaur and Kanyakubja, Sarasvata Brahmins are supposed to be of Aryan stock who had settled on the banks of the Sarasvati.

The number of bavanjai has outgrown the original number of fifty-two. Char-ghar is also known as dhai-ghar (two-and-a-half), apparently for the reasons of their proximity within the larger clan and marriages within.

All these sub-castes of the Khatris were to be found in Punjab which then included North-West Frontier Province and other places. The division into groups or their clustering unto sub-castes was on some or the other scientific basis.

The history of the Sikhs is, in fact, the history of the gurus from Guru Nanak to Guru Gobind Singh, and is linked with the history of Khatris. The founder Guru Nanak was a Bedi Khatri of Talwandi, now Nankana Sahib, in Pakistan. His successor Guru Angad was a Tihun Khatri whose original name was Lahna. Guru Amar Das (b. 1479, 1552–74) was a Bhalla Khatri. Guru Ram Das (b. 1534, 1574–81), the founder of the Har Mandir or Golden Temple, belonged to the Sodhi clan of Khatris. Guru Govind Singh, the last guru, traces his descent and that of Guru Nanak in his Granth, *Bachittar Natak*, from Lava and Kusha respectively, the two sons of Lord Rama. Daya Ram, a Khatri from Lahore, was amongst the Panj Pyare transformed into the Khalsa by Guru Gobind Singh in 1669.

Legend goes that Guru Gobind Singh had called for a special assembly of the Sikh followers on the morning of the Baisakhi festival at Keshgarh Fort, Anandpur Sahib. *Sri Gur Sobha*, splendour of the guru, written by Sainapat, one of the court-poets of Guru Gobind Singh, alludes to the guru's intensity on that day and anxious expectations of the assembly. After the morning prayers, the guru suddenly got up with a drawn sword in hand and thunderously exhorted the sangat (assembly) that it was time to show devotion and faithfulness. 'While the entire sangat is dear, which Sikh will give me his head?' the guru roared. There was deafening silence. The guru repeated his call, but the sangat seemed paralysed at this command-request. On the third call, it is said that Daya Ram got up and offered his head.

'O noble king, my head is at your service,' he said respectfully. Guru Gobind Singh took Daya Ram to a tent backstage and re-emerged a few minutes later with blood dripping from his sword. 'I want another head,' the guru thundered. The sangat became even more unnerved now. This time, Dharam Das, a Jat from Delhi, Bhai Mokham Chand, a tailor from Dwarka, Himmat Chand, a cook from Jagannath Puri, and Sahib Chand, a barber from Bidar, came forward to offer their heads to the guru. As the assembly grew restless, Guru Gobind Singh re-emerged from behind the stage with the five men he had presumably beheaded. He then proceeded to initiate the five men, baptising them with *khandedi-pahul*, holy water stirred by the double-edged khanda, sword, to the recitation of sacred verses from the Guru Granth Sahib, and sweetened by patashas, jaggery candies, by Mata Sahib Kaur. This baptism with *Pahul-Amrit*, holy water, touched now by the sword too, transformed the five men into the Khalsa, pure. Guru Gobind Singh then himself chose to be baptised by the Panj Pyare, the Khalsa, further dissolving all differences between him and his disciples, making him proclaim that 'Khalsa is my own image'. Panj Pyare, the five beloved ones, were given a common surname Singh, lion, and were called upon to wear five new distinctive emblems of the Khalsa: Kesh, unshorn hair; Kirpan, sword; Kanga, comb; Kachchha, short breeches; and Kara, steel bracelet.

A few other groups are closely allied to the Khatris and are accepted as a part of the wider Khatri community though they maintain their separate identity, like the Aroras. These include the Bhatias and Soods. According to a traditional account, the Bhatias are the descendants of those Kshatriyas who sought shelter in the town of Bhatner at the time of Parasuram's onslaught. They are divided into eighty-four subgroups. The Soods trace their ancestry to Rama's cook, assumed to be a Kshatriya. Besides Punjab and other parts of northern India, especially UP, the Bhatias were settled in Kutch, Kathiawar, Gujarat, Bombay, and are also traced in Ratnagiri, Khandesh, Thana, Kanara, Sholapur, Belgaum and Poona districts.

The warlike conquerors of one age became astute administrators and moneylenders in the course of history, while continuing with military responsibilities in numerous cases. Historians claim that the vocational takeover from martial to other avocations could be viewed in terms of changing circumstances and adverse situations.

Although the Khatri community in Multan had been influential in trade for centuries, they rose to prominence during the Delhi Sultanate (1206–1526) as agents and bankers to the nobility in Delhi. In the early fourteenth century, Multanis were trans-regional commercial agents for the nobility of the Delhi Sultanate. In this capacity, Multanis were akin to both saudagars (traders) and sahs (moneylenders) but with the difference that they had deep interest in trans-regional trade, which was a defining feature of their commercial activities. A term closely related to Khatri merchants is the seth and sarrafs, both interchangeable terms. Seths and sarrafs are commonly referred to in European sources simply as bankers, moneychangers, and providers of financial services. The position of Khatris in trade is recorded in historical accounts as 'possessing enormous wealth and wielding great status'.

Khatris were the chief moneylenders and capitalists of Punjab province, and also, the chief creditors of the agriculturists and mortgagees of their lands. They had the reputation of being an industrious, energetic, and laborious tribe. They apprenticed their young early and provided them with rigorous training in technical skills, especially for long-distance trade. When they came of age and were ready to set out on their own, they received venture capital, which they returned after being successful. They often became gumashtas, agents, and went abroad for seven or eight years, or even longer. As they belonged either to the extended family or same sub-caste of the Multani firm, its sahs, directors or principals, had a hold on their investment. Gumashtas left their families behind, which also deterred them from absconding with the firm's capital. Historians label Khatris as Punjab's 'great mercantile castes', as the 'most important merchant communities of early modern India', 'like the Jews of modern times or the Greeks under the sway of the Romans'. Historians argue that the movement of the Kshatriyas from soldiers and sovereigns into traders and shopkeepers has a parallel in the history of the Jews. Men of active minds will always find employment for themselves, and this we know from what Greeks became under the victorious Romans, and what they were under the ruling Turks.

Multani merchants dominated trans-Himalayan trade right through the Mughal Empire until the end of the nineteenth century, when the expanding Russian Empire and Afghan wars of the British brought it to an end. Indeed, evidence suggests that Khatris even partnered with rulers, which highlights Mughal motivations to support their commercial ventures both within India and in foreign markets. This support was likely to have been critical to the early establishment of Indian merchant communities in Central Asia during the sixteenth and seventeenth centuries. But that is not to say that the fate of the merchants was bound inextricably to their political patrons. India's power has always been 'soft', not expressed through conquest and military dominance, but in the export of ideas and goods. Khatris played a dominant role in expanding India's soft power through trade. They surely were too busy creating wealth or serving the government of the time, as is also evident from the fact that they had little or no interest in recording their history or contributing to the expansion of India's soft power.

They were equally able administrators then, as they are now. They were also adept in handling military affairs through proper insight, strategy and even by wielding the sword. Names of notable Khatri administrators in the Delhi Sultanate and Mughal period are recorded in memoirs of the rulers and other statesmen. The medieval period of the country's history provides references to Khatris' contribution in the realm of military and administration at the centre as also in the subas and parganas. Akbar's famous minister Todarmal was a Khatri. He evolved a clear and intelligible system of revenue collection. Todarmal's example was equally emulated by Haridas Rai, a Rai-Rayan, who was conferred the title of Raja Bikramajit by Jahangir. Two other Khatris – Diwan Mohan Das and Kishao Das – were conspicuous in the service of Jahangir. Shahjahan too had Khatris at the higher echelon: Jaswant Rai, who was *diwan-i-tan*, as also Sundar Das, who received the title of raja. Dewan Sawan Mal, governor of Multan, and his successor Mularaja, and many of Ranjit Singh's chief functionaries were Khatris. Ayamal of the eighteenth century, Mokham Chand and Chandoo Lal of the nineteenth were eminent Khatri administrators. There is a record of a

Khatri diwan of Badakshan or Kunduz. Having gained the patronage of the Mughal nobles, the Khatris then acquired administrative and military roles outside the Punjab region. According to a Khatri legend of the nineteenth century, they continued their military service until the time of the Mughal emperor Aurangzeb. A large number of their community died during the Deccan campaign. Aurangzeb ordered their widows to be remarried. This created a furore in the community. Khatri community leaders refused to obey it. Aurangzeb terminated the military service of those who defied his diktat.

While they were mainly the principal financiers and traders, the ancient military spirit frequently resurfaced amongst the once royal Kshatriyas and they became able governors of provinces and skilful leaders of the armies. Hari Singh, a Sikh, and the most enterprising of Ranjit Singh's generals, was a Kshatriya, and the best of his governors. Mokham Chand and Sawan Mal were of the same race. Diwan Mokham Chand, a Khatri of Punjab rose to the status of diwan under Ranjit Singh. The list is endless.

The end of the Sikh rule, however, did not mean the complete snapping of the Khatri's participation in Punjab's administration under the East India Company, and later on under the Crown. The fresh air of Western thinking and English education was equally enjoyed by the members of the community who distinguished themselves in different areas – administration, education, judiciary, business, industrial enterprise, public life and institutions. They started venturing into other occupations during the British Raj. The Khatris made their fortune as officials of the government and as traders, sahukars and businessmen often investing their savings in landed property. Many Khatri families held large parcels of land. The village of Bath in the pargana of Gujrat had been purchased by Wadhawan Khatris in the time of Farukh Siyar. Handa Khatris held the zamindari of Daulatnagar proper, Duggal Khatris held the village of Alamgirpur, Bhatia Khatris of Karianwala, while Badhere Khatris were the zamindars of Gujrat and Herat, and

Mehra of Takht-Hazara. Nayyar Khatris held some of the land of the town of Kunja, while the village of Ghartal Khas was owned by Puri Khatris. In Jhang, large parcels of land were owned by Arora Khatris. Batras held land in Shorkot. These instances are suggestive of the Khatris owning considerable areas of land in the towns and villages of Punjab in the early nineteenth century. Handas and Duggals were associated with Daulatnagar and Alamgirpur, respectively.

In many parganas, Khatris were appointed as qanungos, and in villages, nambardar or lambardar, both hereditary positions. Under the Subah system of Emperor Akbar, the sarkar (district) were subdivided into parganas or mahals, serving as fiscal and police units. Qanungos were hereditary custodians of land and revenue records. They maintained schedules of assessment and revenue collection in the parganas. The nambardar was head of the village under the system responsible for revenue collection

Along with varied achievements in the field of administration as also in business and trade, the Khatris contributed equally in terms of intellectual acumen. There were many Khatri religious thinkers, particularly Dial Bhaun and Shamji in Punjab and Maluk Das in the Kara district of Allahabad as also Pran Puri of Kannauj. Among the Khatris of Amritsar, Bhai Sant Singh Gyani was famous for his understanding of the Granth. Bhai Budh Singh was a distinguished Hindi poet in his time.

Khatris were also men of letters – poets, writers, and historians. The list of Hindi litterateurs belonging to the Khatri caste who enriched this rich language is fairly vast. The history of the Khatris in the following centuries adds another milestone in the long journey of their progress in different fronts – from bureaucracy and military service to trade, commerce and industry, and distinction in the fields of science and learning to sacrifice and privation at the altar of the struggle for freedom. The Khatris participated in the freedom struggle in the nineteenth and twentieth centuries. They had a keen desire to be the best in whatever field they chose for their sustenance or creative pursuits.

Historians notice the Khatris not only for their wealth, but also for public service including building temples, gurudwaras, dharamshalas, gurukuls (traditional Hindu learning schools), health facilities and other initiatives for the benefit of the larger community.

The Batra Khatris formed a prominent part of the Khatri community with a rich historical legacy in Jhang. Many members of their clan thrived in urban centres, particularly in Punjab. They were actively involved in trade, education and bureaucracy. Their agricultural enterprises provided sustenance for the community and generated wealth. They played a significant role in the economic, social and political landscape of the region, shaping its history for centuries. Their economic prowess, social influence and political involvement contributed to the development and prosperity of Jhang. As influential merchants, they were patrons of art, culture and religion. They built temples, schools and hospitals, and also promoted education and spirituality within and outside the community. They were the lifeline of Jhang.

The same Batras now faced the harrowing reality of displacement from the very land of their ancestors.

9

Freedom at Midnight

The dirt tracks through the fields finally opened into a motorway. Ram Lal advised Mukhtyar to turn back from here as it was not safe for him and his sons to go any further. Mukhtyar insisted that he wanted to escort them right up to Toba Tek Singh. On Raj Rani's persistence, Mukhtyar reluctantly agreed to head back. Ram Lal embraced Mukhtyar, their embrace filled with unspoken emotions. Kesar Dass was also overwhelmed with gratitude for Mukhtyar who once again assured Raj Rani that he would take care of their property and livestock.

From this point, they decided to take the motorable road to Toba Tek Singh rather than shorter routes through the web of villages. It was dangerous to pass through them in this hostile time. Moreover, the rains would have damaged the dirt tracks and they could not afford to have their carts stuck in slush. The villages located on the road appeared to be deserted. In some, armed men in large numbers guarded the access roads to the village. While Abdul escorted them leading from the front in his jeep, the second jeep crawled behind the four carts. The bullock cart drivers prodded the bullocks to move faster, reminding them that their power was no less than that of the jeep engines. Prompted by their handler, the bullocks charged forward.

It took them two hours to reach Trimmu Barrage near village Atharan Hazari. Till now, their journey had been eventless. Some group members had dropped off on the way to stay with their relatives in Jhang town. It rained sporadically on the way but not enough to affect their progress. Set on the spectacular confluence of the Jhelum and the Chenab, the barrage was a source of canals which irrigated lakhs of acres of land including their farmlands in Rodu Sultan. As they reached the Chenab, they halted at the river's bank.

Kesar Dass and Nand Lal lifted Bebe's lifeless form and gently lowered her into the flowing currents of the Chenab, as women prayed loudly for the Chenab to carry her to a peaceful resting place, where she would find solace. A storm of emotions gripped the family. The inability to give Bebe a proper funeral left them heartbroken, and guilt gnawed at their souls. Women clung to one another as they watched the water carry Bebe away. Gathering their intense emotions, they resumed their journey. It was getting dark and they wanted to reach their destination before dark.

It was already night by the time they reached Abdul's sister's farm located a few kos before Toba Tek Singh. They had covered a distance of about fifty-five kilometres in ten hours. Fortunately, there was no major untoward incident on the last leg of their journey except for a brief incident which caused momentary anxiety. When crossing Malumor, a village a few kos from the barrage, a group of Muslim boys on the roadside jeered at them, shouting 'coward Hindus', and tried to provoke them into a fight. Abdul stopped his jeep to warn them but the stinging expletives continued. Eventually, Abdul's men had to pull their guns out and chase the boys away.

Abdul's sister lived in a large farm estate a few minutes' journey off the motor road. Here, the Batra family diverted from the main road, and other villagers continued to Toba Tek Singh.

The hosts were expecting them but appeared visibly shocked to see such a large number of people. Abdul took Raj Rani inside the house and introduced her to his elder sister, Shakeela, giving a quick summary of events that had forced them to leave Rodu Sultan. Shakeela listened with rapt attention, nodding her head slowly as her brother spoke. After Abdul finished, Shakeela looked at Raj Rani, her eyes glistening with tears.

'You are safe here, Mataji, please consider this as your own home,' she said, her voice reassuring. 'We will get through this together. My house may not be large enough for all of you to sleep inside, but we have plenty of room in the stud farm for all.'

Her face tired from the journey, Raj Rani smiled softly and placed a gentle hand on Shakeela's head. '*Jida dil dariya, udda ghar vadiya* (a house is as large as one's heart),' Raj Rani blessed her host.

Leaving them at her sister's place, Abdul left promptly, promising to return soon with more news.

They had been staying in Shakeela's house for nearly two weeks now. Shakeela was warm and welcoming, her husband Majid Khan and other men of the house were somewhat indifferent but left no effort to make their guests comfortable. The children of the hosts and their guests soon became friends, playing together in the courtyard of a large house.

Majid's house was part of a large estate, standing testament to his status and thriving business of breeding and supplying horses to the British army and the Punjab police. The two-storey house was an imposing structure, blending traditional Punjabi architecture with colonial influences. The ground floor housed a formal sitting area, a dining hall, and Majid's office, where he conducted business with British officers and police officials. The walls were adorned with portraits of prized horses, trophies, and certificates, showcasing his success in the trade. Upstairs, the family's private quarters included spacious bedrooms, a prayer room, and a balcony offering panoramic views of the surrounding stables and training grounds.

The stables were located at the far end of the property, meticulously maintained, and housed dozens of well-groomed horses. There was a spacious courtyard paved with cobblestones, where horses were often paraded for inspection by potential buyers. Beyond were the farmland, a few godowns, a small poultry farm and even a few camels. Majid's army of staff included trainers and caretakers of horses, and those who worked in the farmland. The farm was a symbol of Majid's influence and prosperity.

The women and children were accommodated in the zenana section of the house on the first floor; the men settled in the unused stable. A portion of the shed, used for storing grains, was converted into a makeshift kitchen.

Raj Rani's health had begun deteriorating rapidly after Tulsi Dass's death. She missed him and felt miserable away from her own home, tending to cows and living in her own little world full of household chores and community responsibilities. Shakeela and other women did their best to make them feel at home, but being in a stranger's house for that long felt awkward. The feeling weighed heavily on Raj Rani's health. She and other women offered their help in the household work but there was little to do with the battery of helpers around.

The men too felt embarrassed at having disrupted the normal life of their hosts. Most men stayed up all night to keep a watch, and slept during the day or worked in the farm to keep themselves occupied. Kesar Dass loved being with the horses that had soon become friendly with him. Even Majid's sons joined them in keeping vigil at night with their arms. Majid owned some sophisticated weapons apparently because of his business dealings with the police forces. In all probability, Muslims of the villages around knew about the presence of Hindu guests in the house of Majid but no one dared to come anywhere close to the house as they were aware of Majid's influence in the army and police, and also, of the modern arms.

Kesar Dass had heard no news from Rodu Sultan since they had left the village a fortnight ago. Nor had Abdul returned with any update. The radio did not give much information. Their anxiety kept building. Every moment, they hoped and prayed for the situation to normalise so that they could return to their homes.

But the events that followed the fateful day of 14 August slayed all their hopes of returning to Rodu Sultan forever.

The evening of 15 August was drawing to a close. It had not rained much since the time they arrived in Toba Tek Singh; not in the night at least. The news had arrived in the afternoon that the Union Jack over the old Lucknow Residency, which had never been lowered by day or night, was hauled down quite unostentatiously at sundown on 14 August and sent home to Britain. Jinnah had hoisted the Pakistan flag in Lahore; and Cyril Radcliffe was packing his bags to leave India. There was speculation that he was quite dejected – he had burnt his papers, refused his fee of Rs 40,000 and wanted to leave, never to return. But his actions had already caused irreparable damage.

Kesar Dass climbed on the stable roof carrying the cot he had brought along. He loved spending time on the roof as it reminded him of his own house in Rodu Sultan. The radio also caught a better signal here. Gobind slept by his side as he kept watch at night. If it started raining they would climb down and sleep inside the stable.

He switched on the radio and rolled a tiny knob to catch the signal for any radio station. Last night, they all wanted to hear the news of Independence and other developments, but the signal was poor and they couldn't hear anything. They all prayed for a better connection today. Thankfully, the radio stuttered to life as it caught the signal of the British Broadcasting Corporation's radio station in India. A reporter speaking in Hindustani was recalling in an exciting tone that the independence of India had been announced from the ramparts of the Red Fort. The surging crowd had broken the bounds fixed for them and it was with great difficulty that path could be made for the carriage of Pandit Jawaharlal Nehru and Lord Mountbatten. He narrated how the sky had become overcast with clouds and it had started raining. 'What a good augury for Independence Day!' he said excitedly. And after a few minutes, with a triumphant note in his voice, announced, 'Look, it has stopped raining and there is a rainbow in the sky – what a grand rainbow! And how auspicious it is!'

Hearing the radio come alive, many men climbed on the roof and gathered around the radio. Another voice, which seemed to be that of a British officer, spoke about the palpable joy in the air in the two countries, in India from Independence, and in Pakistan for getting a new country of their own for the Muslims.

The reporter informed that Mountbatten had addressed the Pakistan Assembly on 14 August. Ironically, he paid tribute to the great men, Muslim League leaders, who he stated helped to arrive at a peaceful solution for the transfer of power. There could not have been a more ludicrous statement than this. Equally shocking was his reference to the situation in Lahore. 'Some days ago I went to Lahore. From the reports I had received, I expected to witness a scene of unparalleled devastation. Those of you who have not visited Lahore will be relieved to hear that the destruction is far less than I expected. It amounts to no more than eighteen houses per thousand of the whole municipal area ... I wish to pay my tribute, and ask you to do the same, to those who have saved Lahore from complete ruin ... to the police and fire services, to the soldiers and the civil administration,' he said.

The men on the terrace started hurling abuses on Mountbatten. How could he even think it fit to compliment the police and civil administration in Lahore which had not only turned a blind eye to what was happening but even joined the rioters in committing atrocities against non-Muslims? How could he be so insensitive to the destruction of property or loss of human life? It was no more than a device, a ploy, to underplay the gravity and enormity of what was happening under his stewardship.

The reporter then turned to describe Mountbatten's address to the Constituent Assembly of India earlier that day, which was India's Independence Day. Mountbatten said, 'I know well that the rejoicing which the advent of freedom brings, is tempered in your hearts by the sadness that it could not come to a united India and that the pain of division has shorn today's events of some of its joy.' Again there was no reference to large-scale massacres, migration of people, atrocities against women and children, and the resultant misery and destitution which was evident all around.

By now, the bulletin had switched over to talk about the speech of independent India's first Prime Minister Jawaharlal Nehru, delivered after the Union Jack came down. Select clips from Nehru's speech were played.

The reporter shared that in his message to the press on that day, Nehru stated: 'We rejoice in that freedom, even though clouds surround us, and many of our people are sorrow-stricken and difficult problems encompass us ... We think also of our brothers and sisters who have been cut off from us by political boundaries and who unhappily cannot share at present in the freedom that has come. They are of us and will remain of us whatever may happen, and we shall be sharers in their good and ill fortune alike.'

Jinnah's speech to the Pakistan Constituent Assembly was also played.

Thus, Pakistan was born on 14 August, and India on 15 August 1947.

Independence Day celebrations were going on in Delhi and elsewhere in India, as well as Lahore and all over in West and East Pakistan, unmindful of the conditions in Punjab and Bengal, where people were experiencing a terrible tragedy.

Kesar Dass asked Gobind to inform his mother about what they had heard on the news. A part of him was happy that finally foreign rule had ended, but the thought that they were all now in a different country, distressed him. Till last night, there was still a flickering hope that the award of the Boundary Commission might yet be founded on truth and justice for the minorities in West Punjab. But it was not to be. Their village ... their own village ... the home of their ancestors was now a foreign soil.

The occupants of Shakeela's house couldn't make up their mind whether to celebrate Independence or mourn the partition.

Ironically, the next evening when Kesar Dass switched on the radio, the newsreader had a very different story to tell. He informed that sadly, the euphoria of freedom had lasted barely hours. Lootings and killings had resumed after a short pause. The celebratory shouts of freedom from colonial rule were soon drowned by the cries of lakhs of Hindus caught in large-scale violence in West Punjab. Violent riots broke out on both sides. In Muslim-dominated areas in West Punjab, Hindus were being chased out of their homes and asked to leave for India. In many parts of East Punjab, Muslims were being driven out of their villages.

The reporter went on to state that Mahatma Gandhi had refused to join the Independence Day celebration in Delhi. He had been in Calcutta since 9 August, striving hard to restore peace in the city that was witnessing brutal violence. He pledged to the Hindu minorities in Bengal that he would protect them from the wrath of Partition. On 11 August, Bapu met with Huseyn Shaheed Suhrawardy, the prime minister of Bengal, to convince him to stop violence against Hindus. In return, Suhrawardy asked Gandhi-ji to lend his protection to the Muslims of Bengal. However, when the Hindus found out that Gandhi was with Suhrawardy, the man responsible for the 1946 Calcutta killings, they were enraged. As agitated mobs pelted stones at the residence where Gandhi and Suhrawardy were staying, Suhrawardy took responsibility for the Calcutta killings in 1946 and expressed his regrets to the masses. In

Punjab, Nehru and Jinnah met at Ambala and discussed measures needed to bring peace, order and security to the Punjab and made a joint appeal for peace.

The reporter ended the bulletin with a promise to be back the next day with an update.

The bulletin ended all hopes of returning to Rodu Sultan anytime soon. Sadness and anger loomed in the air as men started discussing their next step. For the first time, they felt a threat to their lives despite the protection offered by Abdul's family. They decided it would be wiser to leave for Kalanor and return only after the situation calmed down. They did not have to wait for long.

10

Kafila

Abdul and Mukhtyar arrived ten days later. Each day after 15 August had only brought depressing news either through bulletin on the radio or Majid's sources. News on the radio was expected to be censored and, in all likelihood, did not reveal the gory details. It was Majid's informants who divulged that the advent of Pakistan was signalled by hundreds of fires raging in various parts of Lahore and Amritsar.

They informed that in Lahore's Anarkali bazar, twenty shops had been gutted, sixty people killed and a hundred injured on 14 August itself. That same night a mob set fire to a gurudwara; nobody knew how many were killed in this attack. A determined campaign to drive out Hindus and Sikhs from West Punjab was well underway. The process of the elimination of minorities had started in Gujranwala, Sargodha and Sialkot. In many places, armed constables were leading the mobs. Hindus started leaving for East Punjab in large numbers.

Majid's informants mentioned that newspapers of the last few days carried unfiltered news of violence. Sir Robert Francis Mudie, who had taken over as the governor of West Punjab on 15 August, had raised concerns about the complicity of the local police. A gurudwara was destroyed and a number of Sikhs, put at between thirteen and twenty-two were killed, in fairly close proximity to a Muslim picket, composed partly of police and partly of military. The newspaper reported that mass murders and arson were taking place everywhere in Punjab.

People arriving in Amritsar and other villages, from Lahore and other nearby places in West Punjab, what was now Pakistan, narrated tales of horror, misery and unbelievable atrocities. This infuriated Sikhs. In and around Amritsar, bands of armed Sikhs killed every Muslim they could find, while in and around Lahore, Muslim gangs, many of them members of the police force, emptied their guns on Hindus and Sikhs. Trainloads of refugees were gutted and turned into rolling coffins. It was estimated that in ten days about 1,000 had died and 600 injured in West and East Punjab. After more than a hundred years of East India Company rule and ninety years of British Raj, the Indian subcontinent had finally achieved Independence. What should have been a moment of crowning triumph after more than a century of freedom struggle was indelibly marred by unimaginable violence and bloodshed.

Both Abdul and Mukhtyar appeared ruffled; this time they had come with four jeeps full of armed policemen. They exchanged quick pleasantries. Abdul requested all except children to assemble in the courtyard.

Trying to sound calm although he could barely conceal his anxiety, Abdul said, 'I have yet again brought terrible news. Hindus and Sikhs are being evacuated from each village … this time with the brutality that we cannot even dare to imagine. Those who resist are being killed inhumanly. Some are being slaughtered just to instil fear. In many villages women have been…' His voice choked. He continued after a brief pause to get hold of his emotions, deciding to leave his sentence unfinished. 'Till now, many Hindus and Sikhs were continuing to stay put, protected mainly by the Muslim neighbours and friends in their villages. But even neighbours and friends are finding it hard to resist the general mood now that these villages are in Pakistan. They don't want to be seen as traitors. They are advising Hindus to leave, to protect their lives. Some may have turned greedy and are eyeing the property of rich Hindu landlords, shop owners and businessmen which they will be forced to leave behind. On the way here this morning, we saw kafilas of thousands of people leaving on foot with their belongings loaded on the carts, all headed to East Punjab. The government is nowhere to be seen. Hindu policemen and employees have abandoned their duties and are leaving with their families. Muslim policemen have joined the mob in the evacuation efforts. Reports of violence and forced evacuation of Muslims from many parts of India are fuelling the raging fire.'

'We understand, Veer-ji, and are grateful for your concern and all support provided by you and your family,' Bhagwanti said with folded hands. She sounded unnerved. Raj Rani did not speak. She had been sick the last few days; her will and determination had weakened. She let Bhagwanti take charge.

'I am afraid it is not safe for you to stay here, not even for a day. The mob can arrive here anytime, they wouldn't spare anyone of us. They will kill all of them if they resist; no number of guns will work,' Abdul said, pointing to members of his family.

'We will plan to leave at once,' Kesar Dass said firmly, his hands folded. Turning to Ram Saran he instructed, 'Puttar, please get the carts out, we will leave at once.'

Bhagwanti turned to Shakeela. 'We are deeply indebted to you for what you have done for us. May Allah shower you with his blessings.'

Shakeela started sobbing. 'You should stay till things get a little better outside. Abdul Bhai only wants our safety but we cannot ignore the call of insaniyat, our home stays open for you.'

Majid Khan shuffled his feet. His discomfort over Shakeela's offer did not go unnoticed by Bhagwanti. 'We must leave, Shakeela.

We don't want to put your lives in danger. *Rabb mehar karega,*' Bhagwanti said, holding Shakeela's hand. Abdul and his family had risked their own lives to save theirs, she could not take advantage of that knowing that if the mob attacked, their protectors were not likely to be spared.

Shakeela began to protest, her face laced with worry but Mukhtyar, who had stood quietly till now, interjected. 'Bharjai-ji, wisdom says this is the time to be pragmatic and leave for a safer place. Abdul and I are willing to fight and give up our lives to protect our Hindu brothers and sisters, but our priority must be preserving lives. Meaningless death serves no purpose. We must ensure your safety, so you can all return to Rodu Sultan when the situation improves.'

Ram Lal stepped forward. Embracing Mukhtyar and Abdul, he turned to address his family and guests. 'Our brothers Mukhtyar and Abdul are right in their counsel. They have our best interest at heart. Let us leave. We thank our hosts for their humanity and courage for taking us in during these difficult times.'

Majid Khan instructed his sons to help load the luggage in the carts, 'Put ten bags each of rice and wheat flour from the godown in the cart … and yes, add a bag of salt and a jar of achar.' Turning to another son, he instructed, 'Quickly get as many onions, potatoes, tomatoes and fresh vegetables from the fields as you can.' He spoke to Kesar Dass, 'Bhai-ji, you can take one of our carts too. You will need one just for the grains and vegetables. From what we hear, help may not be coming soon. But Allah will look after you!'

Outside, as they prepared to leave, Shakeela's eldest son Daniyal took Kesar Dass aside. 'I have hidden a gun under one of the loose wooden planks in the cart. I pray to God you may never have to use it but in case things get ugly you will need it to defend yourself … your women.'

Kesar Dass was moved by Abdul and his family's gestures. Out there Muslims and Hindus were killing one another, but here one could see an example of the highest order of humanity between the two communities.

Abdul and Mukhtyar escorted the Batras to the motorway. As they approached the road, they saw a sea of people, Hindus and Sikhs, all dressed in white, walking along the road. Hundreds of bullock and donkey carts filled with household goods, covered by oil cloth to protect from rain, tagged along. A few tongas were also to be seen with their carriages overloaded with women and children as they took turns to ride. Some old women and small children were seated atop the luggage. Those who did not have carts, carried luggage on their heads. Many carried children or old women on their shoulders. Some had brought their animals along – cows, goats, camels, dogs, and some even horses. The heart-wrenching sight of this sea of humanity filled everyone with fear and anxiety, inciting frustration and anger.

Abdul requested them to wait till he returned. He drove his jeep ahead of the seemingly never-ending kafila. He came back after twenty minutes and drove past them, to check the tail of the column. This time he took thirty minutes to return. 'There are surely more than five thousand people here – men and women of all ages, children and toddlers, many pregnant women. They are all from villages in Jhang, all headed to Lyallpur, hoping to catch a train to India. You should join them from here.'

Abdul and Mukhtyar touched Raj Rani's feet, embraced the men warmly, and quickly drove away in Abdul's jeep, the other jeeps close on its heel, a thousand angry eyes following them.

The Batra family was now on their own. Slowly, their carts merged into the kafila. As they moved ahead, people in small and large groups, at times in hundreds, kept joining the column from the many dirt roads merging into the motorway, all of them hoping to reach across the newly drawn border.

Kesar Dass looked at the sad faces of people around him. They moved ahead in silence, their gloomy eyes revealing the pain of the humiliating exodus from what had been their homes for hundreds of years. The only sound that could be heard was of the wailing of some women and the noise made by children playing, unmindful of the tragedy. No one stopped, not even if the tired children begged their parents to take a break. People exhausted from the long walk fell on the roadside. No one waited for them as the surge of people behind pushed them ahead. Occasionally, a person would collapse from exertion or sickness causing a commotion.

The Batra family stayed together around their six carts. In a few hours, they were somewhere in the front of the column.

Suddenly, it started raining heavily, adding to their woes. Most people kept walking. Only a few rushed to seek cover under roadside trees. Others got busy protecting their luggage from rain. Those travelling in carts covered by tarpaulin made room to squeeze in some women and children. They kept moving without waiting for those who had stopped. Soon, it was dark. The meagre light created by the lanterns held by a few people in front of the caravan did little to help to guide them through darkness and rain. They followed their instincts. People behind simply followed the ones ahead of them.

The men ahead stopped to confer on their next steps before entering the town. Binder took charge and offered his advice, 'I don't think it is safe to stay here. There are many Muslim villages around. We should keep walking.'

'People are tired, they would be hungry and may need to cook. We must take a break and let our elders and children rest. Men can keep vigil,' suggested an elderly man.

'I think we should keep moving. We might find some police or an army post ahead. They might be able to help,' said another man.

'What are you saying? Do you think we can trust any police or army man? What if he turns out to be a Muslim? He will lead us to the butchery instead,' retorted Binder. 'Best to keep moving.'

As they stood talking, a jatha of Sikhs emerged from nowhere. They were hiding in the shadows and listening to their conversation. They were about twenty in number, mostly men but some women could also be seen in the background. All carried swords; many even guns.

'Don't be alarmed, we are one of you,' said one of them in an assuring tone.

Binder went up to them. 'Sat Sri Akal! Are you from Toba?'

'No, we live fifty miles from here. A village next to ours was attacked last night. They were planning to attack ours today. We were warned by some Muslim friends, so we left at once, leaving everything behind. We reached here around sunset and decided to halt for the night. It is not safe to travel in the dark. They pull out any women from the kafila and run in the field. If anyone chases them, they slaughter him mercilessly.'

'Looking at such a large number, they will not dare to attack us but we should stay vigilant,' responded one of the men from the kafila.

Another man from the jatha stepped forward with a suggestion, 'There is a school a few kos ahead where our women and children are camping. It can take another hundred people if we move the desks and chairs out. I suggest the sick and the women with infants spend the night there. We may have some food to feed the children. Men will need to sleep in the open.'

Binder consulted Ram Lal. They agreed to camp in and around the school for the night. Binder climbed a cart and made the announcement of the planned halt. He requested that the decision be relayed to people behind. Many however, chose to continue with their journey.

They reached the school. The bullock carts in the front of the kafila were parked on one side in a field. The school ground was full of slush from the rain. Disregarding any obstacle, the men walked their women, children and the frail inside the school building, till every inch of space with a roof over it was filled. Some women began cooking food in the corridor using hastily improvised fireplaces, fuelled by twigs and branches gathered from nearby trees.

Thick, white smoke curled upward from the smouldering wet wood, dense and slow, carrying an earthy, damp scent. It met the cold rain outside, creating a misty haze as smoke and rain intertwined. The contrast of warm, rising plumes against the cool, falling droplets painted a melancholic scene of nature's elements in harmony. Even in those tense moments, people could not but appreciate nature's magic.

The members of the Batra family took turns to straighten their backs in their carts. The men ate some roasted gram with gur the women had packed. Though they still had plenty of grains and vegetables, they wanted to be miserly with its consumption. It could take them days to reach Kalanor. So food had to be rationed till they reached or before any help arrived. Everyone was hungry but no one complained.

The first night passed without any untoward incident except that it rained relentlessly all night.

Lord Indra, the God of rain, took some mercy on them the next day. The downpour stopped early in the morning and the sky cleared after many days. A bright and cheerful sky infused fresh hope and energy. They resumed their journey. Some were too sick to walk and a few had given in to fate and decided to stay back.

Another long kafila joined them in the morning. Most walked with their luggage, often carrying their children or elders on their shoulders. Some people were even barefooted. They had their own tragic stories to tell. They had been walking for two days carrying their belongings with little rest and food. Almost all of them had to simply run for their lives, leaving behind their belongings, with no time to pack even bare essentials. Their luggage comprised a few clothes and eatables – mostly roasted grams and some handy items. Many elderly people who refused to abandon their dwellings, stayed behind, their fate unknown to the family members who left. A few were unfit to travel long distances and had to be abandoned in the village or on the way. The elders, stoic yet heartbroken, urged their loved ones to go on and save their offspring, and prevent an entire generation of the clan from being wiped out. The anguish of those who had to leave their elders behind was unbearable. Tears flowed from their eyes knowing they might never reunite; a blend of guilt, sorrow, and helplessness wrenched their hearts. Those listening to their soul-crushing tales were moved to tears. Many vowed to take revenge, and some simply screamed out of anger and frustration.

The caravan moved at a snail's pace alongside the narrow road. En route, the countryside presented a picture of desolation, smouldering ruins, empty houses and closed shops. Harvest had either been abandoned or set on fire perhaps by fleeing villagers, Hindus or Muslims. Cattle went astray in search of food. Many could be seen grazing in the fields.

Kesar Dass's cart was in the front with armed men to defend the head of the caravan. The women of the family followed in the two carts behind. The elderly men and children followed them, a few keeping a careful eye on the cart which carried the grains and some vegetables. There had been instances in the last two days where the hungry and desperate had tried to steal the food from their cart in broad daylight.

The day passed peacefully except for reports of one or two people in the kafila having died of some ailment. The dead were hurriedly buried in the fields.

The blue sky was once again covered by monsoon clouds. As it turned dark, a band of armed men in white skullcaps appeared unexpectedly from the fields, blocking their way, brandishing guns and swords. There were about two hundred of them. Kesar Dass and other men also pulled their guns out. Both sides exchanged heated threats. Without warning, a dozen men appeared from the fields on the left. One of them slit open the throat of an elderly Sikh man in the kafila. A fountain of blood shot up as the man held his throat trying to stop the blood. Another man ripped open his stomach, spilling his intestines out. Yet another used his sword to strike at the front left leg of the bullock. All of this happened in a split second. The man who attacked the bullock was now ready to attack Kesar Dass who stood shell-shocked holding the gun, unaware of the danger. His eyes were glued to the dying Sikh man's body flooded in his own blood.

Kartar jumped in time and buried his kirpan in the neck of the attacker, with all his strength. The blade of the kirpan pierced through the throat and emerged from the other end. Without wasting any moment, Kartar pulled the kirpan out. This time the fountain of blood spurted out from the attacker's throat. The other two men turned to run but a bullet shot from the crowd caught one of them in the track. The other man managed to escape. The band of men ahead also disappeared in the fields at once.

A roar of triumph went through the front ranks. A few people stepped forward and lifted Kartar on their shoulders showering praises on him for his valour and heroism. *'Bole So Nihal Sat Sri Akal'* – the earth shook with a clarion call roared by hundreds from the caravan. The dead man was lifted and buried on the roadside. They all said a prayer for the departed soul.

Sitting in the cart, both Ram Saran and Gobind witnessed the ghastly killings. Trembling with fear, Gobind clutched at his elder brother, his eyes frozen in horror as he witnessed the brutal killings. Shock and disbelief numbed his mind, while a deep, gnawing terror settled in his heart. The innocence of childhood shattered, replaced by vistas of violence and loss that would haunt him all his life. Watching the man die on the road, Ram Saran's heart wrenched in pain. He had seen the elderly man around for the last two days. He was a jovial and carefree person. It was tragic he had to die such a brutal death.

As soon as Bhagwanti learnt of the dreadful incident, she rushed to the cart ahead and pulled the two boys out, taking them away from the gruesome sight. So far most people in the kafila had heard of the heartless killings in other parts of Punjab but this was the first time they had watched one themselves and also had to retaliate and kill two men. The women and children in the carts nearby sobbed inconsolably.

Those behind had no clue of what had transpired in the front. They were facing their own ordeal. Many women were pulled out by a group of men with masked faces. When their relatives tried to pull them back, their hands were chopped off with swords. People in the front remained oblivious to the tragedies taking place at the back. Communication from one end took hours, at times, a day to reach the other end of the kafila.

The Sikh boys gathered in the front to discuss how they must stay prepared if those men were to return with reinforcement. Many volunteers stepped forward to offer their services for keeping vigil and to be included in the defence, covering as much of the kafila as they could.

A group of young Sikhs with rifles kept moving on horses along the caravan, offering protection from the flanks; front and rear. But their number was not enough to cover the entire length of the kafila. There were many exposed spots. The most vulnerable were those who fell behind, too weak or sick to walk any further or had simply lost the will to survive.

It started drizzling again. The kafila continued to move forward in anticipation of help arriving. But none was to come.

The kafila was now on the move for the third day. Hundreds of men, women, and children kept joining. They did not even inquire where the kafila was headed. They just moved along. They were on their feet, only a few fortunate had bullock carts or animals to ride. They could not bring much except some clothes and food with them. Many families left in the middle of the night with the clothes they were wearing, and a khes or sheet thrown over their shoulders, and joined the kafila.

Their ordeal was no longer limited to dealing with frequent attacks from fanatic Muslims; it involved dealing with starvation. Those who still had some food left consumed it with care so as to save some for the uncertain days that lay ahead. Bhagwanti was liberal in sharing the leftover grains from the lot that they brought from Rodu Sultan and was given by Shakeela. She gave away a fistful to those who came asking for it, unable to refuse women pleading in the name of their hungry children. But the water they had brought along was running out fast. She told Kesar Dass that they would have to stop at a tube well or well to refill the vessels.

As they approached the next village, Binder and a few young men decided to go and check if there was any well nearby. As they passed the village pond, they saw two bloated corpses floating. A little ahead, they spotted a well not far from the village chaupal. 'Be careful, the water may have been poisoned,' a young man from the group warned Binder as he lowered a bucket to pull out the water. The water smelt horrible. Apparently some dead bodies or animals had been thrown inside although they could see none floating on the surface. They had heard stories that young Hindu men had killed pigs and thrown them in the wells before fleeing so that the water was no longer edible for Muslims who came to live in their village. Muslims had thrown dead bodies in the village ponds so that if Hindus refused to leave or returned, they had no water to drink. In some cases, dead animals were chained to heavy stones before they were thrown in the wells so that those pulling water out would not know it was contaminated.

They needed water desperately so the boys decided to check a few houses in the village. Nearly every house in the village had been ransacked. Every single grain had been taken away. No water could be found anywhere. As they turned to go back, they spotted a small thatched hut in the distance in a field outside the village boundary. It probably belonged to a Harijan who was forced to live outside the village. The boys decided to check it out although it was highly unlikely that there would be any food or water there. To their surprise, they found an old woman lying on the cot inside the hut. For a moment, Binder thought she was dead. But then he noticed her breathing softly. He heaved a sigh of relief. Hearing the noise, the woman opened her eyes but she was too frail to turn her head to look at them. Binder touched her forehead. It was burning from fever.

'We can't leave her like this. Let us carry her.' A well-built boy stepped forward and lifted her carefully. 'You will be fine, Mataji,' Binder assured her. The old woman muttered a few blessings.

As they stepped out, Binder asked her. 'Mataji, would you know where we can find some drinking water in the village?' She whispered something. Binder couldn't hear her. He brought his ear closer to her lips.

'*Mairey manjay thay thalay paani da bharya hoya ghada rakheya hoya hai, par main Harijan haan, shayad tusaan uh paani naa peena chaho*. (There is a clay vessel under the cot filled with water, but I am Harijan so you may not want to drink that water.)'

Binder rushed back inside and brought the matka out. He poured water in the huge brass tumbler Bhagwanti had given him. 'You are like a God to us, Mataji, not an untouchable. This water is a gift of nature. You don't know how many thirsty children will bless you today after drinking this water.'

Eight-year-old Gobind sat huddled with his mother and grandmother in the bullock cart. The air was thick with uncertainty and fear. Young Gobind's heart pounded with a mixture of excitement and trepidation. 'Dadiji,' he whispered to his grandmother, his small hand clutching hers, 'why do Musalmans want to kill us? You promise every time you will tell me soon but you haven't.'

Raj Rani looked into her grandchild's innocent eyes. She masked her own fears, offering a gentle smile. 'We're going to a safer place,' she whispered, her voice steady, though inside, she carried the weight of uncertainty. She continued, 'We are going to my ancestral village, my child, our other home.'

'But why are all these people going with us?' Gobind asked, his voice trembling slightly.

Raj Rani sighed, her heart heavy with the memories of her land and home. How could she tell the boy this young the reasons behind the violence and bloodshed that had forced them to flee their ancestral village. She thought of a convincing explanation. 'The government has redrawn the map and borders of Punjab. Many people are not happy with the new map so they are protesting. Some elements have turned it into a religious issue. It will take some time for things to settle and the confusion around to get over. Till then, we must stay away from our village,' she said softly. She could think of no other answer.

Gobind was not convinced with the answer. 'Why are Muslims staying back and not coming with us? I wish Shakeela Tai's grandchildren could come with us, we have become such good friends,' he said. 'Some boys here say Muslims hate us?'

Raj Rani's expression softened. 'No, my child, that is not true,' she said. 'It is some evil people who want to kill us, not Muslims. There are good people and bad people everywhere.'

'But they tell me terrible stories,' Gobind protested. 'I've heard that they are killing Hindus and Sikhs everywhere, and even Sikhs are killing Musalman.'

Bhagwanti had been listening to the conversation between her child and his grandmother quietly and could no longer hold herself back from responding, hearing the complex thoughts and feelings her son was going through at a tender age. 'Yes, terrible things have been happening but we must not let hatred consume us. People who kill are evil, they have no religion. No religion teaches to kill anyone. We must remember that there are good and bad people everywhere,' she said.

Gobind nodded slowly, his young mind struggling to comprehend the convoluted situation.

'We are all children of God,' his mother continued. 'And God loves us all, regardless of our religion. We must never forget that. Look at Abdul and Mukhtyar Chacha, Shakeela Behan and her family, they are such good people.'

Gobind listened intently to his mother's words, his fear gradually giving way to a sense of hope.

'I understand, Mataji,' he said finally. 'We must not hate the Muslims. We must be cautious of bad people.'

His mother smiled and hugged him tightly. 'That's my wise boy,' she said. 'We will soon be home and all of this will be just a bad dream.'

As the kafila continued its slow and arduous journey towards the border, Gobind and his mother talked about their hopes and dreams for the future. They talked about the village in Kalanor, and the new friends they would make.

Gobind dozed off in his mother's arms.

As the sun rose above the horizon the next day, they saw a small train station in the distance with a dirt track leading to it. They could see a train parked a little afar. A spark of hope lit up their eyes. A jatha was formed to check if the station was abandoned or any staff was around. Surprisingly, the jatha found an elderly Muslim man in a worn-out railway uniform huddled in a corner of the station veranda with his feet tied with a rope. He appeared shocked. Looking at the Sikh boys approaching, he got more terrified and started pleading, '*Baksh deyo, baksh deyo, meri janani bimar aee, merian do chothi bachiyan ve, mainu na maro.* (Spare me, spare me please, my wife is sick, I have two young daughters ... please don't kill me.)'

Kesar Dass stepped forward and assured the old man that they were not going to harm him. Once assured that there was nothing to fear, the old man broke down and recounted events of the last two days. 'The track on both sides of the station was sabotaged by people from my own village. They kept a huge boulder across the railway line and also damaged some fishplates. When I tried to resist, they tied my feet with ropes so that I could not find a way to warn the driver of an approaching train. The train stopped a few yards from the boulder, a few kos from here. Apparently, the drivers saw the boulder from a distance and stopped the train before it was too late. I heard them say that the driver ran out of fear, abandoning the train.' The old man was now sobbing uncontrollably. He once again pleaded with folded hands to spare his life.

Binder, Dhania and the boys decided to go and check if anyone was alive in the train. It took them ten minutes to reach the site of carnage. The gruesome sight made all of them throw up. Hundreds of blood-soaked bodies of Hindu and Sikhs lay alongside the train on both sides of the track. Bodies of women had no clothes on them – most of them had been raped before they were killed. They had been subjected to unspeakable violence and bore the marks of brutal humiliation. Children had been butchered; limbs of men sliced into many pieces. Foxes and vultures had been feeding on them. The stench of the dead filled the air. The ground was stained with blood, and the air heavy with the stench of death. The sight was gut-wrenching. They had not seen anything like this before. All of them stood in silent horror, their hearts shattered by the sheer inhumanity. The grim tableau was a stark reminder of the deep communal hatred that had engulfed Punjab. They were all filled with rage.

They went back and returned with some tools to dig graves and bury the dead. They decided not to tell the others in the kafila what they had seen. It would only instil more fear. They decided to continue and find a safe place to camp some distance away from the sight of the massacre.

Another tragedy struck them the next morning. They discovered that Raj Rani had passed away in sleep during the night. She had been unwell all this time, rarely stepping out of the cart, but she stayed surrounded by her grandchildren telling them stories of their land, people and epics. No one had expected her death.

A sharp pain cut through the numbness that had settled over Kesar Dass during their arduous journey. Already burdened by the weight of displacement and horror of violence, he felt an overwhelming wave of grief and despair. He was consumed by guilt and helplessness, wondering if he could have done anything to save her.

The Batra family pulled their carts aside to mourn Raj Rani's death and cremate her. The men quickly dug a grave and buried her under the cold, indifferent sky; there was no way they could have cremated her with due rituals. A few strangers stopped to comfort them. An elderly Sikh granthi stopped to say a few prayers as they buried Raj Rani. The cries of Bhagwanti, the wailing of relatives, and the whispers of prayers filled the air. Dhania was devastated, he wouldn't stop crying and refused to leave. Nand Lal had to literally drag him to the cart.

Kesar Dass wanted to sit by his mother's grave and mourn, but he knew that he must carry on, not just for himself but in honour of his mother's memory. Her strength must become his guiding light, he thought. He held back his tears. He filled an empty ghada with soil from his mother's burial; he would immerse it in Haridwar, he resolved. He instructed everyone to resume the journey.

Kesar Dass was unable to overcome his grief. The partition had consumed another loving elder of the Batra family, the third in a matter of weeks. The pain from his mother's demise was greater than anything else they were going through. His mother had been a symbol of resilience and comfort. She had been his anchor. Her death felt like the severing of his last connection to a life that once was – a life of home, belonging and stability. He felt a profound emptiness, as if a part of his own soul had been extinguished with her last breath. Tragically, they could neither perform her last rites properly nor mourn her death as traditions required.

Funeral rituals hold a profound significance in Hindu traditions, serving as a bridge between the physical and spiritual realms. These rituals are deeply rooted in the belief of samsara – the cycle of birth, death and rebirth – and moksha, liberation from this cycle. They are not merely ceremonies but sacred acts that guide the soul's journey after death. In Hindu belief, death is a transition rather than an end. The funeral rituals are significant in ensuring that the deceased's soul departs peacefully and progresses towards its next destination. The body, considered a temporary vessel, is cremated and the soul is released from its earthly ties. A cremation is symbolic of returning the five elements (earth, water, fire, air and ether) to the cosmos, aligning with the Hindu philosophy of unity with the universe.

The rituals also provide emotional closure and spiritual support to the bereaved family. Kesar Dass prayed to God to provide peace to her mother's soul, and sought forgiveness for not having been able to perform the rituals: *Rabba, meri maan dee rooh nu sukoon de te menu maaf kar de ke main ohdiyan aakhri rasman nahi kar sakya.* (God, grant peace to my mother's soul and forgive me that I could not perform her last rites properly).

Bhagwanti could not bear the sadness on the face of her husband. She wondered if their horrible ordeal would ever end. There had been no indication of any help coming from Delhi or Lahore. Did their lives matter to the governments in both states and the political leaders on both sides?

11

The Greatest Migration in Human History

As people scrambled to find themselves on the 'right' side of the border, West Punjab saw an exodus of Hindus and Sikhs heading eastwards, while Muslims from East Punjab made their way west. The British had not made allowances for any potential mass population exchanges in their plan for Partition. The ensuing two-way movement of people caught the leadership of the two dominions unawares, pulling the rug from under their feet and invalidating the safeguards that had been notionally built into the plan. Despite this, both the Congress and the Muslim League remained opposed to a formal exchange of population until the end of August, when the sheer scale and intensity of violence forced their hand.

Across the Indian subcontinent, the genocide was as unexpected as it was unprecedented and brutal. The political leadership on both sides remained in denial of the ground reality throughout the month of August. The new governments tried to stop these movements of people. Both states showed rhetorical commitment to plurality and started hammering out the legal and administrative frameworks in their Constituent Assemblies that would be put in place to secure these minority rights. In his very first speech to the Constituent Assembly of Pakistan on 11 August 1947, Jinnah reminded Mountbatten (who in his address had made an oblique plea for treating minorities well) that the treatment of non-Muslim minorities with utmost tolerance and respect for their faith was in Muslim blood, going back to the time of the Prophet himself. He declared that religion had nothing to do with the business of the state and that in course of time Hindus would cease to be Hindus and Muslims would cease to be Muslims in the political sense as citizens of the state. Jinnah had the Muslim League flag adopted as the flag of Pakistan, but with a white strip covering one-third of the flag as a symbol of peace and minorities. Jinnah said, 'Today I trample under my feet all distinctions of caste, colour and nationality … We should begin to work in the spirit of cooperation, forgetting the past, burying the hatchet, so that all these angularities of the majority and minority communities will vanish.'

It was difficult to believe that this was the same Jinnah who so ruthlessly and single-mindedly propounded and pursued the two-nation theory and brought about such a divide between Muslims and non-Muslims. Ironically, his speech calling for tolerance was made in English to seventy million people, of whom merely 10 per cent were literate. Clearly, it did not resonate with Muslims including his followers as the ethnic cleansing continued unabated. The situation in East Punjab was no different.

Even before the ink dried on such pronouncements, the announcement by politicians ceased to be of any importance. By the end of August, ethnic cleansing had reached gigantic proportions. Hundreds of thousands of emigrants were crossing the border daily.

Eventually, at the end of August, governments on both sides realised that the groundswell of migration was beyond their control and they should aid rather than inhibit it. The initial strategy was reversed and it was agreed to facilitate the greatest exchange of population in history – all Muslims in East Punjab were to be evacuated to Pakistan, and all non-Muslims in West Punjab were to be moved to India. Mahatma Gandhi disagreed with the policy at first. He argued in favour of returning and resettling the displaced persons in their original homes. He also feared that the new policy could be exploited both by the majority and the administration on both sides for ethnic cleansing. Jawaharlal Nehru and even Master Tara Singh were not in favour of a wholesale transfer of population.

A transfer of population seemed, from the point of view of the two future dominion governments, much against their own interests. The Muslims in East Punjab were a poor but indispensable part of the community. The Sikhs and particularly the Hindus of West Punjab seemed an almost essential part of the community, especially in the towns. Apart from whether such a decision could have been put into effect successfully, it would have been very difficult for Pandit Nehru and Jinnah to have agreed to a wholesale transfer of population. Others were of the view that with violence escalating and spreading, it was critical to evacuate millions on both sides of the border to safety.

Finally, with an eye on the fratricide, daily mortality figures, and the grave dangers of unorganised and unsupported refugee columns, Gandhi relented in favour of a rapid and organised exchange. The two governments established the Military Evacuation Organisation (MEO) on 1 September 1947 with Maj. Gen. Sardar B.S. Chimni as its commander. The Punjab Boundary Force was disbanded a day earlier. In the beginning, the MEO had its headquarters at Amritsar, but these were later shifted to Lahore for a closer liaison with the Pakistan government. It was decided to set up transit camps for collecting the emigrants in the other dominion, transporting these refugees either on foot or by rail or motor transport, and finally, settling them in the relief camps established in the country of their destination. The two governments opened liaison agencies, the East Punjab government in Lahore, and the West Punjab in Jullundur.

With this, the migration was legitimised and became a state subject. A spontaneous exodus was turned into an organised evacuation operation. Thus, began another unprecedented event in history – the greatest migration ever, supported by the state on both sides.

By the end of August 1947, the whole of Punjab was pervaded with long columns of evacuees. A vast population, cut off by a stroke of Radcliffe's pencil, was on a long march in both countries to cross the border. Over two million Hindus had left West Pakistan for India by now. Thousands joined them by the day. Yet millions were still stuck in the villages and towns waiting for help to arrive. Muslims from different parts of India travelled to Pakistan, wanting to stay in the country of their religion. The trail of dust raised from so many columns blotted out the sun on days rain stopped and the skies cleared. The length of most kafilas often stretched for kilometres, sometimes 70 km long in places. The kafilas of Punjabis coming to India from Lyallpur or Montgomery districts covered up to 240 km at some point. They all walked, only a few fortunate had bullock carts or animals to ride.

Each column was now escorted by military personnel of MEO moving on foot and jeeps. The tide of people was so vast that managing them amongst the chaos created by violence and transition of power was an impossible task. The two governments had agreed that the dominion from which the evacuees were moving out would provide food, water, fodder and protection until they crossed the boundary. They were to be under the care of the dominion receiving them from this point onwards. But that rule was hardly observed. It fell on the MEO personnel to arrange food and water for starving people.

Many people could not walk after a point, they fell sick, their feet had sores or often even fox bites. The MEO provided transport to the physically infirm, pregnant women, small children and old people who were unable to walk. Even then, it was a humongous task to be tackled as the MEO did not have enough vehicles. The government of West Punjab announced that those who had buses, motorcars, or wagon lorries were to hand them over to the government for evacuation. By the middle of November, 1,200 military and 1,000 civilian vehicles were being used to transport evacuees across Punjab.

These kafilas were headed towards main camps set up in Lyallpur, Sialkot, Montgomery, Lahore and Sheikhupura. Subsidiary camps were put up all over West Punjab to collect smaller groups of evacuees before moving them to bigger camps. Large columns of evacuees on the move were to be directed straight to the main camps. They had to be transported further to transition camps set up near the border, and eventually to relief camps in India, by foot, rail or motor, whatever was available.

The MEO faced a huge task of evacuation. Evacuating millions of people walking in hundreds of columns or stuck in thousands of villages, kasbas, dhanis, towns, bars, all over West Punjab was no mean task. In West Punjab, its officers started efforts to identify non-Muslims scattered in villages and move them to subsidiary bases. It was, however, constrained by the shortage of manpower and had to seek help from military personnel who had left their jobs. Local civilian officers acquainted with the area were dispatched to identify non-Muslims scattered in villages and move them to subsidiary bases. It was decided to identify ex-soldiers amongst the evacuees, and give them uniforms to provide security to caravans on the move. A chain of local liaison officers was also created who went around from village to village to find non-Muslims and bring them to nearby subsidiary bases under military escort. They did their best despite the threat to their lives. A similar plan was drawn for evacuating Muslims from India and transporting them to Pakistan. At many places in West Punjab, administrators and police forcibly shifted those who resisted leaving.

The Punjab countryside was suddenly awash with mud due to unusually heavy storms and torrential rains at the end of September. These rains burst the banks of the Beas, destroyed railway bridges and roads, washed away camps and belongings, and even drowned some of the refugees who were caught in the currents. Fear of the descent into a bitter winter followed, and there were concerns that families would freeze or succumb to disease if they kept living out in the open, shabbily dressed in thin cotton clothes or rags.

The unending violence added urgency to evacuation efforts. Up until the middle of August, the worst violence was in the cities. But, by now, violence had become widespread, frenzied and on a scale the country had never previously witnessed. Districts in West Punjab were not the only scene of carnage; many other parts of the country including Bengal burnt. It was as if people had gone mad. There were deserted tracts and towns in West Punjab. The entire countryside had been reduced to a picture of desolation.

Trains were employed in large numbers to facilitate movement of people. Over 673 trains moved over two million across the border and inside India between 27 August and 6 November 1947. Scheduled trains in East Punjab were suspended so that the maximum number of railway carriages could be used for the movement of refugees from Pakistan to India and their dispersal to camps within India. Train journeys had become perilous. Most trains started by MEO carried on an average three to four thousand passengers. Over-spilling trains piled with people and hastily assembled goods were soft targets for attacks. These trains generally carried members of one community only, who were headed in the opposite direction, and they were ideal targets. Wholesale slaughter occurred on trains frequently.

Aircrafts were also employed to evacuate refugees. By early 1947, India had 115 civilian aeroplane run by eleven private companies.

The end of World War II had sparked an unprecedented boom for civil aviation as Indian companies bought cheap aircraft – mostly Douglas DC-3 Dakotas – left behind by the departing US forces. Civilian planes not flying on scheduled routes were diverted to ferry refugees from Karachi to Delhi while a few planes were placed at the government's disposal. Indian aviation companies were overwhelmed by the magnitude of evacuation. Civilian airline operators proved inadequate to cope with the task. Many refused to fly due to risks to aircraft and threat to crew.

Both governments had to rely on chartered British aircraft. Some 170 aviation personnel were flown in from Britain to help. 'Operation India' was thus launched. Between September and December, twenty-one planes – mainly Dakotas – were chartered from eight British companies. These aircraft completed 962 flights covering over 15,00,000 km, evacuating and transporting thousands of people on both sides. Twelve RAF Dakotas airlifted stranded officials. Baggage weighing over 1.5 million pounds was transported between India and Pakistan. They also carried food, tents and vaccines for Muslim refugees stranded at Delhi airfields.

Amidst all this chaos, there were many positive stories. Humanity may have failed but it had not died. Even in those bitter days, when intercommunity relations were at their nadir, a lot of individuals and communities resisted violence. Many risked their lives – and that of their families – to protect friends and even strangers from the other community. A few even died trying to protect their wards or friends. In response to radio appeals and newspaper advertisements inviting donations and other support for the hungry, shopkeepers, housewives and bakers delivered food parcels. In Delhi, the local population baked 280 maunds of chapatis for stranded and starving foot convoys moving from West to East Punjab. Drugs, vaccines and doctors were sent by air as well as by motor transport. Field ambulance units were sent to inoculate refugees before they crossed the border. The Indian Air Force airlifted cooked food as well as foodgrains and ensured other necessities for the stuck and marching columns.

This was not simply a swap of population. In this exchange, Pakistan lost its hardworking Punjabi agriculturists, bankers, merchants, shopkeepers, entrepreneurs and clerks. The wheels had come off the state machinery. In India, similarly, Muslim railwaymen, weavers, craftsmen, and administrators, disappeared in a few months, halting production and trade and crippling the state's ability to function. Most artisans crossed over to Pakistan.

Dhabas sprung up on the Grand Trunk (GT) Road, one of the oldest and longest roads in the subcontinent, running from Peshawar, Rawalpindi and Lahore through Amritsar, Ludhiana and further to Delhi. As millions migrated between India and Pakistan, dhabas emerged as essential stops for weary travellers. These dhabas, often rudimentary mud structures, comprised a simple kitchen, cots to sit upon while eating, and a wooden plank placed across the width of the cot serving as table to place the dishes. They provided food, shelter, and a sense of community to those undertaking the arduous journey. They became important sources of communication. People left messages for their lost family members or relatives of their whereabouts in case their kin stopped at the dhaba to inquire. Over time, some of these dhabas gained fame and became landmarks along the route.

The mass exodus became the greatest and the most tragic migration ever recorded in human history. More than fourteen million people are estimated to have been uprooted from their ancestral homes on both sides. They were not prepared for this calamity. Many witnessed the destruction of their homes and the deaths of loved ones. By the time the MEO stepped in to evacuate stranded minorities, the damage had been done. Over three million are stated to have perished due to violence, hunger, suicide, and disease, although the number of dead and displaced remains a matter of conjecture to this day.

Hundreds and thousands of unfortunate Khatris perished in the conflagration – unwept, unsung, unhonoured, many unremembered. The migration had uprooted them from the habitat they had known for centuries. The traumatic experiences of migration left a deep scar on people forced to migrate, one that was going to last many generations.

The greatest migration in world history left a legacy of untold tales of pain, seething traumas and unspoken loss. Life, as they knew, had changed forever.

12

A Sigh of Relief

The kafila continued to march forward with monsoon rain battering them mercilessly. Both men and beasts were too tired and hungry. Most people were now without food. The cattle were too frail to carry any further or pull the cart for lack of fodder. Some owners had already abandoned or killed their cows. Goats had been slaughtered for eating. The migrants were completely ill prepared to face the calamity.

The unyielding rain not only slowed them down but also made people sick. The fury of the monsoon commands both awe and dread in Punjab. The skies unleash a torrential downpour that transforms the landscape within moments. The rain falls in relentless sheets, drumming against rooftops, streets, and fields with a deafening roar. Rivers swell, bursting their banks, and the earth, parched just days before, becomes a sodden, muddy expanse. The wind howls, bending trees and tearing anything that is not firmly rooted. Villages and cities alike are brought to a standstill as roads flood, and life pauses under the weight of the deluge. Yet, amidst the destruction, there is a raw, untamed beauty. The monsoon breathes life into the land, replenishing rivers, lakes and reservoirs. Fields, once barren, turn lush green, promising a bountiful harvest. The air, heavy with the scent of wet earth, carries a sense of renewal. The monsoon in Punjab is a reminder of nature's power that can both nurture and devastate with equal intensity.

The monsoon of 1947 signalled hard times for the kafila. Many people fell sick from flu and pneumonia. No medical care was forthcoming, even hot water was hard to get by. Dry wood was no longer available to make fire. People started tearing out their bullock carts for use as fuel wood or to make a bonfire to get some warmth for the cold and sick.

It was getting hard to walk in the mush created by bullock carts moving ahead of them. Their clothes were soiled in mud, some of which had been washed away by the falling rain. There was no place where they could stop even for a while, as everything around them was muddy, filled with water. The kafila had turned too large now and probably had about 20,000 or more emigrants. It stretched endlessly for miles. The ever-growing size of the column also slowed down the progress and made communication nearly impossible.

The Batra family had been on the move for five days. They were all exhausted. Narain Dass had fallen sick. He had turned silent ever since Tulsi Dass passed away. Bebe and Raj Rani's passing away had further shaken him. His communication was limited to nodding or shaking his head. Nand Lal was worried about his father's health and took good care of him.

Kesar Dass sat on the cart, staring blankly at the rain battering the road ahead. He was unable to overcome the loss of his mother's demise. He had barely spoken since Raj Rani passed away. Her passing had left a void that no words could fill. Memories of his childhood in the village flooded his mind, each one a bittersweet reminder of her love. He could still feel the warmth of her arms as she cradled him as a child, lulling him to sleep with her fingers gently stroking his hair. He remembered the way she would light the clay stove to prepare rotis. The smell of fresh bread would fill their home. The annual fair in Jhang town was another vivid memory. She would hold his tiny hand tightly, guiding him through the crowds, her laughter mingling with the sounds of folk singers. Now, as he sat alone, Kesar Dass felt the weight of her absence. He longed for his home, his village, his parents, for the comfort of her mother's hand on his head, and his father's affectionate gaze. Tears welled up in his eyes.

His thoughts were interrupted by Gobind pulling at his kurta to get his attention. 'Mataji wants to talk to you,' he said.

Bhagwanti sat inside the canopy of the cart, sobbing. She pointed to the drenched sack of bajra. 'The grains ... they're almost gone. I tried my best all this time to save it from getting doused but the rain has been too fierce. There is barely enough left for a handful of rotis. And the wood – there's nothing dry left to burn. How will I cook anything?'

Kesar Dass sat down on the cart floor, his head in his hands. 'Do we have enough to feed the children for a couple of days?' he asked, looking up.

'Another day or two, maybe. And then what, Lalaji? I have been rationing it already. Gobind keeps saying he's hungry. He doesn't understand. He's just a child. How do I explain to him that there's not enough left for all of us to eat? Ram Saran understands. He passes on even some of his own share to Gobind. But I know he himself goes hungry most of the time.'

Kesar Dass looked at Gobind. He was playing listlessly with a stick, unmindful of the gravity of the situation. Outside he could see Ram Saran walking alongside the tired Ram Lal, supporting him by holding his arm. *He's just a boy, he shouldn't have to carry this burden*, he thought. 'He is strong, Bhagwanti. Stronger than we give him credit for. He knows we're all in this together. Maybe we can find some grains in the next village. We'll get through this. We have to.' This is all he could bring himself to say.

'But what if we don't? What if this is how it ends? Starving on the side of the road?' said Bhagwanti, wiping her tears with the edge of her sari.

'We will find a way, Bhagwanti. We always have. It won't end like this. I won't let it. We've come too far, suffered too much to give up now. I promise you we will find a way.'

Bhagwanti nodded. She felt bad for imposing on her husband who was already reeling under weight of Raj Rani's death. She had been observing him mourn silently. They were both not very expressive of their emotions. Bhagwanti couldn't help but console her husband. 'We all miss Mataji ... I hope you will stay strong, Lalaji.'

Kesar Dass did not respond. His mind was now occupied with the problem at hand – arranging food.

The rain stopped for some time although the sky remained overcast. The kafila reached an abandoned village. Kesar Dass had shared his concern over the diminishing stock of food with Binder. Some armed young men led by Binder went into the village looking for grains and water. Unlike the previous village, this one had not been plundered till now. Most houses and shops were locked. They were unsure if they should break open the locks and look for grains and water inside. That would be theft and even in this moment of crisis they hesitated to break into someone's house or shop. It was also risky as there could be armed people hiding inside who might attack to defend themselves and their property. But they also knew that they didn't have a choice. They couldn't let their people die of starvation or thirst.

After they had overcome the moral dilemma, they broke open the doors of all shops, one after the other. There was nothing inside. They then started breaking into the houses. Finally, they struck luck. In a godown of one house they found half a sack of potatoes and a few bottle gourd which were still fresh. Their eyes lit up. Boiled potatoes would give the children enough carbohydrates. The lauki was just about enough for one meal for a couple of children but more than plenty in the circumstances. They rejoined the kafila and caught up with their spot which had moved away a few miles by now. Kesar Dass heaved a sigh of relief. Bhagwanti couldn't stop thanking Lord Rama. They had some food to survive now.

It was around this time that they heard the news about both governments having agreed to exchange the population and that the military was stepping in to evacuate the migrating people securely. A wave of jubilation ran through from one end to the other of the miles-long column. People broke into dance, women prayed in gratitude to their gods, and cries of *'Sat Sri Akal, Bole So Nihal'* and *'Jai Shri Ram'* filled the air. Children joined the celebration with confused looks on their faces not knowing why everyone was suddenly happy and celebrating. The news of the evacuation plan revived the kafila. The resolve of people to fight adversity became stronger in anticipation of the arrival of help.

The kafila had been moving nearly all day now. The news of impending help had added a momentary spring in the step of even those who were tired and battered. It was evening when they saw the headlights of a MEO truck approaching from the opposite direction, followed by some jeeps. An officer, who wore an olive-green raincoat over his uniform, got down from one of the jeeps. He appeared to be a junior commissioned officer (JCO). He climbed on the top of the truck with a loudspeaker, ignoring the pounding rain.

'We have come to escort you across the border into India,' he announced. A huge uproar of joy and celebration filled the air, drowning the officer's voice. He desperately signalled everyone to calm down. After some effort, the noise mellowed down. The officer continued. 'I understand you are all exhausted and many of you may even be sick. It will take us five days to reach the transit camp across the border if you follow my instructions. If you don't observe the rules it will not only delay us but also expose us to risk as the entire way is filled with danger. One vehicle with my armed men will escort you, and the other will follow the column. We have some packets of food but that will not be enough for all, so please feed the sick and children first. More supplies are on the way. Those who need immediate medical attention should inform any of my soldiers, and we will try to do our best to help. There are doctors at the camp so help is not too far. All of you will stay in the lane. We will pass Muslim villages on the way, no one will threaten or attack anyone or retaliate. No one will react if provoked. Just keep walking silently. We will halt around 5 p.m. every day at a suitable place where the time of departure for the next day will be announced. Although camps are being set up for halt at night, it is unlikely they will get erected soon so we may have to find clear ground for overnight halt. Now, I will repeat the instructions again, please pass them to the people behind you.'

The officer asked men in the front to create a group of volunteers to work with soldiers and serve as communication channels. The truck in which he had arrived left with a few soldiers to replenish food. One soldier was posted every five hundred yards to protect the column.

People were suddenly walking with a fresh burst of energy. Some people were attended to for emergency medical needs. Cooked red beans and water were distributed to as many people as possible, mostly the old, women and children. Instructions were meticulously passed on to people across miles as per the rules laid by the officer. It took nearly an entire evening to bring a semblance of order on the lines of the officer's instructions.

By the time they finished, it was already dark. As there was no place to stop, the deluge of thousands of displaced people started moving again, this time a little assured. The danger was still not behind them. After they had walked for an hour, soldiers frantically blew their whistles and signalled the caravan to stop. A few people in the kafila had fainted from hunger and exertion; they needed rest and some food. The officer instructed that the caravan would camp for the night. Thankfully, the rain had paused. Bullock carts were parked in an orderly manner on one side in the fields. Men and women hurriedly improvised fireplaces with the twigs saved from the previous day. Some women began to cook chapatis, to be served with boiled potatoes and pickles.

The young officer was Padam Singh, a native of Rajasthan. He walked alongside the caravan, talking to elderly men and women, reassuring them of their safety. Kesar Dass walked across to Padam Singh. Both Ram Saran and Gobind tagged along. They wanted to see the army man in uniform from close quarters. A guard standing by stopped them from approaching the jeep. Padam Singh waved the guard to let them come. Kesar Dass conveyed his appreciation to the officer for his support.

'I have brought fresh roti and lauki cooked by my wife.'

The officer thanked Kesar Dass, and offered him a drink. After the entire month of frenzy, he could use a couple of drinks, Kesar Dass thought. He poured himself a large peg. Padam Singh smiled. Both Ram Saran and Gobind settled on a cot placed for Padam Singh.

'I want to express my deepest gratitude for coming to our aid. Your support has given people hope that they can survive this terrible violence. Thankfully, there was no attack on the column today, but the past few days have been incredibly difficult and harrowing for all of us,' Kesar Dass said after taking a large sip of rum.

'It is still not safe,' Padam Singh replied, speaking very softly, as if he was talking to himself. 'I have not seen this kind of maddening communal frenzy in my life. Even with military forces around, raids continue on the moving columns. Yesterday, a column near Lyallpur was ambushed. More than twenty people died, including a soldier. We have been given a shoot-at-sight order after the incident. The villages located on the route of the columns have been placed under curfew. Armoured cars, wheeled carriers and tanks have been deployed in some towns through which columns have to pass to reach the other side of the border. Military personnel have been stationed on rooftops in towns the kafilas will pass to keep a watch. Lahore and Amritsar, where population is getting exchanged, are also under curfew. But for these measures, we would have definitely faced trouble on the way. We cannot, we must not, let our guard down. Anything can happen in this treacherous time.'

Kesar Dass listened in silence.

'How long have you been on the road?' inquired Padam Singh, pouring Kesar Dass another drink.

Kesar Dass recounted the entire episode with a heavy heart, his voice trembling as he recounted the day they returned to the village after the peace committee meeting. 'It has been over a month since we left our village,' he said, his eyes reflecting the weight of the time that had passed.

Padam Singh listened intently, his expression softening with empathy. 'I am truly sorry to hear about your mother,' he said gently, placing a comforting hand on Kesar's shoulder. 'May her soul rest in peace. You are truly blessed to have friends like Abdul and Mukhtyar by your side during such difficult times.' His words carried a warmth that offered a small measure of solace amidst the sorrow.

Kesar Dass nodded again, taking another large sip of his drink. 'We hope to be back in our village soon. Our lands, house and cattle are safe in the hands of Mukhtyar.'

Padam Singh silently nodded, though his thoughts were in stark contrast to Kesar Dass's optimism. He wasn't surprised that Kesar Dass, like most migrants, saw the partition as a temporary disruption. These individuals who had left their homes reluctantly, driven out by the pressures of communal tensions, were clinging to the hope of returning to their ancestral lands. Their villages were more than just homes for them – they were symbols of identity and pride. Many, including Kesar Dass, had left their belongings under the care of friends and neighbours, convinced they would reclaim them once the situation improved.

But Padam Singh knew better. The hatred and brutality he had witnessed in the last few weeks told him another story. He was certain that a return was impossible, at least not anytime soon. The bloodshed and chaos showed no signs of abating, and even if the violence subsided, the deep-seated hatred and division between the communities would make reconciliation unthinkable. The locals, eager to seize abandoned homes and businesses, would stoke fear and unrest to ensure the migrants never returned. Yet, despite these grim thoughts, Padam Singh chose to remain silent, allowing Kesar Dass to hold on to his fragile hope.

Both finished their drink in silence. After a while, Padam Singh spoke, a bit under the influence of the third drink he had drowned. Looking at Ram Saran and Gobind he said, 'Boys, go sleep now, we have an early start tomorrow.' He didn't want the young boys to listen to the disturbing conversation. The boys left, reluctantly.

'In the army, we are trained to fight the enemy, prepared for the worst. Yet, no training could have equipped us for the horrors I have witnessed over the past few months – our own people, driven by hatred, turning against one another. This madness is unlike anything I have ever experienced. Even in war, there are rules, but here, humanity has descended into savagery. I never imagined man could be so barbaric. Every day, I buried hundreds of bodies – sometimes more. We have rescued girls held captive, but only after they had endured unspeakable violence. How could communities that lived side by side for centuries, in relative peace, suddenly turn on each other with such ferocity?' Padam Singh's voice trembled, his eyes brimming with tears. 'This has only exposed the fragility of our humanity, and the depths to which it can stoop and falter,' he added, staring at an empty rum bottle.

Kesar Dass felt tears running down his cheeks. 'Yet, thankfully, there are people like Abdul, Mukhtyar, your soldiers, and yourself who believe in insaniyat, saving lives at the cost of risking their own,' he said.

Padam Singh did not reply. He sat staring at the bottle the two had emptied, in deep contemplation. Kesar Dass waited for him to say something but Padam Singh remained quiet, his eyes fixated on the bottle. Suddenly, he ordered his assistant to fetch another bottle. Kesar Dass rose to leave. He had already had too many, and wanted to sleep. His legs hurt from walking all day. There was yet another uncertain day ahead.

They resumed their journey the next day. Every few kos, they encountered vultures feasting on the carcasses of cattle that had succumbed to exhaustion, unable to continue any further. The air was thick with the stench of rotting flesh, an unbearable nauseating odour. The sight and smell of decay were insufferable.

Sometime in the afternoon, the column came to a grinding halt. 'The kafila will turn right from here and cross through the fields to reach the bank of the Beas,' Padam Singh announced, standing on the jeep's roof.

The kafila changed its direction.

Padam Singh later informed that caravans of evacuees travelling from East Punjab had begun entering Pakistan, and evacuees from both sides had started crossing paths. Wherever groups from the two communities encountered each other, the situation became precarious. Those moving from India felt emboldened after entering Pakistan and began shouting provocative slogans at the Hindu caravans. People from both sides pelted stones at each other. In one instance, a fight broke out between two caravans, resulting in hundreds of casualties on both sides before the military personnel could restore order. The MEO high command decided that different communities should take separate routes to reach their destinations, but inevitably, some still ended up crossing paths.

The next day, the situation nearly went out of hand. Suddenly, they came face-to-face with a column of Muslim evacuees approaching from the opposite side. The two groups, each fleeing their homes in search of safety, found themselves on a collision course. Both equally battered, carried with them the scars of recent attacks – burned villages, looted homes, and the haunting memories of loved ones lost. They bore similar wounds, their faces etched with fear and anger. Both groups were armed, not just with weapons but also with a seething rage born of betrayal and loss.

It was too late to change course. A small number of MEO soldiers rushed to the front but by then the kafilas were nearly eyeball to eyeball. As the distance between them closed, the atmosphere grew tense. Men from both sides stepped forward, their eyes blazing with fury, their hands gripping sticks, knives and whatever makeshift weapons they had scavenged. Women clutched their children tightly, their faces pale with dread, while the elderly tried to calm the rising tempers, their voices trembling with urgency.

Suddenly, a Hindu man ran towards the approaching kafila, his turban askew, shouting accusations, his voice cracking with emotion. 'They killed my brother! They burned my home!' His words were met with roars of agreement from the kafila of Hindus, their collective anger boiling over.

A young man from the Muslim kafila stepped forward, his eyes blazing. 'And what of our sisters? What of our mothers? Your people back there did the same to us!'

For a moment, it seemed as though violence was inevitable. The two groups stood mere feet apart, their hatred palpable, grief and rage threatening to consume them.

Thankfully, Padam Singh, arrived in his jeep with the soldiers. Another jeep full of soldiers, apparently the escort of the kafila of Muslims, emerged from the opposite side. They pulled out their guns and ordered both sides to halt where they were.

'Stop, else I will order my soldiers to shoot anyone who takes one step forward!' Padam Singh screamed, his voice cutting through the chaos. 'Have you all not suffered enough? Will you now spill more blood, create more orphans, more widows?' His words hung in the air, heavy with truth.

The crowd hesitated, the tension still simmering but no longer at its breaking point. An elderly Muslim man emerged from the crowd, his white beard flowing and hands raised in a gesture of peace towards his kafila. Two elderly men from the Hindu kafila stepped forward, their faces lined with exhaustion, signalling their men to step back. The two kafilas, though still wary of each other, began to move past one another, their eyes avoiding contact. The young on both sides were still fuming with rage and continued to hurl abuses. The soldiers did not lower their weapons till the kafilas had crossed.

As the kafilas continued on their respective journeys, the road behind them remained silent, a witness to a fleeting moment when humanity had triumphed over hatred.

Kesar Dass (Lala-ji) in his house in Kurri in the 1970s

Bhagwanti Devi (Mata-ji)

Dayawanti and Bhagwan Dass

Ram Saran, after his post-graduation

Ram Saran's wife Soma Batra, just after her marriage

Jeevan Dass and Sumitra at their wedding

Gobind Lal and Veena Batra at their wedding

A young Bhagwan Dass (Dayawanti's husband)

Bhagwanti Devi (Mata-ji) with a relative

Bhagwanti Devi with her brother and another relative

Gobind (in front) leading the procession to the Assembly as Secretary of Haryana Legislative Assembly

Gobind Lal after becoming a lawyer

Gobind Lal after his appointment as Chairman of Haryana Public Service Commission

Bhagwanti Devi (Mata-ji) with her relatives

Gobind and Veena at their house in Hisar sometime after marriage

Gobind Lal at the UK Parliament while on training in the 1980s

Gobind Lal leading the ceremonial procession on the opening day of the Assembly session

Gobind Lal leading the Governor and Speaker to the Assembly on the opening day of the Haryana Legislative Assembly session

Gobind Lal on the steps of the Parliament

Gobind Lal taking the oath of the Constitution as Chairman of the Public Service Commission

Gobind with the clerk of the UK's House of Lords in London

Kesar Dass with a relative at a family wedding

Kesar Dass's sisters Bassi (right) and Kuki

Lala-ji's brother-in-law (Bassi's husband)

Veena Batra's mother Satya Passi

Kesar Dass with grandchildren Tejinder and Suman (Sumitra's children)

Veena Batra's father S.P. Passi

Veena Batra before her marriage

The Gurukul honouring Gobind Lal for his support

13

India, Finally

The residents of Lahore woke up that morning to the sound of great bustle and movement along the road. For more than three hours, they watched the organised evacuee party of Hindu and Sikhs on its way to D.A.V. College where the main camp had been set up. Men, women, and children with their few movable earthly belongings, hundreds of donkey carts, bullock carts and camels formed the caravan. A flying military jeep patrol shepherded the procession, which was accompanied by lorry-loads of troops of the Baloch Military, which had joined as they approached the tense areas of Lahore.

The route diversion, river crossing, and a sense of panic among the people had slowed them down and they took an extra day to reach Lahore. The Batra family had now travelled for eleven days on foot to reach this camp. The journey had not been less than a passage through the river of fire. Yet, they considered themselves lucky that they were not among the one million killed. All evacuees were hastily crammed in the D.A.V. College camp where local evacuees were also staying, waiting for their final evacuation.

Kesar Dass went looking for Padam Singh. He wanted to thank the officer personally but the officer was nowhere to be found. He learnt that after depositing their kafila, Padam Singh had left to secure another convoy, continuing to address a human catastrophe of unimaginable proportions.

The D.A.V. camp was protected by military pickets. People were starved and fatigued. There wasn't much ration left at the camp, and the migrants had to once again be content with boiled lobhia. Many evacuees were still making their way to these camps from the hinterland. The scene at the refugee camp was one of both despair and resilience, a poignant snapshot of human endurance amidst the chaos of Partition. There were three doctors to tend to the thousands wounded.

It had not rained for two days. At dusk, a few men lit a bonfire in a corner of the college playground. Similar fires had been lit by many other groups. They sat around the fire, its flames casting flickering shadows on the faces huddled around it. The fire provided warmth against the chilly night air, but its light also seemed to illuminate the collective trauma etched on the faces of those gathered. Men, women and children sat close, their tattered clothes and weary expressions telling stories of unimaginable hardship. The air was thick with the scent of smoke and faint aroma of whatever meagre food they had managed to cook over the flames. Everyone had brought whatever food they had to share with others. Punjabis prioritise others' needs and comfort over their own, readily sacrificing their meals to feed others. Often, the best food is left for others and served with love. This culture of giving reflects their deep-rooted values of community, compassion, respect and unparalleled hospitality. This spirit was maintained even during the most telling times of migration.

As more people joined, an elderly man, his face lined with exhaustion, recounted how his village was set ablaze, forcing his family to flee with nothing but the clothes on their backs. His voice trembled as he described the long, treacherous journey, the constant fear of attacks, and the heartbreak of leaving behind a lifetime of memories. A young woman, clutching a sleeping child to her chest, spoke next. Her eyes were hollow, her voice barely above a whisper as she narrated how her husband was killed in front of her during the journey. She had no time to grieve, she said, as she had to keep moving to protect her child. Her story was met with silent nods and shared tears, a grim acknowledgment of the atrocities they all had witnessed. Another man, his arm bandaged from a recent injury, recounted the hunger and thirst that plagued their journey, the days spent without food or water, and the desperation that drove some to even drink from muddy puddles. A young boy, no older than fifteen years, spoke of how he carried his younger sister on his back for miles, refusing to let her go even when his legs felt like they would give up. His bravery drew murmurs of admiration from the group, a rare moment of pride amidst the grief.

As the night deepened, the stories continued, each one a testament to the resilience of the human spirit. As they shared their overwhelming sorrow, a sense of solidarity built among the group. The bonfire became a symbol of their shared suffering and their determination to survive. It also served as a reminder of the homes they lost. As they sat together, sharing their stories and their pain, they found solace in each other's company. With its flickering flames, the bonfire became a space of healing, a place where they could begin to process their collective trauma and find the strength to face an uncertain future.

They had to stay at that college camp for four days. Most men volunteered to help the newly arriving columns by the third day. The women were taking turns to cook and serve whatever grains or food was distributed. Young boys attended to the elderly. Amidst the ruins of their lives, the evacuees in the camp were not just survivors – they became a community bound by shared suffering and an unyielding will to endure.

Kesar Dass, who had also enrolled himself to volunteer, stood at the gate on the third day, waiting to receive a kafila. He had heard that the kafila had many people from Jhang. He saw the column come in around noon. Like their own column, this too was miles long. It was hard to accommodate them in the already crammed camp but everyone generously made room for them.

Ram Lal sat on the floor next to where Kesar Dass stood keenly looking for a familiar face in the incoming deluge of evacuees. He heard someone call his name. The voice sounded familiar. He looked around and spotted Radhe Shyam, the postman from Rodu Sultan, waving at him as he tried to squeeze his way through the crowd.

'How are you, Chacha-ji?' Radhe Shyam asked, bending to touch Ram Lal's feet. 'How is everyone?'

'*Jeonda rah*, I am so happy to see you, Radhe Shyam. We have been worried about you,' Ram Lal said, blessing Radhe Shyam with a long life.

Radhe Shyam sat down next to him. 'The last few days have been a nightmare. Everything changed after you left, Chacha-ji. All Hindu families in the village, who did not leave with you, also left. Only Krishan Lal Halwai, who lives next to the small temple at the far end of the village, refused. He said no one was going to hurt the old man and his wife.'

Krishan Lal was a bawarchi in the house of a British officer posted in Bhopal for a long time. When both his sons grew up, the elder found employment under his tutelage in the same kitchen, while the younger one left for Lahore to try his luck in the film industry. Krishan Lal quit his job and returned to Rodu Sultan. He set up a business of cooking food and sweets at weddings and festivals. His food was popular all over Jhang, particularly in towns, as he could cook many English dishes. His sons never visited them. After he and his wife turned old, they gave away their business to one of their employees and spent time looking after the temple, cooking for the travellers who stopped to stay overnight nearby.

Radhe Shyam continued, 'Some of us sneaked back into the village two days later to feed our cattle. Fortunately, the old couple was unharmed. They told us that after we left, the village was attacked late in the night by a large mob. Mukhtyar and his men put up a good fight, the mob left but not before they had set a few houses on fire near the outskirts. I went around the village to check out, everything seemed to be where we left.' Radhe Shyam sighed. 'We were still trying to comprehend what to do when a band of men arrived suddenly from nowhere in three jeeps. I hid myself behind a heap of hay in one of the houses. All of them were armed with guns. They drove through the village shouting, "Leave or die. All non-believers must leave this holy land of Allah." Some fired in the air. They then sped away towards your house. Mukhtyar and his sons went after the miscreants. A few minutes later I heard gunshots again. The firing went on for a good thirty minutes. It was still on when I left the village.'

Radhe Shyam looked at Ram Lal. His face had suddenly turned stark white, drained of all blood. Looking at Ram Lal's state, Radhe Shyam decided against continuing any further. 'I have to go now, Chacha-ji. I am searching for my wife's younger brother who got separated from us. After that my family will head to Hansi. I will see you somewhere in Hindustan.'

As he turned to leave, Ram Lal inquired in a feeble voice, 'Is Mukhtyar fine? Is our house safe?'

Radhe Shyam heaved a deep breath. He answered hesitantly, 'If you insist on knowing … I was scared, so I slipped out and escaped through the fields. But Sukhi Chand, the pandit, met me a few days later. He told me that he too had hid himself in the fields when the firing started. These men had come to seize your house and property. From where he was hiding, the pandit could see Mukhtyar and his sons firing on the people inside your house. The firing stopped after an hour. He also saw an injured Mukhtyar put Alam's dead body in the jeep and leave. It appeared that they had ran out of cartridges; Mukhtyar lost his son trying to evict them from your house. He is himself critically injured. What a sincere and brave friend you have, Chacha-ji. I was reluctant to tell you but you…'

Ram Lal was no longer paying attention to Radhe Shyam. He was devastated. He was already a broken man, and the news of his friend losing his son and getting injured and that, too, trying to protect his Hindu friend's property, had shattered him. A searing agony gripped his heart on learning that their sacred home, the sanctuary where a thousand memories were forged, had been forcibly occupied. Tears of anguish filled his eyes. A fire of rage burnt within him. Ordinary people like him had become pawns in a larger game of power and prejudice. Suddenly, he felt a piercing pain in his chest. He knew he was having a heart attack. Before Ram Lal could call for help, he collapsed.

Ram Saran sat on the high wall looking at the thousands of unhappy people in the college compound, corridors and even on the roof. He had lost his grandparents and now his beloved granduncle in a matter of days. They had just returned from the shamshan after cremating Ram Saran, escorted by the MEO guard. Funerals of two elderly women who had passed away the same day as Ram Lal were also performed. *How many more will die before their convoy reaches India*? he wondered, torn from within.

He cast a glance at the crowd around him. Apathy, hopelessness and helplessness were written all over their faces. Even the strong and well-built among them had been reduced to sad, miserable wrecks. Only one question weighed on their mind – their land. All these people had their roots deep in the soil – the soil of the canal colonies of the Punjab, which they had transformed into one of the most fertile regions in India with the sweat of their brow. They were being uprooted from their soil, their very own soil. Hearing the tales of suffering over the last two nights and recalling their own, he felt devastated yet grateful to God that his parents and siblings were alive and together.

Crossing the Wagah border a day later was momentous. Moving from the evacuee camp, they crossed the border into a transit camp on the Indian soil. Wagah was a small village located on the G.T. Road between Lahore and Amritsar in the heart of the vast and populous region of Punjab. There was no natural dividing line between the two cities. A border between them was wholly artificial, not just geographically, but also ethnographically. There was a solitary Indian flag flying on a wooden pole and some overturned drums, partly painted white, partly black, kept where Radcliffe had drawn the line. Two army camps had been erected on both sides of this border to facilitate handover of migrants. Nobody checked to see if they had any documents. They were asked to deposit their weapons at the camp office. Kesar Dass deposited the pistol given by Ram Lal, but held back the revolver Majid's son had passed on to him.

Though there was no formal boundary, crossing over to the new India was a matter of solace for everyone. Everyone was relieved at the thought that they were no more in the danger zone. There were shouts of *Hindustan zindabad!* And *Bharat Mata Ki Jai.* More than patriotism, it was an expression of relief that they were out of Pakistan and in India. People sobbed; it was great to be safe, finally.

The work of the MEO stopped at the transit camp. Thereafter, the responsibility of refugees lay with the East Punjab government and the Indian Ministry of Relief and Rehabilitation. Here onwards, the evacuees were to be sent to bigger camps elsewhere in India. This distribution took some time. Most Jhangis who had crossed over were headed to Rohtak. Relatives of Ram Lal left for Nagpur as they had some relatives there. A few relatives were planning to leave for Amritsar and Delhi.

Kesar Dass informed the officials that they wanted to go to Kalanor. Kalanor was like their second home. It was a small and happy village near Rohtak. Not only was it home to Raj Rani's family, even Bhagwanti's two brothers lived there. Many rural areas of Rohtak were in the grip of violence. Curfew had been imposed in many parts. There were no camps in Rohtak and those headed there were instructed to get down in Kurukshetra and stay in the camp till it was safe to travel further. They had to spend the night in the transit camp.

Though the Batra family felt safe and jubilant to be in India, their ordeal was by no means over.

14

An End and a Beginning

The greatest migration in the history of the subcontinent which began in July 1947 continued for months. It was not a mere relocation, but a journey fraught with fear, violence and immense suffering. A near-complete exchange of population was concluded in three months, between September and November in 1947.

Towards the end of November 1947, Swaran Singh, East Punjab's home minister announced in a press conference that there was complete peace in East Punjab, and anyone could go about anywhere in the region without any escort or fear. He confessed that the government and administration had been shocked by the partition, but assured everyone that it had fully recovered and was well-tuned to deliver. He also stated that 32,00,000 non-Muslims from West Punjab and NWFP had been evacuated. Only 258,000 Hindus and Sikh were left in West Punjab; some of them desired evacuation and some did not.

Earlier, in the first session of the East Punjab Legislative Assembly held on 1 November 1947 at Governor-General's lodge in Simla, a motion was moved for passing a resolution expressing sympathy for sufferers of Partition. While communicating its joy at the advent of freedom, the Assembly noted that it was fully conscious that real happiness had been marred by the tragedy of mass killings, lootings, arson, abduction and other inhuman brutality. The Assembly expressed its deep sympathy for the uprooted population of East and West Punjab, who had suffered heavily, and assured that all who had been forced to leave Pakistan for the safety of their lives and honour would be taken care of and everything possible would be done to ameliorate their sufferings. The resolution acknowledged the tragedy and its scale:

> It was, as you all know, on the 15 August, 1947, at 12 in the night that the Constituent Assembly made a formal declaration of independence and of having assumed the reins of Government and it was on this auspicious day that independence was conferred upon each province in the country, as provided in the India Independence Act passed by the Parliament. But at that time no one knew that it would be attended with so much misery, bloodshed, arson and loot. No doubt, there had been riots even in March 1947, but the situation grew worse in the beginning of August, 1947, and from the 11th of August onward the situation became still worse ... none of us had an idea that things would take such an ugly shape. I need not tell you that lakhs of people on both sides have been rendered homeless. Thirty-eight lakhs of Hindus and Sikhs who had their homes and hearths in West Punjab have been uprooted, and so is the case of the Muslims in the East Punjab whose number is about 45 lakhs.

The resolution went on to talk about 'The inhuman treatment meted out to the non-Muslims in Pakistan [which] has created a feeling of retaliation in those who have been evacuated from Pakistan into the Indian Union'. It acknowledged how difficult it was to supress 'the feelings of 38 lakhs of people'. In view of the unprecedented and unparalleled nature of the tragic happenings 'it becomes rather difficult for any government to assure safety to the Muslims desirous of staying on in the East Punjab'. It mentioned that 'these tragedies have eclipsed even the Jallianwala Bagh tragedy' and acknowledged the complete breakdown of transport and communications, postal, telegraph and telephone arrangements. Lamenting the 'sufferings of Hindus and Sikhs of West Punjab or of those belonging to other parts of Pakistan', the resolution said that the government was aware of the criticism directed at it 'for not doing as much as should have been done' and mentioned that there is 'no hesitation in admitting the shortcomings on our part'. It ended by lauding the Punjabis as 'a brave and self-respecting people ... who know how to endure hardships', and who 'can repair their financial losses. But in no case they are prepared to tolerate any affront to their bravery and self-respect.'

The MEO wound up soon after. In its one-year tenure, the MEO had evacuated over four million refugees from West to East Pakistan. It also helped Pakistan authorities in evacuation of an even greater number of Muslim refugees from the Indian side of the border. Though the MEO had limitations, the evacuation of refugees on both sides of the border became smoother after its inception. It maintained law and order to safeguard the refugees once they joined the columns. Despite numerous constraints, the MEO soldiers did their best to achieve desired results. The officers and jawans of the Indian Army deputed with the MEO worked in extremely difficult conditions. Many of them had just returned from their overseas assignment after World War II. Some had not gone on leave for a long time while others were looking forward to demobilisation. Some soldiers themselves were displaced persons and had no information of their families. Nevertheless, they stood up to save the lives of their people. In this venture, many soldiers also died. An army faced with a severe resource crunch, its manpower divided between India and newly created Pakistan, worked tirelessly to save lives.

With evacuation coming to an end, the focus of the government shifted to the provision of relief and rehabilitation for the displaced people.

Soon, the Batra family was on the move again, this time to reach Amritsar railway station. The family had been reduced to an ageing Narain Dass, Kesar Dass, Bhagwanti and their four children; Nand Lal, Shakuntala and their children; two cousins of Shakuntala, and Dhania. Sukhi Chand, the pandit, who had no relative or friends in India, had decided to tag along with Bhagwanti, the most dedicated visitor at the temple back in Rodu Sultan.

They had to let go of their bulls at the station, as the train did not have the means to carry any cattle. The bulls were like family and Bhagwanti's heart ached as she bid farewell to them. Years of shared toil, care and companionship had forged an unbreakable bond. Tears welled up as she looked in their gentle eyes, warmed by their strength, and response to her voice. All of them hugged the bulls one after the other and sought their forgiveness. They handed over the bulls and the carts to the military for their use to transport people from the border to the train station. Her hands trembled as she released them, whispering a prayer for their safety and happiness, hoping they would remember her love.

The train was cramped with the evacuees and their ragged belongings, strewn around in every possible nook. None of them got a seat, but that was the least of their concern after what they had gone through. The only questions hanging on their minds were of identity, and food, housing, and a dignified life.

The new province of East Punjab was barely a week old, when it faced the first avalanche of migrants. It had scarcely come to terms with the fact of Partition, and now had to deal with the rush of evacuees. Providing relief, housing, education, employment to such huge masses was certainly not the first task which the Indian government had envisioned for itself. Food and housing were the most pressing immediate requirements. They also had at hand the enormous task of restoring the morale of shocked and traumatised millions. The machinery of the new Indian administration was far from adequately organised to meet these needs. The unexpectedness of it and lack of preparation made the colossal task even more difficult.

Many refugees found shelter with relatives, but the vast majority had to be provided for. The main concentration of evacuees was in East Punjab, Delhi, United Province, Bombay, Bikaner, Jodhpur and other Rajputana states. Huge tent cities were set up by the central and provincial governments to meet the needs of lakhs of people arriving from across the border. The camps ranged from small temporarily improvised shelters in schools, temples, gurudwaras, mosques and municipal buildings, to vast state-run establishments. Some non-governmental charitable organisations also joined the efforts.

In all, about 160 camps had come up all over the country, providing temporary shelter to lakhs of migrants. In East Punjab alone, eighty-five camps had been set up in Amritsar, Gurdaspur, Jullundur, Ludhiana, Ambala, and a particularly large one at Kurukshetra with a capacity of five lakhs. However, these too were inadequate to accommodate more evacuees who had already arrived by then; and more were expected to keep pouring in. By the end of November 1947, about thirteen lakh evacuees were being housed and fed in these camps. At one point, the total number of migrants from West Pakistan in eighty-five camps in East Punjab alone reached more than seven lakhs. East Punjab looked like an enormous tent metropolis during the final weeks of the year. The Indian government had to resettle some migrants as far away as Andaman and Nicobar.

A population of over a million had been added to the tally of a newly independent nation by now. A budget of ten crores of rupees had been sanctioned for relief.

On reaching Kurukshetra, the Batra family were allotted two tents in the camp. Twelve people had to squeeze into two ill-equipped tents. Yet, it was a luxury after weeks spent on the road, sleeping under the open sky in rain and storms. In any case, they hoped to leave for Kalanor soon.

The camp at Kurukshetra was the largest relief camp in India. It was a proto-city built over nine square miles to accommodate more than a quarter of a million refugees. The camp spread for miles from Kurukshetra railway station to Thanesar on one side and to Pipli on the other. The largest number of refugees in the camp belonged to Bahawalpur state and NWFP. Refugees from West Punjab also constituted a fair proportion while those from Jammu and Kashmir state, Balochistan and Sindh were negligible in number. The government entrusted the camp's administration to the army. Major General Nathu Singh was appointed as the camp's commander.

Arrangements in the camps were scanty. Food was in short supply and largely dependent on government and voluntary relief organisations. Some ration of vegetables, ghee, pulses and clothes was provided without a charge. Additional food had to be bought. Water supply was scant and not enough for drinking or completing daily chores. The Batras did not care much about the condition of tent as they hoped to reach Kalanor soon – to the security of Kesar Dass's mother-in-law's home. They were thankful for the temporary shelter and food. The only time when they felt humiliated was when their women had to wash and bathe in open spaces with no privacy.

Migrants kept pouring in and the camp's population surpassed three lakhs in November 1947. Kurukshetra grew ten times in size in just six weeks from mid-October to the end of November 1947. Sometimes, as many as 25,000 people would arrive, unanticipated, in the middle of the night. The increasing number of occupants caused severe stress on the limited resources. Necessities were in short supply. By now, ration cards had been issued to occupants, and were needed to receive supplies. There were long queues and fights broke out frequently. The government machinery had been expanded enormously to cope with the demands, and the refugees often made up the new recruits.

Moreover, the camps were ill-equipped to deal with the approaching winter. Winter in north India can get harsh, and the temperature often drops significantly. The children and elderly were least capable of coping with the harsh conditions. Medical facilities were woefully inadequate for such a large population. Makeshift clinics set up struggled with a dearth of medicines and healthcare professionals. Volunteer doctors and nurses worked tirelessly, but their efforts to stem the tide were in vain due to the sheer volume of needed care. Each one of the incoming migrants was now inspected on arrival and later vaccinated and inoculated.

Lighting conditions were also poor in the camp. The power house installed in the camp provided electric light only for roads, and there was an equal shortage of kerosene. Even in these testing times, people retained a spirit of hope and faith. Temples and gurudwaras had been improvised in the tents. *Bhagwati Jagran* and *Mata ki Chowki* were frequently organised. These provided opportunities for religious gatherings and discourses, which served to maintain the morale of refugees. Many organisations like the Ramakrishna Mission and the Hindu Mahasabha joined the government efforts of providing relief to the occupants.

Despite all efforts at an organised distribution of quilts and tents, lentils, rice and flour, the camp buckled under the weight of the sheer number of people still moving across the border. The army struggled hard to manage camps while coping with new responsibilities like guarding new borders, evacuating a large population on both sides of the border, curbing violence and transporting people to camps in different parts of the country. However, over months, the chaos settled and camp management improved. The camp city was divided into four smaller towns, each under the supervision of a town commander, who was helped by a number of unit commandants. Each township had its own considerable staff of rationing officers, storekeepers, clerks, typists and record keepers to handle the distribution of supplies. By the end of November 1947, water supply and sanitation arrangements had become better; bathing places and latrines had also been provided. There was some lighting as electric poles were erected in different parts of the site including hospitals, post offices and schools.

In each camp town, three primary schools and one middle school were opened. There was one high school. By the beginning of 1948, the number of schools had increased to seventeen with more than 5,500 students. Students were not charged any tuition fee. Reading and writing material was also provided free to deserving students. Within three months the number of schools rose to thirty-five and the number of students reached more than 18,200. One education officer with some clerks was in charge of the education department, which also had forty-five sub-officers, 238 teachers, 109 clerks and twenty-one peons.

The Indian government and international organisations worked extensively to mitigate the crisis, but their resources were stretched thin. Transporting and settling millions proved to be a mammoth task. The ordeal at the camps highlighted the administrative challenges of immediately addressing the humanitarian fallout of large-scale migrations.

Kurukshetra, the ground of many battles, became a testament to human resilience and the profound impact of the partition. It was a temporary yet significant chapter in the tumultuous lives of evacuees who were compelled to live there. Their hardiness, despite food scarcity, medical emergencies and emotional traumas, was a poignant reminder of the human spirit's ability to endure and adapt even under the most trying circumstances.

The Batras left the Kurukshetra camp after three days, not because violence had ended in Rohtak rural areas, but because the camp had filled to the brim. Migrants were still pouring in and space was needed to accommodate them. The administration thought it fit to let go those who had a place to stay elsewhere. About two hundred people who were headed to different villages in Rohtak formed a caravan. Kesar Dass rented a bullock cart for three days from one of the cart occupants with some money he had managed to save.

On the way to Kalanor they stopped in Rohtak camp for a day to meet people coming from Jhang, hoping to find a familiar face. They were keen to learn anything they could about their village, home, land and animals as occupants of the Karnal camp were mainly from the districts of Jhang, Multan, Muzaffargarh, Lyallpur and other parts of Pakistan. There were around 57,807 people from Jhang.

They did not find anyone from the village but were pleased to meet some distant relatives. After checking on their welfare, they left for Kalanor.

While the Batra family was fortunate that they did not have to stay for long in the camp and bear the pain of living in those inhuman conditions, many migrants had to stay in camps for years. Some camps continued to exist in new forms in the 1950s. In Punjab, many camps were wound up and their inmates dispersed within several years of Partition or deliberately transformed into more substantial housing colonies. The tents were gradually replaced by brick-and-mortar dwellings and refugee colonies emerged from the ashes of the camps in many places.

As soon as the Batra family reached Kalanor, they collapsed on the floor of Bhagwanti's house, many from relief, and others from extreme fatigue after the long trek. Bano and Kaki had already arrived ahead of them in anticipation of their visit. The women started crying, again from relief, and to mourn the deaths of their elders. Quickly, they were served a warm meal of dal, bhindi, roti and chhach, which, though simple, felt like a feast. Eating at home, and with the family, felt like a luxury. Their eyes were filled with tears at the sight of a comfortable bed after months of sleeping in the open. For the first time in months, they could rest without the constant fear of violence.

The initial days were spent recovering from the physical and emotional toll of the journey. Slowly, they regained their strength and composure as they eagerly waited for conditions to turn normal so that they could return to Rodu Sultan. However, immediately after Independence, tensions between India and Pakistan began to boil over a number of issues. The relations between the two countries continued to get worse. Their hopes of returning to their homeland were shattered by the events of the next few months.

In early September, riots broke out in Delhi like never before. In fact, violence started in August but peaked in September. Hindus and Sikhs, enraged by what had happened to their communities in West Punjab, unleashed their anger towards Muslims of Delhi. Homes and hospitals were attacked, shops were looted, and vehicles carrying evacuees and relief supplies were ambushed. The orgy of violence in Old Delhi and Paharganj witnessed heavy gunfire from homes of retired army officers and families desperately trying to defend their homes from the mobs. Hundreds sought refuge in the homes of prominent Muslim leaders such as Abul Kalam Azad, Anees Kidwai and others. Tens of thousands of Muslims were camping out at Purana Qila and Humayun's Tomb. More than three lakh Muslims left Delhi for Pakistan. A furious Prime Minister Jawaharlal Nehru went out himself to try and prevent violence in Connaught Place. It was only after the arrival of Mahatma Gandhi on 9 September that the violence in Delhi started to abate.

Kashmir became another boiling point of tension. Just prior to Independence, Sardar Patel had urged Maharaja Hari Singh of Jammu and Kashmir to accede to India; the Maharaja dillydallied. In October 1947, barely two months after Partition, Pakistan sponsored an invasion of Kashmir using thousands of tribal lashkars from the direction of Abbottabad, backed by trained men from what had become the Pakistan Army after division. Hari Singh was bewildered. He pleaded with the Indian government to send Indian troops to Kashmir to protect them from the invaders. The Indian government decided that Indian troops would be sent only if Kashmir formally acceded to India. Hectic negotiations were held. V.P. Menon, India's defence secretary, flew to Jammu on 25 October 1947, and brought back the Instrument of Accession, signed by Maharaja Hari Singh. With his acceptance, the state of Jammu and Kashmir became an integral part of the Indian dominion on the evening of 26 October 1947, legally, morally and constitutionally. A full-scale war broke out between the two countries.

The exchange of population was nearly complete, riots were reduced to stray incidents of violence, and relief work was gaining ground. This revived Kesar Dass's hopes of returning to their homeland.

But India was shaken again in the very first month of the first new year of independent India. On 30 January 1948, All India Radio announced in the evening news that Mahatma Gandhi had been shot dead as he was proceeding through the Birla House gardens, his slender, brown arms around the shoulders of his granddaughters, Manu and Abha, for his daily prayer meeting message. Bapu, as Gandhi was fondly referred, was a guest in the home of G.D. Birla, the millionaire industrialist. He had come to New Delhi in the midst of the disturbances in India's capital. The assassination of Mahatma Gandhi shocked a nation still coming to terms with the trauma of the partition and its aftermath. Communal riots quickly swept Bombay as the news of the assassination spread.

These events dashed any hope of peace with Pakistan in the near future. It also dampened any chances of displaced people ever returning to their homes. Their struggle for their own home and identity in their own country was going to be a long one. A realisation started dawning upon the Batras that they had become displaced persons, without any address, in their own country.

After having been exchanged like cattle, a new struggle started for the victimised and displaced persons – a struggle for rehabilitation.

15

The Struggle for Rehabilitation

Hindus and Sikhs arriving from West Punjab had to be provided alternative properties, occupation and employment in lieu of what they were forced to leave behind. It was also important for the Indian government to transform the mass of laborious people into a productive population at the earliest.

In September 1947, the Ministry of Relief and Rehabilitation was set up with K.C. Neogy as its minister. The government issued the Punjab Evacuee Ordinance IV of 1947, which was later replaced by the Administration of Evacuee Property Act in 1950. All abandoned properties of Muslims were taken over as evacuee properties under the Ordinance. Houses, shops, vacant sites, kholas (dilapidated houses) and industrial establishments were given to displaced persons on rent to begin with. The Resettlement of the Displaced Persons (Land Acquisition) Ordinance, 1948, empowered the government to acquire any land to build what it called satellite townships for the displaced persons.

Several entirely new townships, such as Faridabad and Nilokheri in Haryana and Kalyan in Maharashtra were developed, and over a hundred suburbs extended, in response to this need. Housing was provided for about 2.25 million urban dwellers, either from quarters abandoned by Muslim evacuees or from new construction. Employment was to be found for wage earners in 220,000 families totalling roughly 1.1 million people. More than 150,000 traders, hawkers and shopkeepers, in families including about 750,000 people, received rehabilitation loans.

The government decided to pay compensation to displaced persons who had abandoned immovable property in West Pakistan, after verifying their claims. The proposal was mooted in 1949. A press communiqué issued on 12 September 1950 declared that the government desired to assure all concerned that the displaced persons will be recompensed to the extent possible for their losses – the extent of the recompense depending necessarily upon the total assets that became available for distribution. Its chief proponent was N. Gopalaswami Ayyangar. The compensation amount was to be derived from a 'compensation pool' which in turn would comprise the 'properties left in India by persons who had migrated to Pakistan, the amount which might have been received from Pakistan as compensation, and such contribution from the Government of India as might be possible taking the general financial position into account'. The Displaced Persons (Claims) Act was enacted in 1950. Displaced persons were asked to file their claim for obtaining compensation on account of material losses suffered due to the partition of the country.

Meanwhile, interim compensation was sanctioned for certain categories of displaced persons who were in urgent need of relief. The interim scheme was later replaced by the Displaced Persons (Compensation and Rehabilitation) Act, 1954. Under it, scaled compensation was prescribed. It gave more to smaller claimants, and less to the bigger claimants.

Rural rehabilitation was a daunting task, considering factors like fertility of soil and means of irrigation. Hindu and Sikh refugees had left behind 43 lakh acres of irrigated land in West Punjab against only 13 lakh acres of irrigated land vacated by Muslims in East

Punjab. Of the irrigated land left behind in West Pakistan by Hindu–Sikh refugees, 25 lakh acres were perennially irrigated as against only 4 lakh acres of such land left by the Muslims in East Punjab. The best cotton- and wheat-producing areas of the canal colonies had fallen to the share of Pakistan. Even elementary information regarding land in East Punjab was not available and there was scarcely any detailed knowledge of the holdings of refugees in West Punjab. Numerous important forests and mineral resources and a large number of important industries, like rubber goods, surgical instruments and sports goods also went to West Punjab, just as the only and the oldest university in the region – Punjab University – as well as a large number of educational, medical, technical, veterinary and agricultural institutions of the province. West Punjab had therefore emerged comparatively far richer in terms of economic and food resources. The problem of rural rehabilitation emerged far more daunting in East Punjab.

The East Punjab government had decided to allot temporary lands for kharif and rabi crops in 1947-48 to groups of peasant families. The government believed it would provide a source of living to rural refugees and ensure that the productive capacity of these abandoned lands was not wasted. Initially, land allotment was made on a group basis. Persons who were close relatives or were bound by ties of friendship formed groups and secured temporary allotments. All displaced agricultural people who owned or held land and were cultivating in Pakistan, were eligible for these.

Claims were invited from displaced agriculturists which were orally verified at tehsil headquarters. The government obtained the original revenue records from Pakistan and re-verified the claims. This sometimes also showed that there was a substantial difference between the land left behind in Pakistan by the incoming displaced persons and that abandoned by Muslims in East Punjab. The latter were smaller. Graded cuts were applied in making allotments to displaced claimants in order to overcome this problem, the bigger holders receiving the largest slab of cuts.

There was a marked difference in soil, irrigation, rainfall and productivity of land in various districts of West Pakistan and those of districts in East Punjab and Patiala and East Punjab States Union (PEPSU). The government therefore decided to evaluate different classes of land on the basis of a comparable unit of value. The unit devised for land resettlement operations in East Punjab and PEPSU was given the name of 'standard acre'. The 'standard acre' represents a unit of value based on the productivity of land. An acre which could yield ten to eleven maunds of wheat was given the value of sixteen annas and termed one 'standard acre'. The physical area of a standard acre thus varied and all classes of land in all assessment circles were given a valuation in annas so that they could be measured easily in terms of standard acres.

Kesar Dass and his cousins submitted their applications for allotment of land to the rehabilitation department, with proof of ownership of land back in Rodu Sultan.

Kesar Dass and Nand Lal had opted for allotment of land in Hisar, even though many from Jhang and Muzaffargarh preferred to settle in Rohtak. It was mainly Multanis, 58,397 of them, who decided to settle in urban and rural areas of Hisar. People from Lahore and Montgomery were allotted land in Ferozepur; from Rawalpindi, Sheikhupura and Gujranwala in Karnal and PEPSU; from Shahpur and Gujrat in Ambala; from Dera Gazi Khan and Mianwali in Gurgaon; and from Sialkot in Hoshiarpur, Gurdaspur and Amritsar.

The decision to opt for Hisar was driven by the need to avail of group allotment. Land allotment could be sought by persons who were near relatives or were bound by ties of friendship, formed together into groups. Narain Dass had to decide too and had left the matter in the hands of his son, Nand Lal. Kesar Dass and Nand Lal expected allotment of a large tract of land, but such large contiguous pieces of land were not available in Rohtak. Muslims in Karnal or

Rohtak had not left behind such large tracts of land. The department gave them the option to divide their land between Kesar Dass, the heir of Tulsi Dass, Narain Dass and Nand Lal at different locations near Rohtak, Ambala and Gurgaon, but the cousins rejected that option as they wanted to stay together. The other option was to go to UP or Dehradun, or Mewat, but they opted for Hisar where many Punjabi Khatris from Multan had decided to settle. It was better to stay together even if it meant the land was not of their choice, they decided. In the barani areas of Hisar district, the valuation of one acre was four annas; four ordinary acres went to make a 'standard acre'. In ordinary canal-irrigated tracts where the value of an acre was sixteen annas, an ordinary acre was equivalent to a 'standard acre'. The land in Hisar was mostly barren as there was no canal, but to own fragmented land in Rohtak would have been hard to manage, they decided.

They had to undergo unimaginable hardships and daily difficulties in allotment of land. Innumerable trips had to be made to Delhi to deal with the bureaucratic hurdles of the rehabilitation department. The process of land allotment turned into a nightmare of inefficiency and red tape. Each trip to the rehabilitation department was a test of patience. Long queues, unhelpful officials and endless paperwork drained Kesar Dass, emotionally and physically. The lack of clear communication and transparency added to his anguish. The evacuees were considered unwelcome guests and, to an extent, even an imposition. Partition in itself was bitter, but the treatment meted out to them by the bureaucrats was sometimes worse. The frustration was not just his alone; it was shared by countless others in similar circumstances.

It is not that the government was not doing enough. Allottees of land were given assistance by way of agricultural loans for purchasing bullocks, implements, fodder, seed and for the repair of wells and houses. In order to minimise misuse, loans were advanced in kind instead of cash. The rehabilitation process, though well-intentioned, was plagued by inefficiency and corruption. Having lost their ancestral land, home and livelihood, they had arrived in India with little more than hope. The bureaucratic indifference, however, felt like a betrayal. It compounded their sense of loss. Their experiences were entirely at odds with the lip-service and promises of the politicians.

Kesar Dass was anguished at being branded as 'refugee', even in some official communications. It hurt his self-respect. The people who came to India in a helpless state from West Punjab were not refugees, they were natives of this country, born of the soil, brought up in the midst of surroundings in which the rest of the people grew. They were the worst sufferers of Partition. It is not as if they were strangers, coming to seek refuge and shelter with the Indian government.

They decided to leave the comfort of their relative's house in Kalanor and move to Garhsarai village near Panipat where many families from Jhang, including Bhandi's and Veera's, had arrived. The two families had migrated from Multan by train. So horrific had been their journey, it took them seven dreadful days to cover the distance that would ordinarily take less than twenty-four hours. Garhsarai village had largely been abandoned by Muslims who left for West Punjab. As the camp in Kurukshetra spilled over, the government relocated many occupants of the tented city here. After spending a few months with their relatives, Kesar Dass decided to relocate to Delhi till the land was allotted as travelling from Panipat every few days was laborious. Bhandi and Veera had decided to go to Central Province. A relative had informed them that a dairy was up for sale near Chindwara. The government had agreed to give them some compensation as cash. They hoped to settle there.

In Delhi, with some effort they found a place to live for a few weeks in Safdarjung Tomb camp. Most migrants from Jhang were staying there. Bassi, who lived in Delhi, had moved to London with her husband who worked in Burma Oil. A distant relative persuaded the administrator of the camp to let them pitch a tent in the garden for a few days.

Weeks turned into months. Finally, after a struggle of nearly two months, 150 Khatri Punjabis from Jhang were allotted land in rural Hisar. The Batra clan were allotted land in Kurri, a village near Hisar. About 127 were allotted shops or houses in urban areas of Hisar.

'They have allotted us 175 acres for both Nand Lal and me, in Kurri. It is a temporary allotment,' Kesar announced to Bhagwanti one evening, his voice betraying his disappointment. He had come straight from the rehabilitation department after spending the entire day there, just like every day over the last few weeks.

'Temporary?' Bhagwanti inquired.

'Verification of land revenue records in Jhang will take some more time, although on the basis of our documents they are satisfied with the genuineness of our claim. It is just a formality, a letter confirming allotment is expected in a few days. They don't want to lose a harvesting season, so temporary allotments are being made.

'It is much less than what we held back home, is that what is bothering you?' she asked.

'No, I am thankful for what we have been given. I am looking at the challenges ahead. There are no water canals in Hisar like we had back in Jhang. There is no school in Kurri, the Muslim landlord who lived there had no interest in educating his children or the villagers. The nearest school in Hisar is about six miles away. The house allotted to us was that of a Musalman. It has only four large rooms built in a row and it may not be as per vaastu. And, the most troublesome of all is that both the land and the house allotted to us have been occupied by locals. Getting them to vacate may become taxing.'

Bhagwanti realised why her husband felt disappointed. Their troubles didn't seem to be getting over anytime soon. She turned to the little idol of Lord Rama kept on a makeshift table from a wooden crate, and muttered a prayer with folded hands. 'If this is what your will is, My Lord, we accept it with all humility,' she said, addressing the idol.

Turning to her husband, she said, 'If we all get to live together, it doesn't matter if we have less land than before. We will start our life all over again. We all will work hard. I am sure with Siya Ram's blessings, our days will get better soon. Daya is already engaged, she will get married soon. Sumitra will also be soon old enough to marry, so it is all right if they can't go to school any more. Ram Saran and Gobind will help us on the farm. I am sure Rama will ensure that good comes out of this for our children. When do we have to leave?' she asked, prompting her husband to stay optimistic and look ahead as the future might be beautiful.

'In a few days from now,' replied Kesar Dass, feeling a bit hopeful in the light of Bhagwanti's comforting words. 'The department is yet to issue a letter recognising me as nambardar. Kalanor falls on the way to Hisar. You all can stay there for a few days. I will go to Hisar to complete the paperwork. I met the tehsildar of Hisar who is here to attend a meeting. He has agreed to send the patwari along to help us in taking possession of the house and the land in case of resistance.'

When Muslims left for West Pakistan, their urban and rural properties were confiscated by people living in the vicinity of those who had migrated. However, when the government started allotting evacuee property to incoming refugees from Pakistan, the local occupants of the evacuee property were forced to vacate it. This had increased antipathy towards the migrants.

Daya overheard her parents' conversation. Not able to bear the prospect of having to give up her education, she rushed into her mother's arms, sobbing. Her mother consoled her. 'Everything will be fine, have faith in God.'

'I want to go to school, Mataji, I don't want to marry. I want to live with you,' Daya pleaded. Bhagwanti comforted her daughter till she calmed down.

Turning to Kesar Dass, she said, 'No, we will all go to Hisar together, Lalaji. Ram Saran is a grown-up boy. He should be with you to help. And who is going to cook for you in that strange place? We will all go together.'

Bhagwanti was desperate to settle in her own house, big or small. Although her family in Kalanor had been very warm and welcoming, she didn't want to continue to be a burden on them. She was also mindful of Kesar Dass's discomfort with having to live with his wife's relatives for that long. Nand Lal's cousins were also staying with Bhagwanti's brothers or Raj Rani's family. A few other relatives of their hosts who had migrated had also come to stay with them.

Moreover, she wanted to get out of the overcrowded camp at the earliest. She couldn't anymore bear the sight of families crammed into makeshift shelters made of cloth, bamboo and whatever materials they could scavenge. It was cold in Delhi which added to their misery. Sanitation was a major challenge for her, as it was for all women. They had to defecate in the open in nearby fields due to the lack of toilet facilities. Food was neither adequate nor nutritious. She worried endlessly about her children and their future.

Gobind spent all day playing with many boys who had not had a bath for days. She was afraid he might fall sick. Ram Saran had gone into a shell. He stayed quiet and by himself all the time, hardly interacting with anyone. He would leave the camp in the morning and return only before sunset. Daya and Sumitra stayed by Bhagwanti's side all the time, bored. She had taught them to knit but how much could the young girls knit in a day – they had their own dreams. They envied the boys playing around while they had to stay in the confines of the tent. Bhagwanti was scared to let the girls go out as she had heard stories of young girls being kidnapped and deposited in brothels. With their scant resources dwindling fast, and the future of their children at stake, she lived in the daily dread of worse things to come.

She pushed through each day with quiet strength. Bhagwanti found solace in the camaraderie of other women in the camp, sharing stories and supporting one another. She clung to small joys

– a kind word, a shared meal, or the laughter of Gobind playing with friends he had made in the camp. These moments reminded her of the possibility of a better future. But deep within, her heart ached for stability and dignity. She harboured a quiet hope that one day, her family would find a place to call home again.

Ram Saran too overheard the conversation between his parents. He was not happy at her mother's suggestion of him working in the farm. He had no interest in farming; he wanted to open some business of his own. In the two months spent in the camp, he had met many young enterprising boys who had started small businesses and were already making decent money. Some had moved from the camp to rented accommodation in the fort city of Delhi. Others, whose families had been allotted a shop in the city in lieu of that left behind in West Punjab, used the loan disbursed by the rehabilitation department to start new ventures.

But Ram Saran was glad that at least they would finally get to leave the depressing camp life. He hated the camp and spent as much time away from it as one could. Most young residents of the camps slipped out in the morning to return after sunset. They walked around Delhi exploring the old fort city, the parts built by the British, many monuments, and the tents and tarpaulins erected for migrants that dotted open spaces, and many forts, tombs and schools.

The day after, he quietly left the camp for the camp school in Bhogal, which he attended for a few hours every day. That day, he asked his teacher if she could tell her anything about Hisar. The teacher promised to research and let him know.

16

Hisar: An Unfamiliar Terrain

Hisar is an Arabic word for quila. It takes its name from Hisar-e-Firoza, the Fort of Firoz, built by Firoz Shah Tughlaq in the middle of the fourteenth century. Somehow, the word 'Firoza' got dropped from its original name over time. Some historians identify Hisar with ancient Esukara or Isukara, a beautiful and prosperous city of Kuru Janapada, referred to by the Indian grammarian and scholar, Panini. Jain literature also mentions a town, Isukara, in the Kuru country. The city state of Esukara was possibly founded by the Kurus in later Vedic times. With the fall of the Kuru kingdom, Hisar seems to have come under the Nandas and Mauryas. However, there is no definite archaeological evidence to prove it as yet.

The region is closely associated with the political and cultural life of the Bharatas, the Purus and the Kurus – the prominent tribes of the Aryans. Discovery of prehistoric and historical sites at a number of places in the district testify to the antiquity of Haryana. The excavations at Rakhigarhi, Banawali and Seeswal have proved beyond doubt that pre-Harappan and Harappan cultures flourished in the area. The oldest site, Bhirrana, dates back to 7,000 BCE and the largest, Rakhigarhi, is much larger than both Mohenjo-daro and Harappa.

Lying across the route of overland incursion into India, Haryana has experienced many waves of migration over millennia; a notable invasion was led by Alexander in 326 BCE. The area was ruled by Tomara Rajputs at the time of the Ghaznavid invasions. After Lahore's annexation in AD 1020, Sultan Masud, the successor of Sultan Mahmud, advanced towards this region and conquered Hansi Fort. He then marched to Sonipat and defeated its governor, Dipal Hari. While the Tomaras succeeded in recovering these territories, things changed after Lahore fell into the hands of the Ghuris with the fall of the Ghaznavids. The Tomaras were overpowered by the Chahamanas of Ajmer.

After taking Lahore in AD 1186, Muhammad Ghuri encountered the Chahamanas under Prithviraj. Beaten in his first encounter in 1190-91 at Tarain (Traori) in present-day Karnal district, he came back the following year to defeat Prithviraj in 1192. Prithviraj was taken prisoner. During this encounter the important town of Meham of Rohtak district was destroyed. After the battle of Traori in 1192, the Karnal area became firmly attached to Delhi. In 1206, Qutab-ud-din Aibak sat on the throne of Delhi and established Muslim rule in north India.

In AD 1352, Firoz Tughlaq ordered the construction of the fort which was completed in AD 1354. The original town was a walled settlement inside the fort with four gates: Delhi Gate, Mori Gate, Nagori Gate and Talaqi Gate. These gates are no longer in existence but the vicinity in which they stood continue to hear their names. Hisar town sprang up later around this fort.

When Timur invaded north India in 1398, he plundered Hisar. After his departure, the power struggle continued in the region and in 1408-09 Hisar finally fell into the hands of Khidr Khan, the governor of Multan, who subsequently took the throne of Delhi and established the Sayyid dynasty in the early fifteenth century. Khidr Khan ascended to the throne of Delhi as the first sultan of the Sayyid dynasty. He conferred the fief of Hisar on one Mahmud Hassan in reward for his services.

Later, when Bahlol Lodi ruled Delhi, he gave Hisar's fief to his confidant Muhabbat Khan.

The area has been the site of numerous decisive battles in Indian history. Among the most significant of these conflicts were the Battles of Panipat – in 1526, when Babur defeated Ibrahim Lodi and established Mughal rule in India; in 1556, when Afghan forces were defeated by the army of the Mughal emperor Akbar; and in 1761, when Ahmad Shah Abdali defeated the Marathas, paving the way for British control in India. Also important was the Battle of Karnal, in 1739, when Nadir Shah of Persia dealt a blow to the crumbling Mughal Empire.

At the time Babur invaded Hindustan, Hisar was already an important strategic centre of Ibrahim Lodi's empire. Even before the Battle of Panipat in 1526, Babur dispatched Humayun to siege Hisar. Humayun defeated the Lodis. Babur handed over Hisar to Humayun as a reward for his successful maiden military expedition. It was Akbar who made Hisar the headquarters of Sirkar, the revenue division, a level below the Subah or province. In the early years of the eighteenth century, Hisar came under the rule of Nawab Shahdad Khan of Kasur (1707–37). In his time, the condition of the people of Hisar is said to have been one of considerable prosperity. This, however, was not destined to last for long.

In 1795, an Irish soldier in the British Navy, George Thomas, also known as Jahazi Sahib, abandoned his job and travelled to the northern plains of India. Here, he was taken into the service of the celebrated Zeb un-Nissa Begum, more commonly known as Begum Samru of Sardhana. In 1782, for some misconduct, Thomas was reduced in rank, and left her service in disgust for that of Apa Khande Rao, a relative of Mahadji Scindia, and master of the Jhajjar, Dadri and Narnaul territory. Thomas raised troops for the Marathas, and instructed them in the European system of drill. In return, the district of Jhajjar was assigned to him as a military fief. He built a fort, which he named Georgegarh, which was corrupted into Jahazgarh by the people.

When Bawa Rao, nephew of Apa Khande Rao, succeeded his uncle, Thomas asserted his independence, seized Hansi and Hisar, and began to encroach upon the neighbouring Sikh states. Before the close of 1799, he had extended his authority over Hisar, Hansi and Sirsa territory, and a great part of Rohtak. Even the Bhattis paid him a nominal allegiance, though Thomas made no effort to interfere directly with the authority of the Bhatti chiefs over their respective clans. By this time, however, the adventurer, compelled to resort to constant raids as the only means of supporting his numerous army, had made himself so obnoxious to the Sikh chieftains of the cis-Sutlej states that they came together in 1801 to send an embassy to the French general of Scindia's army at Delhi, with a prayer for assistance against their common enemy.

General Pierre Cuillier Perron received the embassy with conspicuous cordiality. The increasing power of George Thomas had roused in him feelings at once of jealousy and alarm. Rejoicing in the opportunity of suppressing a rival whose power, if not checked in time, might eclipse his own, he furnished troops under one of his lieutenants, Louis Bourquin, to act with the Sikh allies. At first, Thomas gained some success, but on the arrival of reinforcements from Delhi, he was compelled to retire to Hansi. Here he was surrounded and, after an obstinate defence, surrendered. Abandoning all his conquests, he retired into British territory, never again disturbing the peace of the cis-Sutlej states. These events occurred in 1802. With the remainder of the Delhi territory, Hisar passed nominally under British rule after the victories of Lord Gerard Lake over the Marathas in the following year.

The area comprising the present state of Haryana was ceded to the British East India Company in 1803. In 1832, it was transferred to the then North-West Frontier Province of British India. Later, in 1858, Haryana became part of British Punjab. Its inclusion in Punjab in 1858 was a punishment for the participation of its princes and people in the Revolt of 1857. Due to the vindictive and repressive policy of the British government, the region remained mostly neglected in the nineteenth century and there was no significant development in the field of education, trade, industry, means of communication and irrigation.

At the time of Partition, Hisar district, part of East Punjab, was one of the three central districts included in the larger Hisar division. It was bounded on the north and north-east by the native state of Patiala, on the east by Rohtak district and the state of Jind, on the south and south-east by the Dadri territory of Jind and the state of Loharu, and on the west, Sirsa, and the terrain of Bikaner.

The district itself was divided into many tehsils – Barwala lay to the north-east, Sirsa and Fatehabad to the north-west, Hansi to the east centre, Hisar to the west centre, and Bhiwani to the south and south-west of Dabwali. The administrative headquarters were situated at Hisar, which lay nearly in the centre of the district.

The Batras started for Hisar early on a May morning, just before sunrise. They wanted to cover as much distance as possible before the sun peaked and the unbearable loo of Hisar started blowing. The families destined for Hansi and Sirsa also joined them. After returning from Delhi, they stayed at Kalanor for a week. Bhagwanti's aunts woke up early and cooked meals for them. Plenty of rotis with pickles and chhaach for children were tiffined in case they felt hungry on the way. It was a full-day journey from Rohtak on bullock carts. They hoped to reach Hisar much before dark and camp in a dharamshala where the tehsildar had made arrangements for their stay overnight. Bhagwanti's family had given them their bullock cart till they got one of their own made; they had borrowed a second cart from a local landholder.

Kesar Dass, Bhagwanti, Shakuntala, Ram Saran, Daya, Sumitra and Gobind sat in the front cart with Dhania behind the bulls. Narain Dass, Nand Lal, their son, Kashmir, and few of his relatives sat in the cart behind. Sukhi Chand had stayed back in Kalanor – the village temple management had employed him for the temple. They had carried a few cots, beddings and utensils for their new home, which no one had even seen so far.

They decided to take a diversion to avoid a few villages in Meham located not far from Kalanor. Meham had a considerable Muslim population before Partition, but most of them had left for Pakistan. However, the Hindu natives of local villages there were not welcoming of the Punjabi migrants. There had been incidents of stoning on caravans passing through their village. Avoiding hostile villages, their tiny caravan reached the metalled road. On the way, two families bound for Hansi bid goodbye to those headed to Hisar and Sirsa.

This was the first time that any member of the Batra family had been to Hisar, which was a large administrative division. Only Kesar Dass had once been to this part of East Punjab a few times in twenty years, first for his wedding, and later with Bhagwanti to visit her parents and relatives. Even Bhagwanti had never ventured in this area. Both had crossed the terrain each time while travelling to Kalanor on train. It was night-time mostly when trains passed this area, so they never got to see much outside.

They were disappointed with the topography of Hisar, which was very different from the welcoming environment of Jhang. There were large tracts of wastelands. Cultivated fields were few. The terrain was largely dry. The effect of the severe famine of 1938 was still visible in the large uncultivated tracts that lay across the vastness of the areas on both sides of the highway. The area of Hisar was known to be prone to droughts, famines and scarcity due to lack of irrigation facilities as well as scanty and erratic rainfall.

Hisar is stated to have been completely devastated during the great famine of 1783. The kharif and grass crop failed, tanks dried up, and wells in many places became brackish. The inhabitants had no choice but to leave their villages and seek food and pasture elsewhere. The famine depopulated the area with peasants abandoning their villages, and dying of disease and hunger. The country gradually became repopulated when things started returning to normal. However, the scars of the famine were still visible. Frequent severe famines occurred in the late nineteenth century when a large number of cattle died and many people left the district. These famines brought great distress to the people.

It was this Hisar that was to become the new homeland of the Batra family, whose ancestors had centuries ago moved to the canal colonies of Jhang, and turned bar land into the most irrigated and rich land of West Punjab. A generation of Batra Khatris had been pushed back by centuries. They had been forced out of the canal colonies to make their home in land fraught with droughts. History had come full circle.

As if reading what was troubling the shocked faces, Ram Saran spoke, 'My teacher told me that in ancient times this area flourished and was prosperous. Somadeva in his *Yasastilikachampu* in the tenth-century AD recorded that the Yaudheya country, which included parts of the Kurukshetra region, was like an ornament of the earth, and was replete with all requisites of good and happy life. Its people had all objects, necessary for the pursuit of dharma and artha, and lived here as if it were heaven. The villages were full of cattle wealth, cows, buffaloes, goats, sheep, camels and horses. There was an abundance of irrigation. Their well-watered fields of krishnabhumi (black soil) were green with harvests and gardens. They yielded such rich harvests that farmers had no space to stack. Their ladies wore rich ornaments. They led a peaceful and quiet life without social frictions, and people respected the varnasramadharma. They were devotees of Kartikeya, the generalissimo of the gods. Rohitaka (Rohtak) was their first capital and the metropolis of the Yaudheyas Rajpura, probably Rajpura, near Ambala in East Punjab, was their second capital.'

Everyone in the cart was impressed by Ram Saran's knowledge. All of them, including Dhania, turned to look at the young boy with admiration. Bhagwanti's face beamed with pride.

'How do you know this?' inquired Daya, looking at her brother lovingly.

'My teacher told me. Her grandfather once served the British education department in Hisar,' replied Ram Saran. 'The Rig Veda, one of the oldest extant texts in the world refers to a river called Sarasvati, which flowed between the Yamuna and the Sutlej. Later texts, like the Mahabharata, describe how the river dried up. The Sarasvati was once a very large river system, fed at times by glacial melt and at other times by heavy rain. After rising from the Sirmur hills of the Himalayas, it is believed to have flowed past what are presently known as Ambala, Pipli, Kurukshetra, Pehowa and Sirsa, before going into oblivion into a large estuary – today the salt flats of Rann of Kutch. It was on the banks of the Sarasvati that the Vedic hymns were composed and recited. The land through which the holy river passed is said to have been as fertile, and the people as prosperous as the land and people of Haryana are. It is here that Lord Krishna preached the Bhagavadgita at the start of the battle of the Mahabharata.'

By now, Ram Saran was unstoppable. 'Even British administrator Charles Metcalfe has confirmed that the village communities here were little republics, having nearly everything they could want within themselves, and almost independent of any foreign relations. In times of trouble, they armed and fortified themselves. When a hostile army passed through this part, the village communities collected their cattle within their walls, and let the enemy pass unprovoked. If plunder and devastation were directed against them, they left, to return and resume their occupations after the enemy had passed. Such was their resilience. They had learnt to live through times of disturbance and convulsion. The change in the course of the river took away prosperity, and everything changed over centuries due to drought.'

Kesar Dass wondered if their ancestors had once lived here and were forced to migrate to find cultivable land in West Punjab.

As they travelled, they observed, on both sides of the road, scanty and sparse trees, mostly unfamiliar to them. Shrubs were in plenty. They also spotted a variety of trees – jand, rohera, khairl, beri, reru, barh, pahari kikar, shisham and neem. Chinkara roamed freely in large numbers in the barren fields grazing on the shrubs. Blackbucks strayed on the road, while the strong nilgai appeared to be present in abundance, its distinctive blue-grey coat, long horns and majestic presence adding beauty to the otherwise uninteresting landscape. Every time the elegant antelope passed by, women bowed their heads in reverence.

The villages looked the same in appearance with one or at the most two phals (entrances). All along, they could see a shivala (Shiva temple) or a thakurdara (Krishna temple). Every village had its johar (pond) in which rainwater was collected for domestic and other use. The houses in the rural areas were mostly identical, all made of mud, and there were no pucca houses.

They saw people gathered around a hookah. The village elders were apparently discussing matters of mutual interest. They also noticed a few sweet shops near Hansi. Here, they stopped to buy a few boxes of peras, a popular milk-sweet of Hansi. They entered Hisar town before sunset. An imposing gate, somewhat similar in architecture to the entrance of the Purana Quila in Delhi, greeted them. They were all wondering what the gate was when Ram Saran spoke again while looking around for more structures he could possibly identify, 'This is Dilli Gate, one of the four gates of Hisar Fort.' Spotting other structures as they passed the east of the town, he said, 'Look there…' he paused to look at his notes and then continued speaking, '…Irish adventurer George Thomas lived here in the late eighteenth century almost as an independent ruler of the tract. What you see there is Jahaz Pul and his house Jahaz Kothi. My teacher told me that the kothi was once a Jain temple. It was later converted into a mosque, before the Irishman started using it as his residence. But no one knows that for sure.'

'Who is an Irishman?' asked Sumitra. She had heard the word for the first time.

'I don't know that,' confessed Ram Saran. 'I was reading from my notes. Probably a British officer ... I really don't know.'

They saw another gate similar to Dilli Gate ahead. 'This is probably Mori Gate. The other two are Nagori Gate to the south and Talaqi Gate to the west,' he said, consulting his notes.

The dharamshala was located near Anaj Mandi, the grain market. Here, the patwari came to greet them. He had brought along some fresh ghiya (bottle gourd) for them. The women set up a temporary kitchen and cooked a meal of roti and ghiya, and served it with pickles.

The patwari, a middle-aged Sikh, carried with him the land records. He apprised them that after receiving an allotment letter issued by the government, he had visited the village a few days back and discovered that the mentioned land was being tilled by some locals. All of them claimed to be in its possession as tenants. He summoned them to his office to verify their claims. Some representations were found to be correct as per the records, other bogus. The tenants who were recorded as such promised cooperation in handing over possession to you as long as you continue having them as tenants. Those who made bogus claims were warned to vacate the land at once, failing which they were told, force would be used for their eviction.

'And the house?' inquired Bhagwanti.

'The house is the only pucca building in the village. It had also been taken over by squatters after its owner left for Pakistan. They left after I threatened to call the military commander and seek his help for evacuation.'

The patwari informed that elders from all communities in the village had assured their assistance and agreed to hold a welcome meeting for the new members of the village community.

The patwari left, thankful for the simple but sumptuous dinner, promising to return the following morning and accompany them to Kurri to help occupy the land and house without any trouble from the natives.

As the sun set, it was pitch-dark outside. There was no electricity connection in the dharamshala. The attendant lit a few kerosene lamps. 'Although electricity was introduced in Hisar town over a decade ago, it is used mainly for street lighting and hospitals. Some public buildings like the railway station also have connections but the supply is erratic and even street lighting continues to rely on kerosene lamps,' the attendant informed.

While the Batra family was relieved to learn that no untoward incident was expected in Kurri, they continued to stay anxious. They waited with bated breath for the next morning.

17

A New Homeland

Kurri – situated a little over ten kilometres from Hisar, on what was then a kachcha (unmetalled) road to Balsamand, and onwards to present-day Rajasthan – turned out to be even more different than they had imagined, nearly in all aspects. They started their journey on a bullock cart soon after sunrise; it took them over one hour, carefully navigating and steering through the potholes on the dirt track. Having rested the previous night, the bulls moved swiftly, goaded by Dhania.

When they reached nearly halfway, the patwari pointed to the right of the road. 'Look there, your land starts from here, and continues as far as your eyes can see, touching the village at the other end. There are a few patches of panchayat land here and there, and some pathways for common use. The rest is yours. The ten-foot-wide piece of land running adjacent to this dirt road belongs to the government.' Pointing to the left, he said, 'This is mostly banjar land owned by the government.'

Excited, everyone looked at the fields which were now theirs. They got down and walked to the fields. Their excitement at once turned into disappointment; the soil appeared productive in many parts but they could also see many large patches of clayey land.

Some parts were even sandy. Coarse grass, and a stunted growth of desert trees and shrubs were the only trace of vegetation. On the left of the track, there were sand dunes as far as they could see. The patwari informed that many times storms pushed the sand hills on to the dirt track, submerging it under sand, only to be cleared after the wind changed direction. They had been forewarned of the state of the land in Hisar and were not expecting anything comparable with their land in Jhang.

Nonetheless, Kesar Dass was devastated. '*Haye Rabba! Aeda kee keresan?* (Oh God! What would I do with such land?)' He could feel that cultivating this land without any irrigation was going to be an impossible task. He was convinced they were up for even tougher times than he had imagined. This was worse land than what he had witnessed on the way from Kalanor.

Noticing the look of disappointment on their faces, the patwari spoke in an assuring tone. 'It is not as bad as it appears. Although it is not comparable with what you may have left behind in Jhang, it is capable of producing an impressive harvest.'

They returned to the cart and resumed their journey. The patwari spoke again. 'Till a few months back this vast tract of land formed the sprawling estate of Ibrahim Khan, a wealthy Muslim zamindar, who lived here with a large family of three wives, their children, and his grandchildren. As overlord of the village and this large tract of land, Ibrahim Khan wielded considerable authority. When communal hatred swept across many parts of India in August, the city of Hisar could not remain unaffected by this frenzy. The majority of the population here was Hindu. Muslims suffered loss of life and property in the violence. Ibrahim Khan left for Pakistan leaving behind everything.'

Shortly, the village appeared in sight. It consisted of many mud houses scattered in the fields close to the village, different from villages they had witnessed on the way. Away from the mud houses, they could see a kothi, a large single-storeyed house built of concrete with a medieval-style architecture. There was no habitation or any other house around it, and only one passage could be seen leading to the house through the clear ground surrounding it from all sides.

The patwari informed, 'Khan was an inconsiderate man. He did not allow anyone to build a house or shop in proximity to his haveli. No one could dare to lay even a single brick in concrete even in the fields. Only thatched huts could be constructed. He did not even permit concentration of huts in one place, they had to be spread all over. Afraid of rebellion, he did not want people to gather in groups to air their grievances and plot against him. He was also a heartless moneylender. He oppressed his own tenants, who were nearly compelled to borrow from him to meet the cost of a marriage or funeral in the family, or even to celebrate their festivals, or more often to pay the lagaan in times of drought. He did not permit villagers to draw water from the only well in the village located inside his house even though it had plenty of water to meet the needs of the entire village. The well water was exclusively used for his household. The poor villagers were forced to trudge miles for water. They all resented him but were powerless against his influence. But Khan did not discriminate on account of religion when it came to tyranny; even his Muslim tenants could not use the water from the well. To him, the well was a symbol of dominance, a means to exert his power over the weak and vulnerable. He left for Pakistan because he feared his own people would kill him to take revenge.'

Kurri was a picture of a feudal set-up with Ibrahim Khan's house dominating the landscape. The villagers must have been happy to see Ibrahim Khan and his family leave for Pakistan, Bhagwanti speculated. They must also be equally apprehensive of the new landlord who had come from a distant place and culture in a country which was now considered to be an enemy state, she thought.

'The villagers celebrated when Ibrahim Khan left,' said the patwari, as if reading Bhagwanti's mind. 'After his Muslim tenants and he left, the other tenants occupied the *khud kasht* (self-cultivated) land and the tracts which were with the tenants. A few broke open the door of Khan's kothi. They enjoyed the house for almost a year till recently. The news of your arrival has revived their fears of old times, but I am sure once they get to know you, they will feel assured and their attitude towards you will change.'

As they approached the house, they could see many villagers – men in white, women in colourful dresses, and children only half clad in clothes – gathered outside the house. The patwari had sent his assistant ahead to announce the arrival of the new incumbents. Seeing them coming, women started singing a traditional welcome song in their native language. The Batras could not figure out the lyrics but were pleased by the welcome. The patwari then called for silence and made a short introduction of Kesar Dass and his cousins.

After instructing some men to help unload the carts and women to clean the house, the patwari and the men left to measure the agricultural land and hand over its formal possession to its new owner. Bhagwanti and other family members stood in silence, absorbing their new surroundings. The children ran into the house to explore their new home.

Bhagwanti stepped inside only after the house had been cleaned. She lit a diya at the entrance, said her customary prayers and drew the swastika symbol on the door, before entering. The house was spacious but it disappointed Bhagwanti, not because it was built in Islamic architecture style, but because it did not meet the Hindu way of living, particularly the kitchen. The entrance to the house was enormous. It was more than twelve feet tall and broad enough to let a carriage loaded to a good height pass through without any difficulty. The two wooden doors had been empanelled with designs and decorated with flowered wrought-iron nails. The doors were closed. A small door had been carved out for people to go in and out. The entrance also opened into an expansive courtyard for social gatherings and ventilation.

There was a large godown on one side of the courtyard. The area next to it was seemingly used to unload the incoming crop or fodder which was weighed or placed in jute bags before being transferred to the godown. Further up, in one corner of the courtyard was a shed where livestock was kept. It was empty but reeked of the buffaloes and goats that inhabited the space not many days ago. There was an empty stable at another end. Hisar was also known for horse breeding. This must have been where the horses were kept. There was no way Khan could have taken the horses, buffaloes and goats with him to Pakistan, Bhagwanti thought. Someone must have taken charge of them after Ibrahim Khan left, she guessed. There was also another shed, open from three sides, which was apparently used for chopping fodder – some chopped fodder was still stacked against the fourth wall. A sturdy chopping machine stood fastened to the ground, but many of its parts seemed missing. Here, in the courtyard was the deep well filled with water that the patwari had spoken about.

Like any traditional Muslim village house, this too featured a simple, functional design centred around family privacy. At the far end of the house were the living quarters with a courtyard of its own. This inner courtyard was an extension of the outer courtyard. The women in the Muslim household required privacy. The two courtyards had been separated by a tall wall. Only a small door allowed access from one to the other. The mardana (men) and zenana (women) living quarters were built in the deeper section on one side of the inner courtyard. They consisted of multiple rooms, mostly of the same size, all built next to one another in a single line, with a common veranda running in front of the rooms. Each room had a small window with iron bars, which barely allowed any daylight into the rooms. Bhagwanti realized that the houses here were built in this manner to keep the scorching sun away and protect them from the notorious loo of Hisar. Doorways were arched with some floral motifs but the work was not intricate; in fact, it was very ordinary. A small prayer area facing Mecca had been built in a corner.

But Bhagwanti did not find any toilet. She learnt that the women of the house went to a field close by to relieve themselves, while men went far away for their purpose. It was not much dissimilar from their house back in Rodu Sultan.

There was a small kitchen but there was no chowki. There was no way she was going to cook out of that kitchen, Bhagwanti decided. She had already made up her mind to build a new kitchen. Her face lit up when she noticed a tandoor dug in one corner of the inner courtyard. They all loved roti and daal cooked in a clay oven.

Large though the house was, it was still inadequate for the Batra family. Bhagwanti couldn't help but compare it with her home back in Rodu Sultan where each room had a good share of sunlight and fresh air. Each part of the house was planned and constructed according to vaastu. Their kitchen was what she missed the most.

There was no furniture in the house; everything had been taken away. A woman from the village, who stood waiting for further instructions, muttered something which Bhagwanti could not follow. It was only a few months later that she was to learn what the woman had said. The furniture and other household items, including kitchen utensils left behind by Ibrahim Khan, had been taken away by some people from nearby villages and sold, she had revealed. They were of no use in their small mud houses.

Bhagwanti and Nand Lal's wife, Shakuntala, decided to set up a makeshift kitchen in the fodder shed till a new kitchen that met their requirement was built. Dhania swept the floor clean. He pulled out water from the well and sprinkled it on the shed floor to settle the dust. A village woman brought mud from the field which was mixed with water to form a thick, malleable paste. The floor was pasted with clay evenly spread across the surface by hands. It was pressed firmly to ensure adhesion and compactness. Bhagwanti and Shakuntala did all this by themselves; not allowing anyone, except Dhania, to enter the kitchen. This was the most sacred place in the house. Once finished, the floor was left to dry naturally, till it resulted in a hard, crack-resistant finish.

They set up a makeshift kitchen in the courtyard to cook the dinner. The water from the well tasted a bit khara (brine) but it was drinkable. Everyone missed the sweet taste of water from the tube well in Rodu Sultan. The men returned just before sunset after measuring the land. The patwari and his assistant were also in a hurry to leave so that they could reach Hisar town before nightfall. It was not considered safe to stay out after it turned dark, they were told, as leopards and other wild animals freely roamed the land at night. All men were served a quick dinner of roti, moong daal, turai (ridge gourd) and pickles cooked by women of the house. The patwari once again complimented Bhagwanti for the sumptuous daal. They all loved the pickle she had brought from Kalanor. Bhagwanti packed some for the patwari, placing it carefully inside a couple of folded rotis. The patwari touched Bhagwanti's feet to seek her blessings.

Nand Lal and his brother occupied the section of the house allotted to them corresponding to the size of their house back in Rodu Sultan.

It was already night. They lit up a few kerosene lamps. Cots were placed in the inner courtyard. Kesar Dass decided to sleep on the rooftop. Nand Lal and a few children decided to join him. They all rolled their gadde (mattresses stuffed with cotton) and carried it to the roof. A narrow flight of steps led to the roof, there was no way to carry a cot. The roof was used to dry crops but not meant for sleeping in summer. The steps would have been a bit wider otherwise. They spread the bedding on the floor. Here, they lay on the floor looking at the night sky. It was full of stars. The twinkling stars mirrored the nights in Rodu Sultan, where the heavens seemed closer, more intimate. A wave of nostalgia washed over Kesar Dass. Memories of childhood – running through fields, the scent of earth after rain, and the comforting hum of village life – flooded his mind.

But for the star-filled sky, Kurri was a complete contrast, as distinct and unfamiliar as it could get. A bittersweet longing stirred within him, mingling joy with a pang of separation. The vast, timeless sky connected him to his roots, evoking both peace and a quiet yearning for the simplicity and warmth of home. He yearned for the familiar sights and sounds of their former home. He longed for a sense of belonging.

The next morning, Kesar Dass woke up to a lot of noise. He discovered that the women were deep cleaning one of the rooms. Bhagwanti was washing its floor with water as Dhania kept fetching buckets full of water from the well. Nand Lal's wife was putting a mixture of cow dung, clay and water on the walls with the help of a local woman who had arranged the dung from the house of the local bania who owned a cow.

'*Kee karendi payeen hai*? (What are you doing?)' he inquired.

'I am converting this room into our puja room. I can't start cooking in my kitchen unless I have done my *griha puja*. Now that we have a house, I might as well pray properly,' she answered, continuing to sweep out the water Dhania was splashing.

Once the cleaning and clay plastering were done, the puja room was purified by lighting dhoop. The idols she had brought from Rodu Sultan were carefully placed on an elevated platform made of one of her iron trunks. Next to them was placed the potli containing soil from Rodu Sultan. After bathing, they all assembled in the puja room for prayers, their first in the new house. The soft glow of the diya placed in front of their gods illuminated the intricate idols and cast an ethereal warmth upon the sacred space. The rhythmic chanting of mantras filled the room. Soon, the air in the house turned thick with the sweet fragrance of incense. The rhythmic clapping of their hands and ringing of bells added a symphony of sound, creating a captivating harmony. In that moment, all their worries faded. The aroma of incense lingered in the air long after the prayers ended. The two idols, remnants of Partition and their roots, were to pass on from one generation to another.

Their next task was to set up a permanent kitchen. Gobind had already made friends with Nanhu, son of a kumhar (potter) from the village. With the help of Nanhu's father, they found a mistri (mason) to construct a new kitchen as per Bhagwanti's liking. The mason lived in the village but worked in Hisar town. He arrived in the evening after returning from his work. Bhagwanti gave him the instructions. The walls were to be made of brick but the floor was to be of clay. The inside of the walls were to be plastered with a mixture of cow dung, yellow clay and water, she instructed. The mason provided a list of materials that they would have to buy from Hisar. He provided them directions to the place where the materials were sold and promised to meet them at the shop the next day.

Next morning, Kesar Dass got ready to leave for Hisar. Bhagwanti insisted on coming along, as did Gobind and Sumitra. 'I need some bartan (utensils and vessels),' she said. 'Also, there is only one cow in the whole village, we need to buy our own cows soon. Ram Prasad, the bania, had come to meet while you had gone to the fields. She says the milk their cow delivers barely meets their own needs but has promised to spare some for us till we buy one of our own. The villagers buy milk from a small dairy two villages further on Balsamand road. The dairyman sends a large dhol (container) with the bus every day. On its way to Hisar, the driver drops the dhol at Kurri with a local villager for distribution. The dhol is loaded back on the bus on its way back. The milk he sends won't be enough for us.'

Kesar Dass nodded. Life without cows and buffaloes was unimaginable for them. Not only because they were accustomed to ghee, curd, butter and lassi in plenty all day, but because, being sacred, cows brought divine blessings and protection to the household. They treated cows as family members. All cows in Rodu Sultan were given affectionate names and adorned with jewellery. Moreover, cows possess purifying qualities; their urine and dung were used for religious rituals and purification ceremonies. Besides, they provided manure, enriched soil fertility and their dung was used as fuel.

Dhania took Kesar and Bhagwanti to Hisar market to buy kitchen utensils. Nand Lal decided they would wait for a few more days for their trip to the bazaar. They found a shop selling utensils not very different from what they used back in Jhang. They bought a few ghara and surahi for carrying water from the well; a few handis for cooking vegetables and pulses; a kadhoni for boiling milk; and biloni for churning curd from one of the series of shops. There were two shops selling metal utensils and vessels made of brass and kansi (bell-metal). She bought a tokni, a vessel for ordinary cooking and carrying water to the fields; a few lotas and gadwas for dipping into water and drinking; four tall brass gilas (glasses); a kachola, a broad shallow bowl or saucer for drinking hot liquids and eating khichri; six thalis; another parat, a larger tray for kneading dough; and a karchhi, a brass ladle. They already had a tawa, an iron vessel consisting of a thin iron plate for baking bread; a karahi or a frying pan, and a few other utensils, all of brass. From a luhar (ironsmith), they bought an iron balti (bucket) for drawing water from the well. They also bought a few articles of furniture – two bedsteads, which the locals called khats, moorhas (cane stools) of different sizes, and a few pidas and patras (small stools). On the way back, they stopped to order some bricks and wooden beams for construction of the kitchen. The mason was waiting for them at the shop.

The shopkeeper promised to send his best artisan to hand-engrave Kesar Dass's name on the utensils, as was then a common practice in all households. The artisan used a small iron hammer and finger-sized chisel in hand to engrave. A few of these utensils and vessels are still intact even after so many years, and in safe keeping of the author as they passed on generation after generation.

They also purchased groceries and vegetables in plenty. The bania's small shop in the village sold only what was needed for cooking the staple food for locals. In fact, food was another problem. The staple diet in Kurri and most villages in Hisar consisted mainly of wheat, barley and gram in summer and bajra in winter. They did not consume pulses in plenty, except *moong sabat daal* (green pulse). The diet of the people was simple but nutritious. Chickpeas were also grown in plenty but mostly for selling, and not as much for consumption. Sattu was the common diet in summer while khichri was that in winter. Dalia was taken all round the year but only by those who could afford to buy milk. A few vegetables like ghiya and turai were grown and were a regular part of people's diet.

The fondness of Punjabi Khatris for food went beyond these. They loved bhindi, baingan and tinda. Also, kakri (cucumber) was a must in summers. The delicious pickle of teet was very common in Hisar but the Punjabis were accustomed to mango and green chilli pickles. Bhagwanti bought a lot of green chillies to make pickles. They had to wait for the mango season, just before the monsoon, to get hold of unripe mangoes. They had enough from Kalanor to last till then. Sugar and ghee were retained by locals for great occasions, and only indulged in as a treat, but for the Batra family, these were ingredients for daily use.

Fortunately, acquiring cows and buffaloes did not pose much problem. There was a large livestock farm in Hisar. In fact, it was the biggest livestock farm in Asia and the second largest in the world. It was started more than a hundred years ago as a camel stud to house and train camels for military purposes. The farm was taken over by the government in 1912 and since then it had been managed by the government. It covered land measuring about 7,000 hectares. Originally, horses, camels and bullocks were bred there. The breeding of horses and camels was given up later as the army purchases slowed. Only bullocks and mules of superior quality for military purposes were being bred. They liked two cows and two buffaloes on the farm. They also liked a pair of bulls but had no money left to pay. They paid some advance to hold their purchase and promised to return a few days later to pay the balance and take the cattle.

A few days later, Bhagwanti and Kesar Dass made a quick trip to Kalanor where they had left their jewellery with the wife of

Bhagwanti's brother. They sold some of her jewellery in Rohtak to arrange some cash to meet the cost of their new purchases.

Meanwhile, they also ordered a new cart to be made by a village khati (carpenter).

Over the next few days, all the villagers came to their house one after the other to pay their respect. They were mostly their tenants but also included labourers who tilled the self-cultivated land. The ways of the villagers were unfamiliar and the dialect difficult to follow. In Kurri, the natives spoke Haryanvi Hindi, making communication with them difficult in the initial days. Another matter of concern was that they appeared wary about the new landlords. All men and women, without exception, squatted on the floor. Even when invited to sit on the cot, they refused. Most were following the tradition set by Ibrahim Khan.

The villagers dressed simply; the clothes men wore were usually made from coarse fabric. The male wore a turban, shirt and dhoti. Their jutis (lace-less shoes), that they would take off before entering the house, were worn and muddy. Their feet, calloused and rough, bore marks of long hours in the fields, exhibiting the physical toll of labour-intensive work. In winters, they wrapped khes around them. The women wore a shirt of gent's style and colourful ghagra. Women of all ages also wore cotton orhna (dupatta) of vibrant colours over the head. Peelia, a sort of headwear (the central part of which was yellow and the rest multicoloured), and chunri were the other important items of dress. Some women wore borla (prepared from beads) on the forehead. Sopli or dupla were used as shawls in winters.

The natives of Kurri were mostly carpenters and potters. There were one or two blacksmiths, barbers and water-bearers. Together, they comprised barely a handful. There were two bania families in the village, one of them operated a small shop, the other was a trader. A few Harijans also lived on the outskirts of the village. The financial condition of the villagers was unstable. Relentless drought made farming an arduous and uncertain endeavour for them. Their meagre earnings were barely enough to sustain their families.

From the land of their Kshatriya forefathers, Kesar Dass had been transported to a nearly alien land. The language, customs and culture of their new surroundings felt alien. Haryanvis also lived in kunba (joint family) often having a common thola (line of ancestors). It was common for several brothers, and occasionally cousins, to live together and farm the land jointly.

As months passed, Kurri no longer appeared as strange to Kesar Dass and Bhagwanti as it did on the first day. Although it was a far cry from the bustling village of Rodu Sultan that they had once called home, they had started to like it. They had also slowly started earning the affection and respect of the villagers. But they could sense that the villagers still perceived them as outsiders who were alien to their culture. When Kesar Dass and Bhagwanti conversed in Jhangi, the puzzled and somewhat amused look on the faces of villagers gave away their feelings of how distanced they felt from their new landlords.

Deep within, Kesar Dass still carried hope that tensions between India and Pakistan would get resolved some day and they would be able to return to Rodu Sultan. He was unable to reconcile that this was going to be their home for the rest of their lives. His longing for the smell of the soil of the land of his ancestors grew only profounder with time.

The weight of nostalgia continued to press down on him as Kesar Dass recalled the verdant fields and abundant harvests they had left behind. Every day, he prayed to Lord Shiva for normalisation of relations between India and Pakistan so that he could return to Rodu Sultan or at least visit his home and fields.

18

Rebuilding Life

Monsoon was around the corner by the time they settled into their new home. Kesar Dass and Nand Lal now shifted their focus to the land. The size of their holding was large. In the Hisar region, the average land belonging to one proprietor was about thirty acres; seventy-five acres would form a large holding. Around Kurri, proprietors held as little as eighteen or nineteen acres. The average holding in other parts was even smaller. By those standards, the landholding of the Batra family was enormous. Cultivating this large tract of land posed many challenges.

The climate of Hisar was dry and characterised by extremes of temperature and scanty rainfall. Without the support of irrigation canals, the land was heavily dependent on the monsoon for water. The year-to-year variability in rainfall meant that agricultural productivity was unpredictable. Periodic droughts often led to crop failures, placing the populace in precarious positions regarding food security and livelihood. Given the semi-arid conditions, farmers typically grew crops that required less water. Bajra, pulses, and gram were common staples. Most farming was for subsistence rather than commercial purposes. Growing food for their own consumption took priority over cash crops.

The land in Hisar in those times had shades of three varied tracts: Chak Hariana, Chak Bagar and Chak Nali (chak means a block of land) – each with its own characteristics, although the nature of land has changed since the canal was built here in the late 1960s. Chak Hariana formed the largest of the three tracts of land occupying the heart of the district. The western Jamuna canal, which ran through the district from east to west, separated this chak into two nearly equal parts. The soil was clayey here, breaking up into large clods requiring abundant rain to saturate it sufficiently for seeding.

In the central part of Hisar, the soil had large patches of sand. Towards the south, it blended gradually with sandy plains and hillocks. Though rich when sufficiently saturated, it produced almost nothing when there were no rains. This chak was inhabited by about 300 villages. Chak Bagar lay to the south of Hisar district, and included the towns of Tosham and Bhiwani. Cultivation in this area was difficult. If there was no rain, there was no crop at all, not even a blade of grass. If it rained too heavily, the sand would wash down from the sand hillocks into the cultivated fields and choke the seed. Camels were used for ploughing. There was no stream or canal in this part of the district. In a few villages the people had kachcha (unlined) wells on the banks of the village tanks, which they used to irrigate a few fields. Masonry wells were not constructed as the water invariably turned brackish. It was considered a waste of money to build wells which might become absolutely useless a few years later. The water became so salty that it was unfit for use by anyone.

Chak Nali owes its name to the fact that during the rains it is traversed by two nalas (streams). It lay on the north of the district that included the towns of Barwala and Fatehabad. The soil was classed for the most part as rausli (loam soil). Only a small portion of the countryside had been brought under cultivation. The uncultivated area was thickly covered with low brushwood which was useful only for fuel. No crop was grown on the northern branch except on land irrigated from one or the other branches of the Ghaggar.

It is this kind of land that the Batra cousins were called upon to cultivate. It was going to be more difficult to till the land than they had thought. The parcels of land they had been allotted were fairly fertile but with no canal, they were going to be dependent on the mercy of the rain for irrigation. Johad (small earthen check dams) and other forms of water-collection structures were employed to harness whatever rainfall occurred during the monsoon but that was not enough to meet the demand of such a large tract of land. The locals did not trust well irrigation alone for their crops. Water level in the wells were at depths ranging between 107 and 133 feet from the surface; and the cost of constructing wells was high. There was neither electricity nor diesel for running the pumps. Well irrigation, which accounted for a third of the irrigated area, was practised with the aid of bullock-driven jhalar (Persian wheels by which water is lifted from a stream or canal). Tube-wells were unthinkable.

They soon realised that rehabilitation did not mark the end of their struggle; it was only the beginning of a daunting task of rebuilding lives from scratch. It was going to be an enormous challenge to get accustomed to this new land which was going to be their home.

The children were going through their own emotional turmoil of displacement. Ram Saran had no desire to follow in his father's footsteps and become a farmer. He wanted to pursue a career that would allow him to make a difference in the world. He had momentarily thought of taking up business as his occupation, but his teacher in the school in Bhogal had a profound impact on him in those few months spent in Delhi. He was now determined to study as much as he possibly could, and become a teacher.

Children's education posed a challenge. Unlike Rodu Sultan, there was no school in Kurri. In terms of education, Hisar district was the most backward in Punjab. There were two Anglo-vernacular middle schools in all of Hisar which were maintained from municipal funds supplemented by district funds. The district had been in the grip of severe scarcity and famines year after year and no attention could be paid to education. The population kept migrating in and out, making education unsustainable. Before the advent of the British, there were indigenous schools which provided elementary education. There were also maktabs (traditional Muslim schools) presided over by the village maulavi (mosque attendant) who taught the village boys passages out of the Quran by rote, as part of his customary duties. There were village schools also where the pandit taught the boys. The maulavis or pandits were not trained; but they were much respected in the society.

No serious efforts were made by the British to improve literacy in the district. In 1843, James Thomson was appointed lieutenant governor of the north-western provinces of India. He directed all his subordinates to encourage people to receive education in indigenous schools scattered across the country. In 1856, tahsildari schools were opened at Hisar and Hansi. After the merger of the district in Punjab in 1858, a scheme was launched to improve the existing indigenous schools and opening new schools.

Ram Saran had already lost one year due to the upheaval of Partition; he was terrified of losing any more. He was convinced education was his only hope for a better future. In the backward village of Kurri, his dreams seemed like nothing more than a distant mirage. He wandered aimlessly around the sand dunes all day, his mind racing with worry and uncertainty. He watched other children playing but he could not bring himself to join in. He was a tall and well-built boy but carried no interest in sports. How could he play when his future was so uncertain? He longed to be back in school, surrounded by his friends and teachers, learning and growing. He couldn't give up on his dreams, no matter how difficult things seemed. As the days turned into weeks, Ram Saran's determination only grew stronger. He inquired from his mother every day when he would be able to go to school. Seeing her son's determination, Bhagwanti was filled with pride. Ram Saran pestered her to talk to Kesar Dass as he was scared of talking about it to his father himself.

In the rural landscapes of Punjab, among the landed Jhangi families, the relationship between father and son was a complex one, woven with threads of respect, affection and unspoken understanding. Sons, imbued with deep-seated respect for their fathers, rarely uttered a word in their presence. This outward silence, however, masked a profound bond. From an early age, sons observed their fathers with unwavering admiration, absorbing their wisdom and values through the subtle cues and gestures that spoke volumes. Respect was the cornerstone of this relationship. Sons were expected to obey their fathers unquestioningly, adhere to their decisions and submit to their authority. This obedience was not borne out of fear but out of a deep-seated belief that their fathers held their best interests at heart. Beneath the surface of respect, lay a deep reservoir of affection. Fathers, though often restrained in their outward expressions, held a deep and abiding love for their sons. They provided them with unwavering support, guided their steps and offered them solace in times of need. As the sons grew into adulthood, the relationship evolved. The sons continued to hold their fathers in high regard, seeking their counsel and respecting their wisdom. Yet, they gradually gained a voice of their own, sharing their perspectives and negotiating decisions with their fathers. Eventually, the father passed on the baton of decision making to the son. In the Batra clan, too, the father–son relationship was a delicate balance of respect, affection and unspoken bonds.

Kesar Dass was hesitant to send Ram Saran to Hisar for his studies. It was too far to travel for the young boy every day, he feared. But looking at Ram Saran's determination, he eventually relented and agreed to send him to school.

Gobind was made of a different mettle. He was growing into a charming boy with sparkling and expressive eyes that reflected his innocence. He had a radiant smile which lit up his face. He was always well-dressed, his hair neatly combed, meticulously parted from the sides. He loved his new home, village and friends. He had made friends with Nanhu and many other young boys from the village. He was energetic and playful, often seen running around with his friends. They often played guli danda or went to nearby villages to watch wrestling and kabaddi matches.

But when he learnt that his elder brother had their father's approval to attend school, Gobind was not the one to be left behind. He too insisted on tagging along. Both boys were admitted to Jat High School in Hisar.

A state transport department bus crossed Kurri every day on its way to Hisar. In the evening, a private bus operated by Krishna Roadways passed through Kurri on its way from Hisar. But their stops at Kurri often did not match the school timings; the boys had to walk back home if they missed the bus for any reason. After a few weeks, Kesar Dass bought Ram Saran a bicycle. The brothers rode seven miles every day to make the trip to school and back home, with Ram Saran pedalling and Gobind sitting on the bar. Later, as he grew taller, Gobind got a bicycle of his own.

The nineteen-year-old Daya was a short but graceful and confident girl. Her expressive eyes sparkled with curiosity, and her radiant smile lit up her face. She was a bundle of love – always busy caring for everyone in the family, particularly her brothers. She too was desirous of studying further but there was no school for girls in Kurri, and it was not safe for a girl to travel to Hisar. Daya felt torn and conflicted when her parents started discussing about advancing her marriage. Her heart yearned for education, but she was not one to disobey her parents. In less than a year after they arrived in Kurri, Daya was married to Bhagwan Dass Arora, who was serving in the Punjab government.

Three years younger to Daya, Sumitra looked upon her elder sister as her ideal. Seeing her sister get married, Sumitra too lost interest in school and waited for her turn to get married in a few years.

Bhagwanti devoted herself to rebuilding the life of her family. She was a strong person, a woman of substance and immense love. She had embraced her three stepchildren with the same unconditional love and care she showered upon her own daughter, Sumitra. Her life revolved around her family, and she dedicated herself to ensure their happiness and well-being. Her children grew up feeling cherished and secure, knowing they had a mother who loved them deeply.

She understood the delicate dynamics of a large family made of her own and of her husband's cousins and their families. Being the eldest amongst the women folk in the family, Bhagwanti looked after her extended family like her own. Her days were filled with selfless acts of care for her family. As in Rodu Sultan, she woke up early to feed the cows, prepare meals, ensure each child's favourite dishes were included, and helped the boys prepare to leave for school in time. Her life was a testament to the power of love and the beauty of a selfless heart.

Daya gave birth to a son in December 1949. Kesar Dass and Bhagwanti had become grandparents. They were thrilled with the arrival of the first grandchild in the family. They named him Satish.

Monsoon arrived with clockwise precision every year, but passed by without enough rain to change the fortune of their land. The Batra cousins tried every possible way to improve the state of the land but the stubborn terrain refused to change. They put to use all the skills they had learnt in Jhang to their new circumstances, but nothing worked. The unforgiving land was a far cry from the fertile soil of their ancestral home in Rodu Sultan. Every day, the men left for the fields at sunrise and worked hard till sunset, eating two meals, one before leaving and the other after returning from the fields.

The weight of the tough land continued to press down on Kesar Dass, constantly reminding him of the verdant fields and abundant harvests they had left behind. One day, frustrated, Kesar Dass resigned to his fate and trudged back home in the afternoon, his weary limbs heavy with exhaustion. He made up his mind to sell the entire land and buy a smaller patch near Karnal.

Bhagwanti noticed the lines of frustration etched on her husband's face when he entered the house. She immediately sensed why he was sad and upset but decided to wait till the evening to raise it with him. She knew well that her husband would like to be left alone in such times to introspect and regain his composure and resilient zeal. He would be fine soon, she assured herself.

In the evening, like every day, both sat on the roof watching the sun set over the dunes. The shifting sand dunes never ceased to mesmerise them. They saw their barren fields glow in the light of the dipping sun. 'You seem troubled,' Bhagwanti inquired, her voice laced with worry. 'The fields have taken their toll on you today?'

Kesar Dass sighed deeply. He replied, his voice heavy with emotion, 'I give up, Bhagwanti. This land is beyond me. It is a constant struggle to coax a meagre crop from this unforgiving earth. I wish we could go back to our village.'

A wave of sadness washed over Bhagwanti as she shared her husband's pain. She had witnessed her husband toil hard every day but without much result and could feel his dejection.

'I know,' Bhagwanti consoled him. 'It's hard to forget the land of our ancestors. But we must not dwell on what we have lost. We have each other, our children, our relatives, and together we will build a new life here.'

Kesar Dass nodded slowly, his eyes meeting hers. The unwavering love and support in her gaze gave him solace. 'You are right, Bhagwanti,' he said. 'We have each other, and that is enough.' It was a rare expression of the love that he held for her.

They sat in silence for a moment, lost in their thoughts. The dim light from the kerosene lamps cast flickering shadows on the walls below, creating a cosy ambience. They also reminded them it was dark. The scent of freshly baked chapati wafted from the kitchen, filling the house with a sense of warmth and comfort. Sumitra was cooking dinner.

'Come, dinner is ready,' Bhagwanti said, rising from her seat. 'Let us forget our troubles for now. I am sure God has better days in store for us.'

Kesar Dass smiled and followed his wife to the kitchen. As they sat down to eat, they engaged in light-hearted conversation, sharing stories of their day. Bhagwanti recounted an amusing incident involving the mischievous Gobind, while Kesar Dass described an encounter with a stubborn farmer. Laughter and love filled the air, momentarily dispelling the shadows of the past. Kesar Dass realised that the pain of displacement would always linger, but with his family by his side, he could face any challenge that came their way.

After dinner, they all sat together on the rooftop to watch the stars, and in them see the reflection of Rodu Sultan. In the tapestry of their lives, the memories of Rodu Sultan remained constant, vibrant threads, but they started to get interwoven with the bond that was starting to develop with Kurri. As the stars twinkled above them, Kesar Dass and Bhagwanti knew that their story was far from over. They would find ways to cope with their trauma and rebuild their lives.

19

A Hope Shattered, Decades of Struggle

Abdul's letter towards the end of the year 1950 jolted Kesar Dass into reality, shattering his hopes of returning to Rodu Sultan someday. His eyes welled up as he read the letter. Their ancestral land and home in Rodu Sultan had been allotted to a Muslim family which had migrated from Gurgaon. The symbol of his family's heritage, and a testament to generations of hard work and sacrifice, was gone. The thought filled him with a deep sense of loss and helplessness. Anger simmered beneath his grief – anger at the injustice of it all, and at the sheer audacity of those who had taken away from them what was not theirs. The idea that strangers now walked on the ground where his ancestors had toiled, where he had played as a child, and where his family had celebrated festivals and milestones, was unbearable. It felt as though a part of his soul had been ripped away. In his heart, he always knew something like that would happen but he chose to live in denial, hoping against hope, to return to his home and fields.

The harrowing journey to India, the relentless struggle to survive, and the constant fight to rebuild their lives had not allowed him to grieve since the time they had left Rodu Sultan. Abdul's letter activated a sleeping volcano filled with months of suppressed pain. It jolted him into confronting emotions he had long buried, even denied. The letter stirred memories of his mother's warmth, his uncle's guidance, and the vibrant community they had lost. It brought back the anguish of abandoning their home, cattle and friends, symbols of a life that had been torn apart by the madness of Partition. So far, he had been too consumed by the urgency of survival to grieve properly. Now, Abdul's words forced him to acknowledge the depth of his loss. He was filled with a tumultuous mix of grief, regret and unresolved sorrow.

Kesar Dass felt a profound sense of guilt for not having mourned his loved ones adequately. He was overwhelmed by a deep sadness, not just for his personal losses, but for the collective tragedy that had uprooted millions. Abdul's letter became a catalyst for Kesar Dass's mourning. It was a painful yet necessary reckoning, a step towards healing the wounds that Partition had inflicted on his heart and soul. The letter also evoked a bittersweet nostalgia for the shared humanity and friendships that once transcended religious divides, now shattered by violence and displacement.

Sitting on the rooftop of their new home that evening Kesar Dass and Bhagwanti watched the sun set behind the ever-changing sand dunes. As the wind swept across the vast expanse, it sculpted the dunes into new shapes and patterns. The golden waves shifted seamlessly, like a living canvas, with ridges and curves forming and dissolving in a rhythmic dance. As the golden rays dipped below the horizon, it cast long shadows across the unfamiliar landscape. Shadows played across the slopes, highlighting the intricate textures created by nature's hand. They found a reflection of their own life in the shifting sand dunes, of their displacement from the land of their ancestors and home, and from one part of a united nation, to the other of a divided country. And despite the turmoil raging in his heart, his anger at the turn of fortunes, he also realised that someone on the other side of the border was probably going through the same emotions at being uprooted from the land that Kesar Dass now called 'home'.

Kesar Dass couldn't sleep that night, burdened by the weight of loss.

Years went by. Kesar Dass and Nand Lal struggled and strived to rebuild their lives all over again, from the start, brick by brick. As time passed, they began to adjust to their new circumstances. While the memories of their lost homes lingered, they gradually made new connections and found a sense of belonging in Kurri. Narain Dass passed away a year after they arrived in Kurri. Although he remained quiet and uninterested in the affairs of the land, his presence as the eldest in the family provided strength. Nand Lal's relatives had also settled in Kurri. Over time, they rebuilt their lives, creating a future for themselves and their families in a land that had initially seemed so foreign. Nand Lal and Shakuntala were blessed with another son, whom they named Darshan.

Bhagwanti missed the ritual of her visits to the temple twice a day. There was not a single temple in Kurri when they arrived. Ibrahim Khan allowed Hindus to pray only at home. There were temples in Hisar, but not many. Shiva worship was very common and Shiva temples or shivalas were to be found in the district in large numbers. People visited shivalas generally on Mondays and worshipped the deity by pouring milk and water on the linga enshrined in it. Fairs were also held at many shivalas on Shivaratri day in February/March. The Hindus of Hisar were in no sense orthodox but followed traditional Hindu beliefs.

The temple had been a sanctuary for Bhagwanti where she could seek solace and commune with the divine. The absence of a temple dedicated to her beloved Lord Rama in the village troubled her. Recalling the temple in their village in Jhang, Bhagwanti's heart yearned for the familiar melodies of hymns that wafted through the village every morning and evening. She missed the serene ambience of the temple in Rodu Sultan, where she spent countless hours lost in devotion. As days turned into weeks, Bhagwanti's longing intensified. She yearned for a place where she could offer her prayers, chant sacred mantras, and feel the presence of her beloved deity. The absence of a temple felt like a gaping hole in the fabric of her existence. Tears would well up in her eyes as she imagined herself standing before the idol of Lord Rama in Rodu Sultan, pouring her heart out in supplication.

She raised the matter with Kesar Dass one day. 'We should build a temple for the villagers. With Ibrahim Khan gone, the village deserves a temple.'

Kesar Dass brushed aside her demand. 'We have so many other pressing matters. We must wait.'

'The village has struggled so much. Lord Rama's blessings will change the fortunes of this backward village,' she persisted.

Kesar Dass was not convinced that spending resources on the temple was the right thing to do at that point of time. But Bhagwanti's faith refused to be extinguished. She continued to persist till Kesar Dass relented. He assured her that he would speak to his cousins.

The thought of constructing a temple seemed like an insurmountable task but the cousins were welcoming of the idea. It was decided to build a small temple of Lord Rama on a piece of their land just outside the house. Together, the Batra family pooled the money for the construction. Skilled masons and artisans from Rajasthan were hired, bringing with them their centuries-old knowledge of temple architecture. The artisan and engravers worked tirelessly over a year, shaping stones with precision and carving intricate designs into the walls. As the temple began to take form, they went to Jaipur to order an exquisite idol of Lord Rama, Sita and Hanuman, crafted from the finest marble.

When the idols arrived, the villagers gathered around the idols, their faces radiant with joy and devotion. The idols were adorned with garlands of fragrant flowers and placed in a temporary shrine until the temple was completed. The sthapana (consecration) ceremony was a momentous occasion for the entire village. Bhagwanti, dressed in her finest attire, performed the sacred rituals with unwavering devotion. The air was thick with the scent of incense and the chanting of Vedic hymns. As Bhagwanti invoked the divine presence into the idols, the villagers witnessed a profound transformation. The marble figures seemed to come alive, their eyes sparkling with a divine radiance. Tears of joy streamed down Bhagwanti's face as she felt the overwhelming sense of Lord Rama's presence.

After the temple was officially consecrated, the villagers streamed inside, eager to offer their prayers and seek the blessings of Lord Rama, Sita and Hanuman. Bhagwanti's heart overflowed with gratitude as she beheld the fruits of her unwavering faith and the unity it had fostered within the community.

Word of the newly built temple spread far and wide. Devotees from neighbouring villages and towns flocked to pay homage to Lord Rama and witness the beauty of the temple's architecture. Bhagwanti's dream had not only come to fruition but had also become a beacon of spirituality for the entire region.

In the years that followed, the temple became a central part of village life. It was a place where people gathered for daily prayers, religious festivals and community events. The temple became a symbol of hope, harmony and the enduring bond between humanity and the divine.

Bhagwanti spent a good amount of time serving the temple and its devotees, ensuring that the flame of devotion burned brightly for generations to come. Although a priest had been hired, Bhagwanti took it upon herself to ensure all rituals in the temple were followed with precision. The temple had become a turning point in Bhagwanti's life. Although not old enough for that, she became Mata-ji of the village. Even her own grandchildren started addressing her with that title.

A woman of remarkable dignity and generosity, Mata-ji transformed the lives of the villagers in Kurri through her benevolent approach, earning her the revered status of a godmother, especially among the women and children. She was Mata-ji to all, old and young. She made time to understand the villagers' struggles, needs and aspirations. She approached them with humility and empathy, which immediately endeared her to everyone around. She had the ability to connect with people on a personal level. Mata-ji celebrated their joys and shared their sorrows, becoming a pillar of support for many.

Her home was always open to those in need, and she often mediated conflicts within the village with wisdom and fairness. Her kindness and selflessness earned her the trust and admiration of the entire community. Her generosity knew no bounds. She also funded the construction of a well in the village and encouraged women to be economically independent, transforming the lives of many women and giving them a sense of purpose and confidence. Over time, Mata-ji became a symbol of hope and resilience to the villagers. The women of Kurri, in particular, saw her as a mentor and protector, someone who had their best interests at heart. At the same time, Mata-ji continued to remain the anchor for her own family.

After Ram Saran finished his school, Kesar Dass tried to discourage him from studying further, and persuade him to work on the family land. Ram Saran was determined to join college and study further. But there was no degree college in Hisar. Ram Saran left for Aligarh, much against the wishes of his family. There, he took admission in Aligarh Muslim University (AMU), a premier educational institution of the country. He worked at a petrol pump to earn some extra money to pay for his overheads, as the money order he received from home barely met his college and hostel fees. He was determined to become a teacher.

The country started emerging from the shadow of foreign rule after Independence. With nation building gathering momentum, many opportunities were opening up. A number of new schools and colleges started opening in Hisar. A part of the Lahore Veterinary College was shifted to Hisar in 1948 and became the Punjab Veterinary College; a government college and the Dayanand College came into being in 1950; and another college, Fateh Chand College for Women, opened in 1954.

Gobind had aspirations to make most of the opportunities the new India offered. He too was determined to study further. But Kesar Dass wanted one of the sons to be around to look after the land. This time he did not relent and refused to pay for Gobind's college. One day, Gobind ran away to his sister's marital house in Ferozepur and took admission in a college there with Daya's support. Eventually, seeing his wife sad every day, Kesar Dass relented, and Gobind moved back to Hisar and joined Dayanand College. He cycled nearly ten miles every day from the village to reach the college. Many times, if it turned dark on return, Gobind would spend the night on a tree to escape from jackals and other wild animals that roamed in the barren land stretching from the village to Hisar. After graduation, Gobind joined the law department in Panjab University Chandigarh to pursue a bachelor's degree in law.

Sumitra got married to Jeewan Dass Arora, another Jhangi. His parents Amir Chand and Tulshi Bai had migrated from village Jaivan in Jhang and settled in Kurri. Jeewan Dass, a hard-working and happy-go-lucky young man had set up a motor repair workshop in Delhi. The couple settled in Delhi's Kalkaji.

With Ram Saran and Gobind deciding to pursue higher studies, and both his daughters having left for their husbands' homes, the house in Kurri, which had just about started bustling with their laughter and energy, grew quieter. Though proud of their children's achievements, Kesar Dass and Mata-ji couldn't help but feel a sense of loss. As time passed, Nand Lal's children, like their own, left the village in search of education and better opportunities, leaving behind a way of life that had sustained their ancestors for centuries. The arid lands surrounding the village demanded relentless toil under a scorching sun, yet yielded little in return. The departure of their children marked the slow decline of a tradition that had once thrived in Jhang.

Initially, Kesar Dass felt a sense of loss and confusion when his sons chose professions different from the family's long-standing agricultural heritage. For generations, his family had tilled the land, finding pride and identity in the rhythms of sowing and harvesting. Agriculture was not just a livelihood but a way of life, a connection to the earth and to their past. With his sons deciding to pursue education and careers outside of farming, Kesar Dass felt as though a vital link to his heritage was being severed. As time passed, his feelings began to shift. He recognised the changing world around him and the increasing challenges of sustaining a livelihood through agriculture. He started to appreciate the determination in Gobind's eyes and his desire to carve out a future that offered stability and opportunities village life could not provide. Slowly, pride began to replace his initial disappointment. He realised that their pursuit of education was not a rejection of their roots but an evolution, a way to honour the family's legacy by adapting to a new era.

Mata-ji found solace in her cows who were like an extended family. Her mornings, earlier spent in the kitchen preparing choicest dishes for her children, were now spent in the cowshed. She would wake up at dawn and head to the cowshed where she lovingly prepared fresh fodder, mixing it with grains and jaggery, ensuring that her cows received the best care. As she fed them, she would hum traditional folk songs, her voice soothing the animals. Bhagwanti often spoke to her cows as if they were her companions, sharing her thoughts and reminiscing about her children. In the evenings, one of the village boys would take the cows to graze, while she meticulously cleaned the cowshed, and milked the cows with practised hands. The rhythmic sound of milk filling the pail was a comforting ritual.

Both parents felt immensely proud when Gobind enrolled as an advocate in November 1962. The entire village came to congratulate them; he was the first from the village to pursue higher education and become a lawyer. Gobind started practising at the district court in Hisar. He rented a room in the town, where he lived during the week. He visited Kurri on Sundays and holidays to spend time with his parents. He had also bought a second-hand scooter.

Ram Saran visited his parents as and when he could. After completing his master's, he decided to pursue his doctorate. There he met Soma Devi, younger sister of a widowed co-student also pursuing her doctorate. He started teaching in a university in Sikar, Rajasthan, in the meantime. With the intervention of their guide, he decided to marry her. Soma Devi was also from a family displaced from West Pakistan which had settled in Aligarh. After some time, Ram Saran quit his job and set up a factory of brass hardware.

With the prospects of his sons returning to their village no longer a possibility, Kesar Dass lost the zeal to toil hard. If his children were not interested in farming, who should he work hard for in the farm? He had little interest left in the land. As moneylenders, they rarely bothered to charge interest or penalty, often shifting the repayment dates and mostly adjusting them in parts from the crop share. Most of their time was spent in the service of God and the villagers.

Kesar Dass had received notification of his appointment as lambardar, and permanent allotment of land, a few weeks after they had arrived in Kurri. As lambardar, he wielded a position of authority and responsibility within the village, often acting as an intermediary between the government and the local community. His role granted them additional power and influence over village affairs. The power was further amplified by his role in maintaining law and order, ensuring compliance with government policies, and distributing resources. The position made him a key figure in shaping the socio-economic dynamics of the village. Additionally, his own stature as a large landlord, compassionate and benevolent, enhanced his standing within the community. This dual role – official and communal – made him a central figure in the village's governance and daily life. His influence extended beyond formal duties, and often shaped the cultural and political fabric of the community. His selfless actions and ability to connect with individuals from all walks of life made him a beloved and trusted figure. Recognising his deep connection with the community and his ability to sway public opinion, local politicians began visiting him to seek his blessings and support, knowing that his endorsement could strengthen their credibility and appeal among voters. Chief among them was Bhajan Lal who went on to become chief minister of Haryana after the state was formed.

Kesar Dass's influence was not rooted in his own political ambition, but in his genuine desire to serve others. He and Mata-ji became the elders of the village, ever willing to help. Out of respect for them and in deference to their generosity, the villagers started addressing Kesar Dass as Lala-ji. The couple became Lala-ji and Mata-ji for the village.

In 1953, the Punjab government enacted the Punjab Security of Land Tenures Act, fixing a ceiling on landholdings and utilising the surplus area for resettlement of ejected tenants, landless labourers and small landowners. The ceiling fixed for the landholdings was thirty standard acres for local owners and fifty standard acres for displaced persons from Pakistan. It strengthened the rights of tenants. Rigorous terms added made eviction of tenants nearly impossible. Unfortunately, taking undue advantage of this law some tenants of Kesar Dass turned unreasonable and stopped disclosing the actual produce. A few even became hostile. Kesar Dass was left deeply hurt.

In 1956, the Hindu Succession Act, was passed, recognising the right of daughters, mother and the widow to inherit the intestate property simultaneously. Till then, the right of inheritance was vested only in the male descendants. Similarly, the daughters and their issues had no customary rights to succession but were entitled to maintenance and to be suitably betrothed and married. The daughter now had as good a claim to her father's property as a son, provided the father did not debar her by law and that too in the case of self-acquired property only. However, generally the girl did not claim any part of the intestate property but in the absence of a brother, she usually retained her right to property. Lala-ji wrote a will bequeathing the house in the village and his share of land to Mata-ji. He had already provided for his daughters at the time of marriage but continued to support them financially till he was alive, a tradition that Mata-ji and Gobind continued.

Gobind married Veena Passi in 1964. He fell in love with the twenty-year-old stunningly beautiful girl while watching her perform on stage in college during a cultural festival. Initially, Veena's father, Prof. S.P. Passi, a renowned professor of physics, refused to give his daughter in marriage to a village boy. Her mother, Satyawati, was not prepared to let her daughter live in a village. Many members of the Passi family had relocated to Jullundur in Punjab a few months before Partition. They were originally from Amritsar. S.P. Passi eventually settled in Hisar where he served as the principal of Dayanand College. Finally, Veena's parents relented. An elegant and charming girl, Veena spent her life looking after her husband, children and caring for them even after they had grown up. An independent person, she travelled around the country by herself, mainly for pilgrimage or to visit places of religious importance.

Over time, Kesar Dass became a quiet and introspective figure. The brutal violence, communal riots and mass displacement had shattered his spirit. The trauma of seeing neighbours turn against each other, families torn apart, and villages set ablaze left an indelible mark on his psyche. The memory of the long, arduous journey fraught with the fear of being persecuted on the way was still painfully etched in his mind. He had lost loved ones, his ancestral home, and the sense of belonging that had defined his identity. He continued to carry the weight of grief, leaving him withdrawn and unable to articulate his pain. He found solace only in silence. Partition had uprooted him physically but it could not sever his connection to his past.

This was compounded by the struggle to produce good crops from an arid land. Even after all these years, he longed to visit Rodu Sultan, only to touch the soil, to soak the landscape of Jhang, to feel the draught of cool breeze from the canal, to gaze at their home from the distance knowing he may not even be allowed to step in, to sit on the floor of the classroom where he once studied, to walk through the bazars of Jhang, and to just inhale the air of Rodu Sultan which carried elements of his ancestors' sweat.

Every few years, as a tradition, Kesar Dass's six sisters would reunite in Kurri with their children. The siblings spent time together rekindling childhood memories. Laughing and crying, they reminisced about their days in Rodu Sultan. The children of some of the sisters stayed back in Kurri for higher studies in Hisar. For many years after Independence, most other towns in Haryana did not have institutions of higher education. Lala-ji married off many his nieces as was then customary. Being the only brother, it was his responsibility to ensure that all his sister's children were cared for from the proceeds of the land.

His eyes reflected the unspoken sorrow of a generation scarred by the violence and displacement of Partition. His silence spoke volumes, a testament to the enduring trauma of those tumultuous times. He found some relief in watching the sand dunes in which he saw grains of sand that had probably flown from Jhang to Hisar.

20

A New Era and the Gurukul

The fortunes of Kurri turned after the construction of the Bhakra Nangal Project (completed in 1963) and the irrigation canal reached Kurri in 1964. The arrival of water alleviated the struggles, leading to agricultural turnaround. The construction of this canal was Prime Minister Nehru's dream project for a modern India. He poured the first bucket of concrete for the construction of what was conceived as the world's highest straight-gravity dam in 1955. Although the importance of irrigating vast tracts of land was realised nearly half a century before Independence, the project evolved at a very slow pace. Partition had brought only 20 per cent of the canal system of undivided Punjab to India's share with 50 per cent population. The Upper Bari Doab Canal between the Ravi and the Beas and the Sirhind Canal in southern Punjab came to India's share. Until the Bhakra Canal arrived, the districts of Hisar, Fatehabad, Sirsa and neighbouring regions remained arid.

The various channels providing irrigation to Hisar district were constructed between 1954 and 1966. The government started lining different channels in the district. An irrigation system originating from the Bhakra mainline discharged water into these regions. The Bhakra mainline canal entered the Hisar district near village Balyala in Tohana tehsil. This transformed life and agriculture in the Hisar district from an arid region to an agriculturally and economically prosperous one. The dam's waters were no less than that of the Ganga erupting from Shiva's locks for the people of the Hisar belt.

With the introduction of the Bhakra canal, cropping showed a marked upward trend in the district. The intensity of cropping, which was as low as 71 per cent, improved to 115 per cent in 1964-65 and to 143 per cent in 1977-78. The cropping pattern also changed. Till 1965, barley, bajra, gram and fodder crops covered a major area, but with the advent of irrigation, the percentage area under barley and bajra started decreasing and that of rice, wheat, cotton, sugarcane and oilseeds increased. The major crops of the district became jowar, bajra, cotton, sugarcane, rice and pulses in kharif, and wheat, gram and oilseeds in rabi. Cotton, oilseeds, gram and bajra became the principal crops of the district.

The advent of canal irrigation also brought big chunks of barren and parched lands under cultivation. A district which was marked by recurring droughts and famines slowly became one of the most agriculturally developed districts of the state. The extensive canal irrigation introduced by the project caused rapid changes in water table configuration. The water level rose by two to seven metres in the Hisar area between 1974 and 1978. The canals provided a more reliable water source, enabling farmers to cultivate water-intensive crops like wheat and rice. Agricultural productivity improved dramatically, leading to better food security and economic stability for the rural population. The district which earlier grew only coarse grains, now boasted of being the cotton belt of Haryana.

The Haryana Agricultural University was established at Hisar, only a few kilometres from Kurri, bringing spectacular transformation in the age-old agricultural economy of the district. Asia's biggest and the world's second-largest livestock farm was also built in the district.

With the implementation of the rural water supply scheme, non-availability of water slowly became a thing of the past. Piped water supply was made available to many villages and dhanis, including in Kurri over the years that followed.

Bhagwanti believed that it was a manifestation of Lord Rama's blessings for building his temple, and praying to him.

Kurri was renamed Aryanagar, symbolising a fresh start and alignment with broader socio-political changes in India. Agriculture became the mainstay of Aryanagar's economy. Villagers started growing water-efficient crops, particularly millets, pulses, and pearl millet, aligning with typical semi-arid agro-economics. The availability of reliable irrigation moved the village from dependency on erratic monsoon rains to a more predictable and productive agricultural regime. This enhanced agricultural growth brought economic prosperity to Aryanagar, improved the standard of living and enabled better infrastructure development within the village. Aryanagar village witnessed a transformation in social dynamics with increased emphasis on education, migration for employment opportunities to urban centres, and improved connectivity.

The changing destiny of the village did not make much difference to the fortunes of the Batra family. Kesar Dass was getting old; he did not have the will or strength to start a new phase of life as a farmer. The two sons had embarked too far on their new paths to turn back. Gobind, however, found time to spend with his family and look after the land.

With the canal arriving, land became valuable; some tenants turned greedy. Land disputes with some tenants started leading to tension in the village, exposing the lives of Lala-ji and Mata-ji to danger. The 'refugee' tag for Kesar Dass and his clan became more profound in the village, giving voice to what had remained unsaid so far.

One day, Lala-ji was surprised to find Swami Devanand-ji Maharaj walk into their house, unannounced. He was one of the most renowned Arya Samajists of Hisar district. He was accompanied by his disciple and a farmer.

Named as Lakshman Dev by his parents, Devanand-ji was born in 1908 in a well-to-do family of Matarshyam, a village ten kilometres from Hisar town. His parents were Kumhars by caste and farmers by profession. He acquired some knowledge of Hindi through non-formal education at his native village. When he desired to acquire more knowledge from a Brahmin, the latter refused to teach him as the boy was an outcast. This incident left an indelible imprint on the young mind of Lakshman Dev who did his best to improve his knowledge on his own. He was married to Vedwati who belonged to Sri Ganganagar district of Rajasthan. They had four children.

Lakshman Dev adopted the profession of agriculture to earn his livelihood. He also opened a khadi shop at Hisar, but it was not profitable.

He was a popular figure among his fellow villagers who often invited him to settle their disputes. Keeping his impartiality in view, he was appointed the sarpanch of his village. The turning point in Lakshman Dev's life came when he joined the Arya Samaj Movement. When the historic mass movement, Hyderabad Satyagraha, was launched by the Arya Samaj in 1939, he played a vital role in making it a success. During the language agitation of 1957, he also courted arrest. As the days rolled by, Lakshman Dev grew discontented and wanted to serve his people in a much better way. He decided to give up his family life so that he could devote himself to others wholeheartedly. With this end in view, Lakshman Dev took sanyas in 1959 and adopted the name of Swami Devanand Saraswati. He devoted the rest of his life in promoting the cause of the gurukul system of education.

After Swami-ji had been offered hot milk and shakarparas, he said, 'Lala-ji, I was passing through Kurri. I stopped for some time on the bank of the canal for sandhyopasana. An inner voice told me I must set up a gurukul in this village. I inquired from a farmer who owned the land near the canal. He guided me to your house.' Swami-ji folded his hands and requested Lala-ji and Mata-ji, 'I beg you to donate land for establishing the gurukul in the village.'

The history of gurukuls is the history of India's education system. The word 'gurukula' or 'gurukulam' is made up of 'guru' and 'kula', translating to 'the lineage/clan of the guru'. The gurukul system has been recorded as the earliest form of imparting organised education. Gurukuls enjoyed state patronage under most dynasties in India. They flourished well up to the eighteenth century till the British started introducing an alternative education system. It is a type of residential schooling system in which the shishya lives with the acharya or guru (teacher), who feeds him, teaches him, and treats him as one of the family. The shishya helps the guru in his day-to-day work and learns from his conduct as well. Gurukuls acted as the main centre of learning in ancient times.

In gurukuls, brahmacharis (students), or satyanveshi parivrajakas from far-off places used to come to complete their education. The developed forms of such gurukuls were Takshashila, Nalanda, Vikramshila and Valabhi University. In these universities, students from far-off places came to study. Many famous rishis/gurus who are mentioned in the Indian epics Ramayana and Mahabharata had famous gurukuls. Rama and Krishna also studied in gurukuls under Maharshi Vashishtha and Sandeepani respectively. Maharishi Vishwamitra, the teacher of Lord Rama and Lakshmana taught them the usage of devastras (celestial weapons) for use in warfare. He guided them in defeating the powerful demons. Sita took refuge at the ashram of Maharshi Valmiki and gave birth to Luv and Kush; he taught them the shastras and the art of using weapons. He also wrote the Ramayana. Guru Dronacharya was the guru of all the Kauravas and Pandavas of Mahabharata fame. His gurukul was situated somewhere near present-day Gurugram, the town which also gets its name from Dronacharya's gurukul.

However, the gurukul system faced challenges from the continuous persecution and destruction at the hands of Muslim rulers.

Lala-ji and Mata-ji readily agreed to donate the land. It was an impromptu decision made on the request of Swami Devanand-ji Maharaj.

'It will be our privilege to serve the Arya Samaj,' was all that Lala-ji said.

'How much land do you need?' Mata-ji inquired.

Swami-ji was surprised by the response of Lala-ji and Mata-ji; he did not expect that they would agree so readily. 'One-and-a-half acre on the bank of the canal,' he replied hesitatingly, not sure if he was asking for too much.

Lala-ji looked at Mata-ji. Their eyes met briefly. Lala-ji knew the answer from the look in Mata-ji's eyes.

'We will be honoured to donate one-and-a-half acres. You may pick the site of your choice, Swami-ji,' Lala-ji replied graciously.

Mata-ji and Lala-ji also promised to donate about two thousand rupees, a princely sum in those days, for construction of the gurukul. Later, the members of the Batra family collected the promised sum and handed it over to Swami-ji.

That is how one-and-a-half acres of prime cultivable land next to the recently constructed canal was donated for building the gurukul. It was Mata-ji and Lala-ji's way of supporting the Arya Samaj which encouraged a great number of Hindus to be drawn to the fountain of Vedic lore.

Gurukul Aryanagar was established on Chaitra Shukla Pratipada Samvat 2021 corresponding to 13 April 1964 amidst the sound of holy Vedic mantras. On the foundation day, eleven brahmacharis took admission and, as per the wish of Swami-ji Maharaj, teaching and learning started according to the gurukul system. The construction of buildings and the arrangements for its administration also commenced.

At the age of seventy-seven, Swami Devanand breathed his last on 20 May 1985 at Fatehabad, near Hisar. A motorcyclist under the influence of alcohol hit Swami-ji, fatally injuring him. Swami Devanand was one of the rare Arya Samajists of his region who went to the extent of becoming a sanyasi.

Even today, Gurukul Aryanagar stands as a reputed gurukul of India. The website of the gurukul records, 'The sacrifice of respected Mata-ji and respected Lala-ji is exemplary and praiseworthy. May God grant them eternal peace.'

Mata-ji and Lala-ji continued to support the gurukul throughout their life. This tradition was continued by Gobind and Veena. After their death, the author and his wife are attempting to continue the tradition of their ancestors.

21

Shifting Sand Dunes

Merely nineteen years after their migration in 1947, and less than a year after the author was born, the sand dunes shifted yet again. Punjabi-speaking Khatris rehabilitated in the north-western part of the state of Punjab found themselves amidst another disruption. Many parts of the districts of Ambala, Hisar (including Aryanagar, Rohtak, Hansi, Sirsa), and other places, where Punjabi Khatris had settled, were partitioned from Punjab, and made part of the new state of Haryana created on 1 November 1966. The Punjabi Khatris, just about starting to find new roots, were relegated to the new state of Haryana, dominated by Jats and other communities.

Arriving in India had brought a sense of relief despite the unfamiliarity of terrain, culture and people, although this relief was accompanied by an overwhelming melancholy. The nostalgia for the home they had left behind was acute, and the realisation that they might never return was heart-wrenching. But over two decades spent in Hisar, they had reconciled and let go of most of the bitterness of displacement. A process of reconciliation had started. They had integrated into the new social landscape, bridging numerous divides while navigating mutual suspicions and prejudices.

With yet another partition of Punjab, though this time peacefully, their lives once again shifted, relegating them from Punjab to Haryana by a stroke of another executive order.

In 1947, thirteen out of twenty-nine British districts of Punjab in undivided India came to East Punjab's share, which was renamed Punjab (India) on 26 January 1950. In 1948, the former princely states were organised separately as Himachal Pradesh and PEPSU, the latter merging with Punjab in 1956.

Soon after independence, the question of division based on linguistic units cropped up. The Akali Dal started pressing for the claim of the Punjabi language as the sole official language of the new state of Punjab. In April 1948, Master Tara Singh, as the president of the Shiromani Akali Dal, demanded Punjabi Suba, a separate state for the Punjabi-speaking population. Since Punjabi was the primary language of the Sikhs, the language problem was intertwined with religion. The demand was rejected.

The Akali Dal did not have enough muscle in the legislative assembly but their politics was to back whoever agreed to enable Punjabi as the official language of the state. Master Tara Singh led a vigorous campaign in 1948-49. The initial role of the legislators from the Haryana region was limited to acting as a pressure group to counter the Akali Dal. The Akalis, who were now a part of the government, were in a fix.

The Hindu Mahasabha of Punjab and the Arya Samaj of Haryana region wanted safeguards for the Hindi-speaking people of Punjab. Hindus of Punjab feared that if the state split, creating two smaller states on a linguistic basis, Punjabi-speaking Hindus on both sides would come under Jat dominance in the 'new' states. As a safeguard for their own interests, Punjabi-speaking Hindus raised the slogan of Maha Punjab, which was meant to include some areas from Rajasthan and UP as well. Thus came up a division among the legislators and their political parties based on communal affiliations. Hindus and Sikhs, united before the partition of 1947, and united against Muslims (except, of course, those in the Unionist Party), now formed two separate religious and political camps.

Notably, historically, there was never a direct demand for a separate state of Haryana; it only emerged as a counter to the Akali Dal's assertion to create a Punjabi Suba. In 1925, Pirzada Mohammad Hussain, a Muslim League leader from Delhi, had advocated the demand for separation of Ambala division (Haryana region) from Punjab and the expansion of Delhi province. It was later supported by the Muslim League, perhaps motivated by communal and political considerations. Some leaders in Delhi also made a request for an enlarged province of Delhi, uniting the Hindi-speaking region of Punjab with it. The Delhi Provincial Congress Committee too raised this demand the same year. The desire was to have the same type of partially democratic set-up for Delhi as in other provinces.

In 1928, an all-party conference in Delhi again demanded the expansion of the boundaries of Delhi. The report of the provincial redistribution committee of the Congress also lent its support and expressed the view that the separation of Ambala division from Punjab would solve a number of political problems of the province. One of the motivations was to wean away the Hindu Jats of the Haryana region from the Unionists. But the demand failed to gather much support in the Haryana region of Punjab.

Sir Chhotu Ram, a tall leader from the region, and Deshbandhu Gupta, a Delhi-based Congress leader from Haryana region, supported this demand. Sir Chhotu Ram voiced his support for the Haryana Prant in his presidential address to the Jat Mahasabha at Agra in 1929, but it was mainly in opposition to the separation of Ambala division from Punjab and its merger in Delhi before the Indian Statutory Reforms Committee in 1930. He believed that the separation of Ambala division would have converted Punjab into a predominantly Muslim province. Deshbandhu Gupta supported Sir Chhotu Ram in 1932, stating, 'The Hindi-speaking region had never been a part of Punjab. For the development of this region, it was necessary to separate it from Punjab and ... a new state should be created.' He demanded a 'Greater Delhi' with Haryana as its part, not Haryana as a separate state. When the organisational map of the Congress was redrawn in 1939, Haryana region was a part of the Punjab province.

As a countermove to Master Tara Singh's demand, Jats and their allies in the Haryana region raised the slogan of Vishal Haryana and Maha Dilli, which intended to include, besides the Ambala division of Punjab (Haryana region), Delhi, western UP, and parts of Rajasthan. The natives of the districts which now form part of Haryana had been feeling neglected – that they were not being given due importance in Punjab. This Hindi–Haryana struggle was primarily led by the Jat leaders, although some Arya Samajis supported them too. This struggle and counter-struggle marked the next one-and-a-half decade of Punjab until the formation of Haryana.

In 1953, the Indian government established the States Reorganisation Commission tasked to demarcate provinces on a linguistic basis. The Haryana Prant Front formed by some parties, headed by freedom fighter Pandit Shri Ram Sharma and twenty-three Congress MLAs, raised the demand for a separate Haryana before the States Reorganisation Commission in 1954. The demand was raised in the Lok Sabha by Pandit Thakur Das Bhargava and Chaudhary Ranbir Singh, and by Prof. Sher Singh and Chaudhary Devi Lal in the Punjab Vidhan Sabha in 1954. There was no mass movement for the demand of Haryana Prant although Haryana Prant Front organised well-attended political meetings at Samalkha, Sonipat and Rohtak in 1955. Most of the participants included the articulate sections of the peasantry and educated persons, affected by the economic, political and educational backwardness of Haryana region.

The Akalis were asking for a Punjabi Suba, but they were against the creation of Haryana. They had agreed to separate from Punjab only the districts of Rohtak, Gurgaon and Mahendragarh, where Sikhs had no presence, and merge them with UP or Rajasthan, converting the rest of Punjab into the Punjabi Suba.

On 23 September 1965, the Government of India constituted the Shah Commission, a parliamentary committee, to consider the partition of Punjab under the chairmanship of the then speaker of the Lok Sabha, Sardar Hukam Singh. The commission gave its report on 31 May 1966. The report recommended that the Punjabi Suba would be formed of Punjabi-speaking population from the districts of Gurdaspur (except Dalhousie, Balun and Bakloh), Amritsar, Kapurthala, Jullundur, Ferozepur, Bathinda, Patiala and Ludhiana; the tehsils of Sangrur district (Barnala, Malerkotla and Sangrur); Ropar tehsil of Ambala district; tehsils Dasuha, Hoshiarpur and Garhshankar, Anandpur and the development blocks of Nurpur Bedi, villages Kharabagh, Samipur and Kalseh of Una Block and village Kasauri of Una tehsil of Hoshiarpur district.

Hisar, Mahendragarh, Gurgaon, Rohtak and Karnal, tehsils Narwana and Jind (Sangrur district), and tehsils Kharar (including Hadigarh Capital Project), Naraingarh, Ambala, Jagadhri (of Ambala district) were to form the Hindi-speaking state of Haryana.

The hilly areas, such as Simla district, Kulu, Kangra, Lahaul Spiti were given to Himachal Pradesh. The development blocks of Gagrat and Una (excluding the villages of Kharabagh, Samipur, Bhabhour and Kalseh), village Kasri from tehsil Una (Hoshiarpur district), tehsil Nalagarh (Ambala district), enclaves Dalhousie, Balun and Bukloh in Chamba district, and the hilly areas having cultural affinity with the people of Himachal Pradesh were merged with Himachal Pradesh.

A boundary commission was constituted to give effect to the partition of Punjab. In September 1966, the Parliament passed the Punjab Reorganisation Act; the state of Haryana became the seventeenth state of independent India in November 1966.

The name Haryana was not familiar to people in many parts of the country before 1966. There are also differences in opinion on the origin of the name amongst historians, but the antiquity of the area in history is not disputed. It appears in the Mahabharata as well as in the legends on ancient coins, especially those of the Yaudheyas. The name can also be traced to the ancient Rig Veda, where Hariana is used as a qualifying adjective with the name of a king, Varuraja.

There were frantic political developments in Haryana politics since the beginning of the state's formation as Jats asserted their right to govern the state. After the formation of the state in November 1966, Dharma Vira was appointed as the first governor of Haryana. It was decided not to hold elections in the new state at that time. An interim government was appointed comprising legislators from the Punjab Legislative Assembly, who were elected from the part of Punjab that now formed Haryana. Bhagwat Dayal Sharma was made the first chief minister of the state.

Jats asserted their right to govern the state and refused to accept a non-Jat as their chief minister. Appointment of a non-Jat leader antagonised the Jats and other senior political leaders from Haryana. Professor Sher Singh, Devi Lal and Lehri Singh, being in the opposition, were naturally not in the race for the chief ministership. But Ranbir Singh, Rao Birender Singh, Hardwari Lal and Suraj Mal of the Congress, all senior to Bhagwat Dayal Sharma, expected to be the rightful candidate for the seat of chief minister.

The fault lines in Haryana politics developed rapidly in the next few months. The politics of Haryana came to be dominated by the Jats. Punjabi Khatris were relegated to the fringes in Haryana's political space with very little voice or representation in politics or the state assembly.

The election to the state assembly was announced within weeks of the formation of the first government, to be held in 1967 along with the general elections in the country. Jats tried to secure a majority of seats by defeating non-Jat candidates in the constituencies of their dominance, voting for non-Congress Jat candidates. In caste arithmetic, Jats secured the numerical majority, for, even within the Congress, they were the single-caste majority. Congress won 48 out of 81 seats in the state assembly, and seven out of nine seats in the parliamentary election. Bhagwat Dayal Sharma was once again sworn in as chief minister, as a choice of Congress leaders in Delhi.

The selection of Bhagwat Dayal Sharma once again made Jat leaders sore. Many senior non-Jat leaders of the party also felt humiliated. Rao Birender Singh, who had been a minister in Punjab, was especially annoyed over the decision. The Jats had not forgotten the defeat of Professor Sher Singh in the 1962 election at the hands of Bhagwat Dayal Sharma when he was handpicked by Sardar Partap Singh Kairon, the then chief minister of Punjab. The appointment of Bhagwat Dayal Sharma as chief minister sharpened suspicion of the Jats that the Congress was an anti-Jat party, a party of the Brahmin–Bania combine.

The revolt came within months of the formation of the new government. Jats combined with the landowning legislators of the other castes including Ahirs, Gujars and Rors. But the Jats were not able to agree on any name. Within days of the formation of government by the Congress in 1967, Congress candidate Dayakishan was defeated by Vishal Haryana Party candidate Rao Virendra Singh in the election for the Speaker of the legislative assembly. Dayakishan got 37 votes and Rao Virendra Singh got 40 votes, due to internal strife that had developed within the Congress party. Devi Lal, Rao Birender Singh and Siri Chand along with ten other MLAs crossed the floor. Bhagwat Dayal Sharma's government was brought down and he had to resign just after thirteen days of being sworn in as chief minister. In his place Rao Birender Singh, who was the leader of the United Front, became the new chief minister but even he could not remain in power for long as he was unable to get along with the Jat leaders.

In November 1967, Rao Birender Singh's government was dismissed on the basis of the report of the governor and President's Rule was imposed in the state. This was an indication of the times to come in the political landscape of Haryana, where Jats and non-Jats jostled for power. Punjabi Khatris mainly supported both the Congress and the Jana Sangh.

In the mid-term poll held in 1968, the Congress got 48 seats out of 81. The non-Congress combination could not show any unity or vision and voters again opted for the Congress. Wiser from the fall of the Bhagwat Dayal Sharma government, the Congress this time decided to have its chief minister from the majority caste of the Jats. Bansi Lai, a Jat, was chosen to become the chief minister. The rule of majoritarianism was put in practice in Haryana. The state was not to have a non-Jat chief minister for a very long time.

Bansi Lal's ministry was shaky because of regular defections but he managed to complete his term. He was re-elected as chief minister after the 1972 Assembly elections and continued till 1977. Devi Lal had in the meanwhile quit the Congress before the 1972 Vidhan Sabha elections. The Janata Party was formed in 1977 at the national level and its units were established in various states including Haryana. Devi Lal joined the Janata Party, which in Haryana consisted of six main factions: Bharatiya Lok Dal, Jana Sangh, Congress (O), the Socialists, the Congress for Democracy (CFD) and Arya Sabha. When elections were held in Haryana in June 1977, the Janata Party won with a thumping majority of 75 seats out of 90.

When Devi Lal formed the ministry, there were more than one aspirant for a birth in the ministry from each faction which made the task of ministry-making difficult, more so because the Janata Party leadership in Delhi decided that the size of the ministry should be limited to 10 per cent of the total strength of the assembly which meant there were to be only nine ministers in Haryana. Dissidence in the party led to Devi Lal's resignation on 25 June 1978. Bhajan Lal was elected as the next leader and administered the oath of office on 28 June 1978.

The rise of Bhajan Lal was a turning point in Haryana's power politics; it marked the end of Jat dominance. This was no small achievement on the part of Bhajan Lal. What non-Jat leaders from Sri Ram Sharma to Bhagwat Dayal Sharma could not achieve, despite their long struggle, Bhajan Lal accomplished in less than ten years of his political career. This also posed a challenge to the majority community that turned fiercely hostile to him, never relenting in its fury against him. The contest between Bhajan Lal's foxiness and Jat fury shaped the power politics of Haryana for over two decades.

After the split of the Janata Party in 1979 which led to the fall of the Janata government headed by Morarji Desai at the Centre and installation of Charan Singh's minority government in his place, Charan Singh and his followers including Devi Lal formed a separate party known as Lok Dal. The Lok Dal became the champion of the Jats of Haryana. Devi Lal went on to become the deputy prime minister of India in the V.P. Singh government. In the state, Devi Lal's place was taken on by his son Om Prakash Chautala on 2 December 1989.

Caste had become central to Haryana politics by now. Out of ninety constituencies, in forty there were a sizable number of voters belonging to one caste. Nearly half of these were dominated by Jats, five by Ahirs, four by Punjabis, two by Rors, five by Banias, and one each by Bishnois, Gujars and Sikhs, and three by Muslims. In these constituencies, a major section of the dominant caste voted for the candidates of their castes. Another seventeen constituencies were reserved for Scheduled Castes and Scheduled Tribes; four were dominated equally by two castes. Brahmins by and large voted for the Congress and Jats for the Lok Dal. Punjabi settlers were almost equally divided between the Congress and the Bharatiya Janata Party (BJP), which was formed in the year 1980. Keeping in view their business interests, they switched their loyalty to either of these two parties. The Banias and the Scheduled Castes oscillated between the Congress and the Lok Dal. The political parties allotted tickets to their candidates taking the caste composition of the constituencies into account. This held true in the formation of the ministry too.

Aryanagar then was a part of the Adampur constituency of the legislative assembly. Bhajan Lal had begun his very interesting career in politics from Adampur as a village sarpanch. He gradually became the chairman of the Panchayat Samiti and was also very active in the Congress party's district unit.

Bhajan Lal was a Bishnoi. His father, Khiraj Ram, was born in Koranwali village of Bahawalpur district of Sindh (now in Pakistan), who came and settled in village Mohammed Rohi in Hisar after Partition. The legend goes that the founder of the Bishnoi sect was born in 1451 at Pipasar in Bikaner, in a family of Punwar Rajputs. When he was just five years old, he used to take his father's herds to water at the well, and had for each head of cattle a peculiar whistle, which it knew and recognised. At the sound of his whistle, the cows and bullocks would come one by one to the well, drink and go away. One day a man named Udaji happened to witness this scene, and, struck with astonishment, attempted to follow the boy when he left the well. He was on horseback and the boy was on foot, but galloping as fast as he could, he could not keep up with the boy's walking pace. At last, in amazement, he dismounted and threw himself at his feet. The boy at once welcomed him by name, though he had seen him for the first time. The bewildered Udaji exclaimed, 'Jambhaji' (omniscient), and henceforth the boy was known by this name.

On attaining manhood, Jambhaji left his home, and became a fakir, or religious mendicant. It is said that he remained seated upon a sand hill called Samrathal, in Bikaner, for a time period of fifty-one years. In 1485, a famine devastated the country, and Jambhaji gained an enormous number of disciples by providing food for all who would declare their belief in him. He is said to have died on his sand hill, at the good old age of eighty-four, and to have been buried at a spot about a mile away from it. His tomb remains to this day. Jambhaji was and is still worshipped by his followers as an incarnation of Vishnu. They avoid taking life of any sort, and should any animal be accidentally killed, they bury it. Bishnois are also found in some numbers in the Sirsa district. In Hisar, they held ten villages as proprietors. They were good cultivators, and of thrifty, careful habits. They preferred camels to cattle, using them even for agricultural purposes.

In 1968, Bhajan Lal successfully contested from Adampur constituency. Bhajan Lal was genial, pleasant and informal, and enjoyed life. He could be sugar and honey when he felt it would serve his purpose, but on the whole he had learnt to live by his wits. After the Emergency in 1977, when elections to the Lok Sabha were announced, Bhajan Lal joined Jagjivan Ram's Congress for Democracy. He fought on the CFD quota of the Janata Party ticket and entered the assembly. In June 1979, Bhajan Lal's ascension to chief ministership also had the blessings of Prime Minister Morarji Desai.

The Punjabis gravitated towards Bhajan Lal, who became the camp opposite of the Lok Dal although he managed to take some Jat leaders along, mostly those who were disgruntled with Devi Lal. It was not until the year 2014 that the Punjabi Khatris had a chief minister of their own in Manohar Lal Khattar of the BJP. Khattar served as chief minister for nearly ten years.

The political division of Jat versus non-Jat was compounded by a subtle political and social narrative perpetuated by some politicians that the new state constituted the homeland of the 'sons of the soil', its main linguistic group and those who were born here; Khatris were outsiders. There were whispered demands of preference for 'sons of the soil' in state policy, a demand claiming special treatment on the basis of place of birth and conferring benefits, rights, roles and responsibilities, which may not apply to others. This was not the Punjab of independent India the Batras had lived in for two decades, nor was it the history of the people of Haryana they had come to know or heard of in folk tales.

22

The Last Days

Lala-ji had always been a man of few words. After the trauma of Partition, his silence became more pronounced. Having turned into a refugee in his own country, Lala-ji was left a broken man with little interest in material life. Not being seen as a 'son of the soil' after the creation of Haryana hurt him deeply. He felt homeless in his own country. It was unfair to his ancestors who had over the centuries loyally contributed to the country's economic progress.

Only Mata-ji realised the pain of her husband, and the sadness in the few words he spoke.

Both felt disillusioned, yet they had an unshaken faith in God and humanity. They spent the rest of their lives in philanthropy. Over time, they sold parcels of land, piece by piece, to provide for their sons whose needs were increasing. They also sold land to donate for many social causes.

They frequently went on pilgrimage to Haridwar, the holy city dating back to the time when Brahma created the world. Here, they donated money to purchase a piece of land on Kushaghat near Har Ki Pauri, and donated generously for building guest rooms for Punjabi Khatris who visited Haridwar from all over India. A room in the building was given to the pandas as well. Pandas are the record-keepers of Hindu lineage. In a practice dating back a long time, Punjabi Khatris, on their visit to Haridwar or Pehwa in Haryana, customarily record the names of the dead and existing family members in bahis (scrolls) which are maintained by pandas. These registers comprise a unique treasure trove of sociological data. Visitors to Haridwar can trace their genealogical record with reference to the family's name, place of origin, and date of a recent visit. The pandas have a system of indexing known only to them. Most of these handwritten scrolls have been maintained by over twenty generations of pandas, making it a popular family business in the region. Nowadays, pandas are in charge of designated registers categorised by original districts/villages of a particular family's ancestors. Their leaves are getting discoloured with age and whatever indexing they use, is in the minds of the pandas. The Genealogical Society of Utah, USA, has microfilmed some of them.

Lala-ji never claimed ownership of the building in Haridwar. Ram Saran and Gobind were told not to count it as family property.

A ritual Lala-ji observed all his life unfailingly was to watch the sand dunes every evening from his rooftop. After the Bhakra Canal became functional, land became fertile, and villagers became prosperous. Many built concrete houses, some with more than one floor. Because of changing land conditions, sand dunes along the road also moved away gradually, over years. Lala-ji could no longer enjoy their uninterrupted view from his rooftop. He changed the ritual and began going on a walk every evening two miles away from the village. He would sit there for an hour observing the dunes in silence till Dhania, who accompanied him, reminded him it was time to return. Dhania himself was nearing sixty years by now.

One day, while walking to the dunes, Lala-ji noted that Gawarias, a group of nomads, had set up a dera (camp) near the village. He had heard a lot about them in Jhang. This tribe lived even before the period of the Buddha. They were merchants of inland trade, who carried goods on carts, by camels, donkeys and bullocks on the trade routes known as Laman Marg. They could normally make a good thirteen kos (twenty-six miles) a day. When Silk Road trade was at its prime, they also transported goods from different parts of India to Multan from where these were traded onwards to other countries. The Banjaras were frequent visitors to Jhang and familiar with its geography and people. The railway destroyed the trade of this community except in mountain tracts. These people started settling on the outskirts of the villages and took to varied occupations.

Lala-ji's eyes lit up at the sight of a camp. *Here is hope for some news of Jhang,* he thought. He instructed Dhania to inform the head of the group that he wanted to meet him. The head of the tribe appeared promptly. He was an elderly man with a weathered face that spoke of experience and wisdom. His eyes were deep-set and expressive, reflecting a keen intelligence and a compassionate nature. He wore the traditional Banjara attire – angarkha, a long, flowing robe, salwar, loose-fitting trouser and a colourful turban.

'I am Rakoo! What can I do for you?' he said, folding his hands in greeting.

Lala-ji returned his greetings with folded hands.

'When were you last in Jhang, sardar? Lala-ji asked.

The sardar thought for a while trying to recollect something. 'Two years back I think, but why do you ask?'

'Tell me about my Rodu Sultan or about any place in Jhang … anything. I have been waiting for all these years to hear from someone who has walked on the land of my ancestors in Jhang,' Lala-ji said, his eyes welling with tears.

Rakoo thought for a moment, trying to absorb the strange request. After a long pause, he spoke. 'We went to Kabul two years ago. As you might be aware, no one asks us for any documents on the India, Pakistan or Afghanistan border, we just make an entry in a register at borders. We have been crossing borders like this for centuries. Like every time, we passed through Jhang to stop at the Sufi shrines. The shrine of Heer there is my wife's favourite.'

Lala-ji remembered the shrine of the celebrated lover. Jhang was Heer's hometown. Unlike other shrines, the soul interred in the shrine belongs not to a saint, but a woman. In the cultural world, she is the Heer of the celebrated lovers, Heer and Ranjha. Lala-ji recalled having heard their legendary tale from his mother.

Lala-ji's thoughts were interrupted by Rakoo calling out his name. 'What happened, Lala-ji? Are you fine? I have been talking for the last few minutes but it appears your mind was elsewhere. Do you want me to repeat what I said?'

Lala-ji folded his hands in thanks. 'No, Sardar Rakoo. Your opening words transported me to Jhang. My thoughts travelled all over Jhang in the last few minutes. Love is love, one can love another person, and love one's land. When you spoke about the love of Heer and Ranjha, I could see my fields, still vast and stretching endlessly, becoming golden under the sun, the canals crisscrossing the landscape like lifelines ... I even saw many cattle grazing in the fields.'

It was late but Lala-ji was determined to observe the daily ritual of going to the sand dunes. He sat there recalling his days spent in Jhang. Reflecting on the repeated displacements experienced during the partition and subsequent division of Punjab, he likened their life to shifting sand dunes – constantly moving, unstable and devoid of permanence. The initial upheaval during Partition forced them to abandon their ancestral home, leaving behind a lifetime of memories, possessions, and a sense of belonging. The division of East Punjab rendered them a minority in the new state, reminding them they were not sons of the soil.

The traumatic events of 1947 uprooted them from their cultural and social moorings, thrusting them into an uncertain future; in 1966, without having to relocate, vastly different political and social circumstances were thrust upon them. The metaphor of shifting sand dunes captured the essence of their existence – constantly adapting to new environments, yet never finding solid ground to call home. Each move eroded their sense of identity and continuity. The constant need to adapt had left him yearning for stability and a sense of belonging. Just as the sand dunes are shaped and reshaped by the wind, Lala-ji felt that their life too was at the mercy of forces beyond their control.

Lala-ji passed away in sleep that night. It was 10 April 1982.

He was cremated in a crematorium built on the land, merely a furlong away from the sand dunes.

It was Lala-ji's wish that his ashes be mixed with the handful of soil he had brought from Rodu Sultan, and immersed in the Ganga.

Mata-ji was engulfed in a profound sense of loss and sorrow after the passing of Lala-ji, her companion of fifty years. His death left a void that felt insurmountable. Lala-ji left carrying the weight of the trauma of Partition – a pain that never fully healed. His sadness, a constant shadow, was a testament to the scars left by the violence, displacement, and loss of their homeland. Even in her own sorrow, Mata-ji felt a deep empathy for his suffering, knowing how it shaped their lives together. Yet, she also felt a quiet pride in the resilience he showed, building a life amidst the ruins of their past.

She felt a mix of loneliness and relief – relief that his pain had finally ended, but loneliness in his absence. His presence had been her anchor for half a century. She found herself reminiscing about their shared moments of joy and hardship, and the strength they drew from each other. Mata-ji's grief was tinged with gratitude for their enduring bond, even as she prepared to navigate the unfamiliar terrain of life without him.

But gradually, with Lala-ji gone, Mata-ji also lost the will to live. Gobind tried to persuade her to relocate to Chandigarh, and later to Delhi, and live with them. But she politely declined each time.

Mata-ji passed away on 13 June 2011. A prayer meeting was held in the village. The turnout was overwhelming, with nearly every household represented. Villagers of all ages, dressed in traditional attire, gathered to pay their respects. Farmers, artisans and shopkeepers paused their daily routines to join the gathering. Even those who had moved to nearby towns returned to honour Mata-ji's memory. Elders shared heartfelt stories of Mata-ji's kindness and wisdom, while women listened intently, absorbing the legacy of their beloved guide. The meeting ended with a collective pledge to uphold her values of compassion and service.

23

An Inheritance of Loss

After decades of struggle, Ram Saran and Gobind embarked on the long journey of recovery and success. In their days of struggle, they adjusted to their new lives. Deep within, they knew that their family's story was not over, that they would find a way to endure and perhaps even reclaim what had been taken from them. Both battled hard with the immense psychological toll of displacement, of being driven from their ancestral place, witnessing atrocities, and loss of multiple family members. They worked tirelessly to build new communities and forge new lives. Once insecurities of survival were behind them, they were determined to pursue success. The rags-to-riches story came after the 1970s.

Ram Saran left the village to pursue studies. He toiled at a petrol pump and took up menial jobs to pay for his own education. After graduating from Jammu University, he moved to Aligarh where he obtained a master's degree, and later, a doctorate in Hindi, from AMU, under the guidance of eminent Prof. Goberdhan Shukla. The topic of his dissertation was 'Manas Ke Ram'. There, he married Soma Devi, who was pursuing a doctorate in Sanskrit. He later taught in Sikar, Rajasthan, but returned to settle permanently in Aligarh after some time. In 1963, Ram Saran quit his job and ventured into the hardware business in Aligarh, a city with a rich history of craftsmanship. In the initial days of struggle, he himself carried bags of hardware to sell to wholesale traders in Delhi's Chandni Chowk. With his hard work, he turned his small enterprise into a flourishing business, set up a factory, and began exporting to Britain and many European countries. He soon became a prominent citizen of Aligarh.

As a child, Ram Saran had witnessed a period marked by violent communal strife and his family struggle. Despite the personal trauma he endured during this time, Ram Saran did not harbour any ill will against anyone. He chose a path of inclusivity and reconciliation, which defined his life and work. His life serves as an inspiring example of secularism in practice, where his personal experiences of loss and suffering were transformed into a commitment to peace, understanding, and shared grief. Ram Saran's legacy is a reminder that humanity and compassion can triumph over prejudice and hatred.

He passed away on 16 October 1988, three decades before his younger brother's demise in 2018.

Their daughters Manisha, Charu, Babli and Richa, and son Vikram live a happy and prosperous life, making their parents proud. Manisha, the eldest child (born, 27 July 1958), is married to a businessman Subhash, who is also Gobind's brother-in-law (Veena's brother). Subhash once worked in Indian Oil. The two now live in Aligarh, Uttar Pradesh. Their elder child, a daughter, Shweta (born, 12 February 1978), is married, and lives in Bareilly, Uttar Pradesh. The couple lives in Kanpur in Uttar Pradesh. Their son Samir (born, 23 January 1987), married, lives in the USA.

Charu (born, 3 December 1963), who arrived after Manisha, is the most liberal and outspoken grandchild in the Batra family. She is married to Dr Navneet Thakral, who has a flourishing practice in Deoband in Uttar Pradesh. They lost their son, Ankur (born, 12 March 1989), tragically when he was merely twenty-six years old. Deeply shocked and traumatised, Charu is trying hard to go back to normal life even after many years. Her daughter, Anouska (born, 11 August 1994), the eldest child, is a free-spirited girl. She works as a business development lead for a global investment corporation. She is amongst my favourite nieces. Anouska lives in Mumbai. One of the warmest individuals I have come across, Charu is the bond that keeps her siblings and cousins glued.

Vikram (born, 7 October 1965) is the third child of Ram Saran and Soma. He married Deepali, a devoted wife and mother. She is a staunch follower of Sri Sri Ravi Shankar. After Vikram lost his father, he worked tirelessly to sustain the business his father had toiled hard to build. They too live in Aligarh. Their elder child Viraat (born, 14 September 1993) – both, an engineer and management graduate by qualification – now supports the family business. Their daughter Vaibhavi (born, April 1999) is a lawyer in the making.

Babli (born, 11 March 1969), the fourth child of Ram Saran and Soma, was deeply attached to her father. She went into depression after Ram Saran's death. An emotional and sensitive child, she is differently abled from her siblings. She married Kishan Pruthi. Babli raised her child with love and courage. Her son Nitish (born, 20 September 1996) is a chartered account and works with a global firm.

Richa a.k.a. Mini (born, 28 August 1971) is married to Saket Uberoi, a businessman. They live in Kanpur, in Uttar Pradesh. Their daughter Riya (born, 14 October 2000) has just completed her master's in business administration in marketing and sales.

Dayavanti and Sumitra got married young as was customary then. Both lived a happy life bringing up their children well. Dayavanti passed away in 2013. They had five children – Satish, Shashi, Harish, Rashmi and Sunil. Satish and Harish passed away fairly young.

Satish (born, 15 December 1949), the eldest grandchild of Lala-ji and Mata-ji, is survived by his wife Gulshan and children Honey (born, 30 September 1976) and Money (born, 6 January 1979). Harish, his younger sibling, has also passed away. He is survived by his wife Kanta and children Tanu (born, 25 May 1982) and Nidhi (born, 24 February 1984). Kanta lives in Faridabad in Haryana. Shashi, the younger sister of Satish and Harish, lost her husband Rajeev Chaudhry. Her sons are Vishal (born, 2 February 1979) and Varun (born, 14 February 1983). Shashi lives in Gharaunda in Haryana. Rashmi, the younger daughter of Daya and Bhagwan Dass, is married to Virendra Satija and lives in Chindwara in Madhya Pradesh. Her children are Bikesh (born, 2 September 1984) and Astha (born, 3 July 1988). Sunil (born, 13 July 1963) is the youngest of the five siblings. He also lives in Faridabad with his wife Tarun. His children are Lokesh (born, 7 October 1990) and Juhi (born, 6 February 1997).

Sumitra passed away in 2005. Her son Tejinder (born, 15 October 1964) is a successful businessman in Delhi. After Jeevan Dass passed away in 2003, he takes care of family business. His elder sister is Suman (born, 7 July 1959). Tejinder married Sushma. Their son Dhruv (born, September 1994) is a lawyer practising in Delhi. Their daughter Muskan (born, January 2001) is pursuing law after graduating from Delhi University.

Gobind a.k.a. G.L. Batra went to become a persuasive advocate, an able administrator, refined writer, eloquent speaker, caring husband, doting father, and a caring grandfather – all bundled into one man. His journey from a small village in Haryana to holding many high positions in the government at the centre, and in the state, makes an inspirational story.

A diehard patriot, in 1971, when war broke out between India and Pakistan, G.L. Batra, then a young lawyer, stepped forward and joined the RSS's efforts as a volunteer. In 1972, G.L. Batra joined the Government of Haryana as a public prosecutor. He became district attorney in 1978. As a special public prosecutor, he represented the state in several intricate trials including the sensitive Nirankari murder case. In 1991, he resigned as district attorney and was appointed deputy advocate general in Punjab and Haryana High Court at Chandigarh. During twenty-two years of impeccable practice at the Bar, he distinguished himself as a lawyer and public prosecutor of great repute.

In 1988, he was appointed joint secretary in the Lok Sabha Secretariat, the Lower House of Indian Parliament. Soon after he joined, he was assigned the task of studying subject-based parliamentary committee systems. He spent weeks in Britain's House of Commons and House of Lords to acquire a deep understanding of their committee system. After returning, he was instrumental in successfully seeing through the birth of the departmentally related standing committee in the Indian Parliament, formally inaugurated in March 1993. His contribution drew accolades from a host of national leaders. G.L. Batra was promoted as additional secretary in 1991. His contributions are well-documented in the Parliament. He was in-charge of the parliamentary committees during an eventful period which witnessed the 73rd and 74th constitutional amendments, the reports of joint committees on the securities scam, fertiliser subsidy, the committee to inquire into the conduct of Justice Ramaswamy, and many other historical events.

In light of his reputation as an officer with unimpeachable integrity, G.L. Batra was appointed chairman of Haryana's Public Service Commission in 1994. During this period, he was unanimously elected and re-elected as national chairman of the Body of Chairmen, State Public Service Commissions, India. After his retirement, Batra served as an executive director of Delhi's leading Batra Hospital where his rich administrative experience helped the hospital improve its efficiency and branding.

G.L. Batra remained firmly rooted to the ground despite holding high public offices in his stellar career spanning over thirty-seven years. He remained a people's man all the way. Having grown up in a village, he understood the problems of rural India. He spent his entire life in the service of the country using the positions held by him for the welfare and upliftment of people, and touched countless lives in his public and personal life. His affection for Aryanagar ran deep. He worked for the betterment of its people till he breathed his last.

Remarkably, in his private and public life, G.L. Batra never experienced any form of discrimination from the establishment, which reinforced his trust in the broader framework of governance at both central and state levels. He demonstrated an extraordinary capacity for forgiveness and understanding, even towards those who sought to undermine his progress. Among his detractors was a powerful Jat chief minister who, in a bid to exert control, terminated his services when he refused to relinquish his position as secretary of Haryana's Vidhan Sabha, so that the chief minister could appoint his favourite to the important office. The Punjab and Haryana High Court stayed the chief minister's arbitrary decision on Batra's petition.

Despite this blatant attempt to sabotage his career, Batra harboured no ill will or resentment against that chief minister. His focus remained steadfast on his principles. He maintained that as long as the state did not engage in discriminatory practices, it did not bother him if some individuals, from whatever caste, harboured disdain for him or for any displaced persons, even if that individual was the chief minister of the state. He fought fearlessly for his rights. His unwavering faith in the system and impartiality allowed him to navigate adversities without bitterness. In this approach, he followed the traditions set by his parents. Batra continued to support the gurukul all his life, financially and otherwise. He passed away on 29 May 2018.

Both his sons, Sumant (the author) and Hemant, built successful professional lives, earning global acclaim.

Hemant (born, 15 August 1967), the younger son of Gobind and Veena, married Preeti, herself a lawyer. The two live in Gurgaon in Haryana. Their son Vedant (born, 12 October 1995), eldest of the two children works in USA, while daughter Yashna (born, 11 September 1997), a budding lawyer, works in one of the country's top law firms, after graduating in law from London.

My bundle of joy, my wife Asha, is a lawyer, a film historian and a social entrepreneur; son Dev (born, 3 February 2003) has just finished his graduation in global luxury hospitality from Le Roche Switzerland and is presently working with a leading hotel in Dubai; and daughter Siya (born, 12 December 2006) is studying law in one of India's leading law schools, Jindal Global Law School. Asha and I live in Delhi.

This resilience of Lala-ji and Mata-ji's children stemmed from a deep cultural and spiritual wellspring. While many displaced persons could not let go of the bitterness of displacement, for many, there emerged a process of reconciliation. Their achievements reflect the community's commitment to excellence and its ongoing legacy of leadership, and serves as a reminder of the resilience and contributions of ethnic communities from West Punjab now living in India or spread across the world. The remarkable stories of accomplishments of successive generations is a testament to the enduring human capacity to create positive change. They serve as a testament to the transformative power of migration and the importance of community in shaping history. They remain an influential and respected community in present-day India, carrying forward the legacy of their forefathers.

Epilogue

Even after nearly eight decades, Partition remains a living memory and an unfinished history, its spectre looming large over the three countries – India, Pakistan and Bangladesh. The traumatic division of India, mass migration, marked madness and massacres that accompanied it, inflicted great suffering on a scale rarely seen in human history. It was a catastrophe on an unimaginable scale for the displaced people.

Millions of Punjabi Khatris uprooted from their land and homes arrived in India with nothing but the clothes they wore. They had to take shelter in relief camps which served as their homes, often for years. The Punjabis of West Punjab were enterprising and laborious who slowly stitched their life together with their unwavering courage. Incoming migrants arrived with different occupational histories. Some set up small businesses, which were to flourish in years to follow, or found small jobs and worked hard, ending up holding many key posts in the central or state governments.

The Khatri Punjabis distinguished themselves in nearly all spheres of life including giving two prime ministers and a few chief ministers to the country. Many, including my father, went to hold high constitutional offices. There have been Khatri heads of the armed forces, judiciary, and executive, in the post-Independence period. Their roles in literature, science, and music have also been specific and prominent. The flamboyant Punjabi personality also found expression in the country's Hindi film industry, with a string of actors, from the 1940s onwards, such as Raj Kapoor, Dev Anand, Sunil Dutt and Rajesh Khanna to name a few. Wherever they lived, whatever they did, they created an indelible mark and became a well-established and respected community.

The Jhangi families which migrated from rural areas of West Punjab, like my grandparents, had to go through a greater suffering. Their occupation was mainly agriculture. They left behind large tracts of rich agricultural land and wealth, reaching India with the bare minimum possessions. They were rehabilitated by providing them with banjar land in the areas of Punjab bordering Rajasthan (now in Haryana). With no rivers or canals for irrigation, they had to strive harder to make new life. Jhangis are a resilient lot. Over time, many found ways to cope with their trauma and rebuild their lives all over again. My eyes well up at the very thought of the trauma and suffering they had to undergo in those horrific times. Imagine the pain of losing nearly everything one fine day, and the courage it would have taken to start all over again.

My grandfather, Kesar Dass a.k.a. Lala-ji, died sad and hurt at being labelled a refugee all his life, in his own country. He was not considered a 'son of the soil'. This stripped him of his sense of belonging and rootedness. The hurt never healed. There was no overt discrimination, but socially, a deep-rooted resentment festered against those who had come to East Punjab at the time of Partition. He never complained. Only my grandmother understood his silent suffering. She knew that his sadness stemmed not from any official discrimination but on account of the unspoken hierarchies and prejudices of society which refused to treat her husband and children as sons of the soil. This unexplainable social ostracisation compounded his trauma of Partition, making it difficult for my grandparents to reclaim their dignity.

But this did not seem to bother my grandparents beyond a point; they continued to work for the benefit of the villagers.

They donated land next to their house to build a temple; 1.5 acres of nahari land for building a gurukul, where children from Kurri and neighbouring villages study the Vedas and undertake *gau sewa* even today. A part of land was also donated in Haridwar to build a guesthouse on a famous and busy ghat for Punjabi Khatris visiting Haridwar to perform last rites of their beloved, and an ashram near Kalanor.

Lala-ji passed away silently in 1988, his face carrying the same sadness in death. I was among the nearly entire village who gave shoulder to his bier. His small but stout, lifeless form was heavier than his appearance suggested. Was it the added weight of the burden from years of suffering and sadness from Partition and its aftermath?

My grandparents never spoke to us much about the unimaginable adversities. My questions to them were mostly met with stoic and tense silence. Only when pestered would they hesitatingly tell some anecdotes enough to send a chill crawling down the spine. I could hear in their silence echoes of the pain of having been uprooted from their home, the violence they witnessed, and the elders they lost. Perhaps they preferred silence because they did not want to offload their baggage of dreadful memories on us. But their silence hung in the air of our house in Kurri (now Aryanagar), where my grandfather was rehabilitated. I grew up in this house for most of my childhood interpreting that silence intuitively.

They did not blame anyone except their own fate for their loss and sufferings. '*Bura waqt haee*' (it was a bad time) is all that they would say. If probed further, they would simply ignore the question or change the topic. So, we seldom asked. They did, however, feel angry and betrayed by the political leadership of the time for having conceded to Partition. They did not hold the entire community of Muslims responsible for their tragedy, as their Muslim friends and co-villagers assured their safety and protected their properties till they could. 'It's all gone, there is no point in remembering,' they would tell us, and yet, they remembered and grieved in silence.

Mata-ji told her children stories of the many Muslims who risked their own lives to protect their Hindu and Sikh neighbours during the violence. She told them about the many Hindu and Sikh families who had hidden their Muslim friends and strangers in their homes, and of the doctors who, irrespective of their personal faith, treated wounded Hindus and Muslims. They were not prejudiced against any community. Her legacy remains as that of love, empowerment and unity, proving that the real meaning of life lies in serving others with a gracious and generous heart.

Their children – my father and his elder brother Ram Saran – the next generation of the displaced persons, went on to make a mark and achieve distinction in their respective fields. My father, G.L. Batra, younger son of Lala-ji, held high offices in the government including a constitutional position, a privilege only few are able to earn. A true patriot, my father dedicated his life in the service of this great nation. After he superannuated, he devoted a significant time to the village, perhaps to be around places that carried memories of his parents.

Unlike Lala-ji, my father did not carry any sadness when he died in 2018. He recalled the few years of childhood he spent in Rodu Sultan lovingly. He too spoke only little about his experience of Partition. He missed Jhang, his language, and the time spent in the village back in Jhang. He regularly listened to the folk songs from Jhang by popular singer Attaullah Khan on audio cassettes, lost in nostalgia. The only remorse he often expressed was about not having been able to ever visit the home of his childhood in Rodu Sultan. Being a government servant, circumstances did not permit him to travel to the country with which India's relations were hostile.

Sadly, my father inherited the refugee tag. Sharnarthi. It hurt him for not being accepted as the son of the soil. But he accepted that as an aberration of the few ill-informed and ignorant people compared to the vast majority who did not differentiate even if they viewed us as outsiders. He was consoled because the state never discriminated against him.

Though seventy-eight years have elapsed since Partition, the crisis it created is yet to be relegated to the pages of history. Punjabis who migrated continue to be dubbed as refugees even today. So much so that an association of displaced persons from West Punjab had to submit a representation to the then chief minister of Haryana, Manohar Lal Khattar, himself a refugee from Jhang, to pass a law declaring illegal the use of the word refugee or sharnarthi for the emigrants from West Punjab.

Like my father, my brother and I have had unfettered opportunities. Never once were we discriminated against for my father having migrated from West Punjab. From Kurri to Chandigarh, and then to Delhi, we have both made big in our profession. When I look back to the days spent in the village, I can't thank God enough, and the people of my country, for everything we are, and have today – accomplishments, fulfilment and happiness. I certainly have not been made to feel a refugee, although in many aspects of life, we are still considered an outsider. This behaviour towards us manifests in many ways. But, inspired by my father, I have taken it in stride and treated it as an aberration.

Partition was not just a political event; it was a human catastrophe. The prosperous and proud people of West Punjab had to suffer an unimaginable tragedy. The marks of sufferings of our elders still weigh on our minds, and in the hearts of many displaced people I have spoken to. The trauma of displacement is intergenerational. Like a family heirloom, the pain of migration has been carried generation after generation. The ordeal experienced by the displaced generations continues to reverberate through their descendants. Even after nearly eight decades, the dramatic events of 1947 stay central to identity in the subcontinent and continue to influence how the people of these countries envisage their past, present and future. The stories of those who survived this ordeal are now part of the collective memory and identity of the Punjabi people. Memoirs and oral histories have ensured that the trauma of the migration is documented and remembered, fostering a sense of identity and continuity.

My children were born in Delhi. For them, the history of their ancestors is as good as blanked out. They don't carry any great sense of deprivation. They are suitably placed to provide a closure to this dark chapter in our history so that future generations of displaced persons do not have to endure the pain experienced by generations before them. But, the haunting nature of trauma keeps repeating itself, often against their will. Millions of Indians opposed to Partition still believe it was avoidable. They are unwilling to forget what they perceive as a betrayal of the majority Hindu population by some leaders. The trauma of Partition remains an unresolved issue. There is, however, hope in the resilience of love, and its power of healing.

This book is a humble missive to young Punjabi Khatris and future generations of my tribe. While it is vital to remember the sufferings of our ancestors, their struggle and resilience, and draw strength from them, it is equally crucial that we don't forget both the deleterious and upbeat experiences of the period. The adverse and destructive episodes will remind us of the sacrifices our ancestors made for us, the positive and upbeat experiences will provide us a perspective and strength to approach legacy issues constructively.

Key Characters

Name	Relationship
Kesar Dass	Son of Tulsi Dass and Raj Rani; author's grandfather
Tulsi Dass	Kesar Dass's father
Raj Rani	Tulsi's Dass wife, Kesar Dass's mother
Bhagwanti	Kesar Dass's second wife; Gobind's stepmother
Shanta	Kesar Dass's deceased first wife
Ram Saran	Kesar Dass and Shanta's elder son
Dayavanti	Kesar Dass and Shanta's elder daughter
Sumitra	Bhagwanti's daughter from her first marriage
Gobind	Kesar Dass and Shanta's younger son, and youngest child
Ram Lal	Husband of Tulsi Dass's youngest sister Nirmala Devi
Nirmala Devi	Tulsi Dass's youngest sister, Ram Lal's wife
Narain Dass	Tulsi Dass's younger brother

Name	Relationship
Nand Lal	Narain Dass's son. Kesar Dass's first cousin
Shakuntala	Nand Lal's wife
Bebe a.k.a. Sudarshan	Widowed stepsister of Tulsi Dass
Kundan Singh	Sudarshan's late husband
Kartar Singh	Son of Sudarshan from Kartar Singh
Dharam Pal	Husband of Ram Lal's sister
Satish Chand	Tulsi Dass's cousin
Santosh	Ram Lal's daughter
Binder	Tent house owner
Sukhi Chand	The village priest
Radhe Shyam	Postman of Rodu Sultan
Patwari	The officer who helps Kesar Dass and Narayan Dass with possession of house and land
Krishan Lal	Halwai
Padam Singh	JCO of MEO
Abdul	BDO of Jhang
Shakeela	Abdul's sister
Majid Khan	Shakeela's husband
Mukhtyar	Ram Lal's Muslim friend in Rodu Sultan
Ibrahim Khan	Owner of evacuee property (land and house) in Kurri allotted to Narain Dass and Kesar Dass
Dhania	House help from childhood, treated as a family member, mainly looking after the cattle.

Name	Relationship
Nanhu	Gobind's friend in village
Veena Batra	Gobind's wife
Sumant Batra	Elder son of Gobind and Veena Batra
Hemant Batra	Younger son of Gobind and Veena Batra
Soma Batra	Wife of Ram Saran
Manisha, Charu, Vikram, Babli, Richa	Children of Ram Saran and Soma
Rajender	Ram Lal's son-in-law
Alam (oldest) Qadir (youngest) Nazir	Mukhtyar's sons
Rakoo	Head of banjaras/wanderers who travelled from one place to another
Krishan Lal	Cook

Bibliography

TITLE-BASED REFERENCES

'About Us.' Gurukul Aryanagar. https://gurukularyanagar.com/About.aspx.

'Chapter XX: Rehabilitation.' In Rohtak District Gazetteer.

'First-Hand Account of Delhi During Partition in 1947.' United Service Institution of India. https://www.usiofindia.org/publication-journal/first-hand-account-of-delhi-during-partition-in-1947.html#:~:text=As%20the%20partition%20of%20the,side%20were%20gathered%20in%20camps.

'History of Banjaras.' Banjara Community Blog, June 2018. http://banjaracommunity.blogspot.com/2018/06/history-of-banjaras.html.

'Jhang.' Pak Visitors. https://pakvisitors.wordpress.com/jhang/

'JJ Singh: Indian Businessman Helps Millions Get US Citizenship.' The Better India, 2022. https://thebetterindia.com/282581/jj-singh-indian-businessman-helps-millions-get-us-citizenship/.

'Memoir: Men of Yesterday.' *The Friday Times*, 14 August 2022. https://thefridaytimes.com/14-Aug-2022/memoir-men-of-yesterday.

'Milwaukee Braces for 50,000 Arrivals and Trump After Shooting.' *Mint*, 15 July 2024. https://www.livemint.com/news/world/milwaukee-braces-for-50-000-arrivals-and-trump-after-shooting-11721000903841.html.

'The Haryana Urban (Control of Rent and Eviction) Act, 1948.' *Laws of India*. https://lawsofindia.blinkvisa.com/pdf/haryana/1948/1948HR8.pdf.

'The Jhang of Sultan.' *Dawn*, 14 April 2013. https://www.dawn.com/news/1020449/the-jhang-of-sultan.

'Twentieth-Century India: An Overview.' *Education About Asia*, Association for Asian Studies. https://www.asianstudies.org/publications/eaa/archives/twentieth-century-india-an-overview-2/.

'We Used to Be Brothers: Partition 1947.' Introduction.

'Why Was British India Partitioned in 1947? Considering the Role of Muhammad Ali Jinnah.' University of Oxford. https://www.history.ox.ac.uk/why-was-british-india-partitioned-in-1947-considering-the-role-of-muhammad-ali-0.

AUTHOR-BASED REFERENCES

Aiyar, Swarna. 'August Anarchy: The Partition Massacres in Punjab, 1947.' *Journal of South Asian Studies*, 18, no. s1 (1995): 13-36. https://doi.org/10.1080/00856409508723242.

Alluri, Aparna, and Gurman Bhatia. 'The Decade That Changed Delhi.' *Hindustan Times*. https://www.hindustantimes.com/static/partition/delhi/.

Ansari, Sarah. 'How the Partition of India Happened – and Why Its Effects Are Still Felt Today.' *The Conversation*, 10 August 2017. https://theconversation.com/how-the-partition-of-india-happened-and-why-its-effects-are-still-felt-today-81766.

Arrian. *Anabasis of Alexander*. Translated by E. Iliff Robson. Cambridge: Harvard University Press, 1929.

Awan, Maqbool Ahmad. 'Rise and Fall of the Unionist Party in the British Punjab (1923-47): A Theoretical Study.' *Journal of the Punjab University Historical Society*, 33, no. 1 (January–June 2020): 21-39.

Bagchi, Sanjoy. 'The First War with Pakistan.' Review of *War and Diplomacy in Kashmir 1947-48*, by C. Dasgupta. *Economic and Political Weekly*, 37, no. 27 (6-12 July 2002): 2709-2712. http://www.jstor.org/stable/4412323.

Baines, J.A. 'The Aroras of South-western Punjab'. In *The Imperial Gazetteer of India*, edited by W.W. Hunter, Vol. X, Multan to Palhallil. Second Edition. London: Trubner & Co, 1886.

Bharadwaj, Prashant, and Rinchan Ali Mirza. *Displacement and Development: Long Term Impacts of the Partition of India*. Preliminary draft September 2016.

Brass, Paul R. *The Politics of India Since Independence*. Cambridge: Cambridge University Press, 1994.

Burton, Antoinette. 'Foreword.' In *The Indian Partition in Literature and Films: History, Politics and Aesthetics*, edited by Rini Bhattacharya Mehta and Debali Mookerjea-Leonard, xvi. London and New York: Routledge, 2015.

Campbell, George. 'The Ethnology of India'. *Journal of the Asiatic Society of Bengal*. Calcutta: C.B. Lewis, Volume No. XXXV, Part I to V, 1866.

Caruth, Cathy. *Unclaimed Experience: Trauma, Narrative, and History*. Baltimore and London: Johns Hopkins University Press, 1996.

Chakravarty, Pallavi. 'Post-Partition Rehabilitation of Refugees in India'. NMML Occasional Paper, History and Society, New Series 46. Nehru Memorial Museum and Library, 2014.

Chawla, Muhammad Iqbal. 'Mountbatten's Response to the Communal Riots in the Punjab, 20 March to 15 August 1947: An Overview.' *Journal of the Royal Asiatic Society*, 26, no. 4 (October 2016): 683-706. https://doi.org/10.1017/S1356186316000225

Cunningham, Alexander. *The Ancient Geography of India*. London: Trübner & Co., 1871.

Cunningham, Joseph Davey. *A History of the Sikhs*. London: John Murray, 1849.

Curtius Rufus, Quintus. *The History of Alexander*. Translated by John Yardley. London: Penguin Books, 1984.

Dahiya, Bhim S. *Power Politics in Haryana: A View from the Bridge*. New Delhi: Gyan Publishing House, 2008.

Dalrymple, William. 'The Great Divide: The Violent Legacy of Indian Partition.' *The New Yorker*, 29 June 2015. https://www.newyorker.com/magazine/2015/06/29/the-great-divide-books-dalrymple.

Dalrymple, William. *The Anarchy: The East India Company, Corporate Violence, and the Pillage of an Empire*. Bloomsbury Publishing, 2019

Das, Mahen. 'My Memories: Lahore 1937-1945.' *India of the Past*. http://www.indiaofthepast.org/mahen-das/life-back-then/my-memories-lahore-1937-1945 2.

Dhulipala, Venkat. 'Rallying the Qaum: The Muslim League in the United Provinces, 1937–1939.' *Modern Asian Studies*, 44, no. 3 (2010): 603-640. https://www.cambridge.org/core/journals/modern-asian-studies/article/abs/rallying-the-qaum-the-muslim-league-in-the-united-provinces-19371939/8468C5AFE0DD63CAB799922671ED3511.

East Punjab Legislative Assembly Debates – 1 November 1947. Vol. 1, no. 1: Official Report. Chief Reporter Punjab Vidhan Sabha, Chandigarh.

Eglar, Zekiye. *The Economic Life of a Punjabi Village*. Introduction by Beena Sarwar. 1961., April 2008.

Elliot, Henry Miers, and John Dowson. *The History of India, as Told by Its Own Historians: The Muhammadan Period*. London: Trübner & Co., 1867-1877.

French, Patrick. 'Indian Independence in 1947: Seeing Partition in a New Way.' *TIME*, 14 August 2016. https://time.com/4421746/margaret-bourke-white-great-migration/.

Gatrell, Peter. *The Making of the Modern Refugee*. Oxford: Oxford University Press.

Godbole, Madhav. *The Holocaust of Indian Partition: An Inquest*. New Delhi: Rupa Publications India, 2006.

Government of India, Archaeological Survey of India. *Gazetteer of the Jhang District*, 1883-84. Lahore: Printed at the Arya Press by Ram Das, 1884. Archaeological Library, Accession No. 30636, Call no: R910.3095473G/P.D.G./Jha.

Grewal, J.S. 'Seventy-Five Days to Partition (1 June–15 August 1947).' In *Master Tara Singh in Indian History: Colonialism, Nationalism, and the Politics of Sikh Identity*. Oxford University Press, 2018. DOI:10.1093/oso/9780199467099.003.0015.

Grewal, J.S. *Master Tara Singh in Indian History: Colonialism, Nationalism, and the Politics of Sikh Identity*. Oxford: Oxford University Press, 2018. https://doi.org/10.1093/oso/9780199467099.001.0001.

Hardy, R. Spence. *A Manual of Buddhism in Its Modern Development*. London: Partridge and Oakey, 1853.

Hasan, Mushirul, ed. *India's Partition: Process, Strategy and Mobilization*. Oxford in India Readings: Themes in Indian History. New Delhi: Oxford University Press, 1993.

Hunter, William Wilson. *The Imperial Gazetteer of India*. Oxford: Clarendon Press, 1881.

Hunter, W.W. *The Imperial Gazetteer of India*. Vol. X, Multan to Palhallil. Second Edition. London: Trubner & Co, 1886.

Ibbetson, Denzil. *Panjab Castes*. Lahore: Superintendent, Government Printing, Punjab, 1916.

Jain, Sanjeev. 'Wounded Souls: 75 Years After India's Partition, Survivors' Trauma Has Still Not Been Recognized.' *The Conversation*, 7 September 2022. https://theconversation.com/wounded-souls-75-years-after-indias-partition-survivors-trauma-has-still-not-been-recognized-188692.

Jaswal, Chandini. 'Braving Betrayal, Tragedy, and Partition.' *Museum of British Colonialism*, 10 November 2023. https://museumofbritishcolonialism.org/braving-betrayal-tragedy-and-partition/.

Joginder, S. 'Partition of the Punjab 1947: Dispersion of Agriculturists of West Punjab and Their Resettlement in East Punjab: A Case Study of Namdhari Sikhs.' In Proceedings of the 69th Session. 2008.

Juneja, M.M. *History of Hisar from Inception to Independence (1354-1947)*. Modern Book & Co., 1989.

Kadian, Arjun Singh. *Land of the Gods: The Story of Haryana*. Rupa Publications, 2021.

Kamran, Tahir. 'The Unfolding Crisis in Punjab, March-August 1947: Key Turning Points and British Responses.' *Journal of Punjab Studies*, 14, no. 2 (2007): 1-20. https://punjab.global.ucsb.edu/sites/default/files/sitefiles/journals/volume14/no2/kamran.pdf.

Kohli, Pranav. 'The Many-Faced Afterlife of 1947.' *The India Forum*, 31 May 2023. https://www.theindiaforum.in/history/many-faced-afterlife-1947.

Lahori, Muhammad. *History of Sargodha*. Lahore: Sang-e-Meel Publications, 2010.

Levi, Scott C. Caravans: *Punjabi Khatri Merchants on the Silk Road*. Penguin/Portfolio, 2016.

Levi, Scott C. *The Indian Diaspora in Central Asia and Its Trade, 1550-1900*. Leiden: Brill, 2002.

Marino, Elisabetta. 'A Legacy of Loss: No Return Address: Partition and Stories of Displacement.' *Testo e Senso*, 26 (2023): 29-38. Università degli Studi di Roma Tor Vergata. https://doi.org/10.58015/2036-2293/674.

McCrindle, John Watson. *Ancient India as Described by Megasthenes and Arrian*. Calcutta: Thacker, Spink & Co., 1877.

Milo, Imilo. 'Between Two Worlds: 8 Challenges as a Second-Generation Immigrant.' *Medium*. https://imilo.medium.com/between-two-worlds-8-challenges-as-a-second-generation-immigrants-4fe556e48fa7#:~:text=Internalized%20shame%20and%20societal%20oppression,born%20into%20an%20immigrant%20family.

Moon, Vasant, ed. *Dr. Babasaheb Ambedkar: Writings and Speeches*. Vol. 8. New Delhi: Dr Ambedkar Foundation, Ministry of Social Justice and Empowerment, Govt. of India.

Mosley, Leonard. *The Last Days of the British Raj*. London: Weidenfeld and Nicolson, 1961.

Nanda, Reena. *From Quetta to Delhi: A Partition Story*. New Delhi: Bloomsbury Publishers India, 2018.

Nesfield, John C. *Brief View of the Caste System of the North-Western Provinces and Oudh*. Allahabad: North-Western Provinces and Oudh Government Press, 1885.

Panayi, Panikos, and Pippa Virdee, eds. *Refugees and the End of Empire: Imperial Collapse and Forced Migration in the Twentieth Century*. De Montfort University, Leicester, UK.

Pargiter, F. E. *Ancient Indian Historical Tradition*. Oxford University Press, 1922

Parmar, Sandeep. 'The Workings of Refugee Memory.' *Refugee History*, 23 August 2017. http://refugeehistory.org/blog/2017/8/23/the-workings-of-refugee-memory.

Punjab Boundary Commission. 'Radcliffe Award: Report of the Punjab Boundary Commission.' Exported from Wikisource on 2 July 2021.

Punjab Legislative Assembly Debates. Vol. 1, No. 1, 1 November 1947. Official Report.

Puri, Baij Nath. *The Khatris: A Socio-Historical Study*. New Delhi: M.N. Publishers and Distributors, 1988.

Rathore, Riya Singh. 'Embracing "Refugee-istan": A Look at Delhi's Refugee History and Why It Must Continue.' *Economic and*

Political Weekly. https://www.epw.in/engage/article/embracing-%E2%80%98refugee-istan%E2%80%99-look-delhis-refugee.

Rose, H.A., Denzil Ibbetson, and Edward Douglas Maclagan. *A Glossary of the Tribes and Castes of the Punjab and North-West Frontier Province*. Lahore: Printed at the Civil and Military Gazette Press by Samuel T. Weston, 1911.

Salim, Ahmad. 'Partition, Violence and Migration: The Case of Miana Gondal.' Sustainable Development Policy Institute, 2003. https://sdpi.org/sdpiweb/publications/files/Partition-Violence-and-Migration-The-Case-of-Miana-Gondal (W-85).pdf.

Sandhu, Akhtar Hussain. 'Communitarian Response to the Lahore Resolution of 1940 in the British Punjab: An Analytical Discourse (Part I).' *Al-Hikmat*, 31 (2011): 21-39.

Sarila, Narendra Singh. *The Shadow of the Great Game: The Untold Story of India's Partition*. New Delhi: HarperCollins Publishers, 2005.

Sengupta, Debjani, ed. *The 1947 Partition of India: An Anthology of Writings*. New Delhi: Worldview Publication, 2024.

Seth, Moti Lal. *History of the Khattris*. 1904.

Seth, Moti Lal. *A Brief Ethnological Survey of the Khattris*. Agra: Khattri Hitkari Association, 1905

Sethi, Jatinder. 'My Memories of Lyallpur.' *India of the Past*. Accessed 25 March 2025. www.indiaofthepast.org.

Sherring, Matthew Atmore. *Hindu Tribes and Castes*. Calcutta: Thacker, Spink & Co., 1872.

Shuaib, Haroon. 'Jhang: Mysticism of Rivers and Deserts.' Youlin Magazine, 14 December 2021. https://www.youlinmagazine.com/article/jhang-mysticism-of-rivers-and-deserts/MjE1MA==#google_vignette.

Shukla, Rajeev. *Scars of 1947: Real Partition Stories*. New Delhi: Penguin Random House India, 2022. https://www.amazon.in/Scars-1947-Real-Partition-Stories/dp/0670095672.

Singh, Joginder. 'Partition of the Punjab 1947: Dispersion of Agriculturists of West Punjab and Their Resettlement in East Punjab: A Case Study of Namdhari Sikhs.' In IHC: Proceedings, 69th Session, 2008; Modern India.

Singh, K.S., ed. *People of India: Haryana*, Volume XXIII. Edited by M.L. Sharma and A.K. Bhatia. Anthropological Survey of India. New Delhi: Manohar, 1994.

Singh, Shivani. 'Capital Gains: How 1947 Gave Birth to a New Identity, a New Ambition, a New Delhi.' *Hindustan Times*, 24 April 2018. https://www.hindustantimes.com/delhi-news/capital-gains-how-1947-gave-birth-to-a-new-identity-a-new-ambition-a-new-delhi/story-e0GfoFrhwStTU2910v5DrJ.html.

Siwach, J.R. 'State Politics in Haryana.' *The Indian Journal of Political Science*, 48, no. 4, Golden Jubilee Number: State Politics in India (Oct.-Dec. 1987): 526-540. Published by Indian Political Science Association. http://www.jstor.org/stable/41855336.

Steedman, E.B. *Report on the Revised Settlement of the Jhang District of the Punjab, 1874-1880*. Lahore: W. Ball, 1882.

Sutton, Deborah Ruth. 'Masjids, Monuments and Refugees in the Partition City of Delhi, 1947–1959.' *Urban History*, 50, no. 3 (2023): 468-485. https://www.cambridge.org/core/journals/urban-history/article/masjids-monuments-and-refugees-in-the-partition-city-of-delhi-19471959/72CF91AB4678C508FE897F92284442B2.

Tandon, Seeta Ram. *History of Khatris in India*.

Tariq, Adnan. 'City in Transit: Cross-Migration in Lahore During Partition of India.' Assistant Professor, Department of History, Government Islamia Graduate College, Civil Lines, Lahore. kaziadnan@msn.com.

Varma, Ram. *Life in the IAS: My Encounters with the Three Lals of Haryana*. New Delhi: Rupa Publication, 2017.

Weston, Samuel T. *A Glossary of the Tribes and Castes of the Punjab and North-West Frontier Province*. Vol. II. Lahore: Printed at the Civil and Military Gazette Press.

White-Spunner, Barney. *Partition: The Story of Indian Independence and the Creation of Pakistan in 1947*. New York: Simon & Schuster, 2017.

Yadav, Sneh. 'Partition and Displacement: A Study of Rural Rehabilitation in Punjab (1947-1958).' *International Journal of Advanced Research in Management and Social Sciences*, 13, no. 1 (2025): 42-50. https://doi.org/10.61506/01.00172.

Yasin, Shabana, Mamoona Kanval, and Farzanada Aslam. 'Economic Transformations in British Colonial Punjab and the Feudal Identity of District Jhang.' *Bulletin of Business and Economics*, 13, no. 1 (2025): 42-50. https://doi.org/10.61506/01.00172.

Index

Abdali, Ahmad Shah, xxiii, 181
Administration of Evacuee Property Act in 1950, 169
Afghan wars, 96–97
Ahmadiyas, 23
Ahmadpur, xxvii
Aibak, Qutab-ud-din, 180
Akali Dal, 28, 232
Akali Sikhs, 29
Akhil Bharat Hindu Mahasabha, 20
Alam, Dr Muhammad, 23
Ali, Chaudhary Rahmat, 17
Aligarh Muslim University (AMU), 217
All-India Hindu Mahasabha, 20
All-India Muslim League (AIML), 14
All-India Radio, 46
Angad, Guru, 93–94
Arora, Bhagwan Dass, 208
Arora, Jeewan Dass, 218
Arora Khatris, 99
Aroras, 59, 95
Arya Samaj, 232
Arya Samaj Movement, 227
Attlee, Clement, 2–3, 30
Aurangzeb, emperor, 6, 98
Ayak nadi, xxii
Ayamal, 97
Ayyangar, N. Gopalaswami, 170
Azad, Abul Kalam, 16, 166

Badhere Khatris, 98
Bahoo, Hazrat Sultan (Sultan-ul-Arifeen), 8, 44
Bahris, 93
Baisakhi festival, 94
Balochistan, 16, 37
Bannu, xxi
Barelwis, 23
Batra, Chaudhary Matu Ram, 61
Batra family, 77, 86, 89, 102, 114–115, 117, 124–127, 139–140, 144, 156
  at Amritsar railway station, 160
  construction of temple, 215–216
  father-son relationship, 207–208
  first grandchild, 209

in Hisar, 183–189
household purchases for new housing, 199
importance of cows and buffaloes, 198
Kesar Dass as lambardar, 220–221
in Kurri, 191–202
land allotment to, 172, 174–176
land donation for gurukul, 229
landholding of, 203
letting go of bulls, 160
mode of transport, 208
pilgrimage to Haridwar, 242–243
respect for Bhagwanti, 216–217
in Rohtak, 165, 172
trust with Qureshis, 10
volunteering in refugee camp, 151–152
Batra Khatris, 92–100, 185. *see also* Khatris
Batras, xxviii, 40, 44, 51, 60, 77, 84, 92, 114–117, 126, 138
Battle of Karnal, 181
battle of Traori in 1192, 180
Battles of Panipat in 1526, 1556, 1761, 181
Beas river, xxii, 75, 133, 146, 224
Begam, Zebun Nisan, 181
Bhagavad Gita, 27
Bhagwanti, 43–44, 85–86, 112–113, 120, 123, 126–127, 139–140, 155, 160, 165, 174–176, 183–185, 192, 197–200, 202, 206, 209–211, 213, 216–217, 226, 246–247
Bhakra-Nangal Project, 224
Bhalla Khatri, 94
Bharatiya Lok Dal, 238
Bhargava, Pandit Thakur Das, 234
Binder, 41, 78, 86, 115–116, 121–122, 125, 140
Bishnois, 239–241
Boundary Commission, 48, 57–58, 71, 81, 108
adjustments of Lahore-Amritsar district boundary, 76
boundary between the East and West Punjab, 71–74
district boundaries, 74
eastern boundaries, 72–73
fixing of a boundary, 74–76
southern boundaries, 74
Boundary Commission report, 51
brihat kutumba (the great family), 43
British Broadcasting Corporation, 105

Calcutta Municipal Amendment Act, 1939, 21–22
Caliphate of Baghdad, xxii
Chahamanas of Ajmer, 180
Chaj Doab, xxv
Chand, Sukhi, 153, 160, 183
Chautala, Om Prakash, 239
Chenab river, xxv, xxvii, 102
Chimni, Maj. Gen. Sardar B.S., 130
Chiniot tehsil, xxv
Churchill, Winston, 26
Cis-Satlaj states, xxi
collective trauma, 101–104, 108,

111–114, 145–147, 150–151
communal tension, 3–4, 29–30, 55, 77
attacks on Hindus and Sikhs in rural areas, 79–80
Bengal carnage (Great Killing, 1946), 29–30, 108
cow slaughter and, 79
Multan massacre, 6
Rawalpindi massacre, 5, 7, 10
Congress (O), 238
Congress for Democracy (CFD), 238
Congress party, 3, 7, 22, 26, 28–29, 37, 54, 238–239
Congress Working Committee, 22
Constituent Assemblies, 47, 107, 129, 158
Cripps, Sir Stafford, 26
Cripps Mission, 26

Dahir of Sindh, Raja, xxiii
Dass, Chaudhary Tulsi, 1, 3, 6, 8, 11, 34–35, 37–44, 46, 59–61, 63, 82, 87, 104
Dass, Kesar, 11–12, 33–34, 40–42, 44–46, 51, 63, 66, 68–69, 78, 80, 83–86, 89–90, 101–102, 104–105, 108, 112–113, 115, 118–119, 121, 124–127, 139–140, 144–145, 152, 155, 160, 172–176, 183–184, 186, 196, 198, 200, 202–203, 207, 210–211, 213–214, 218–223, 226, 242, 244–246, 254–255
Dass, Narain, 12, 40–41, 50, 160, 172, 214
D.A.V. College camp, 149–151
Dayanand College, 218, 222
Dayavanti, 34, 249
Delhi Provincial Congress Committee, 233
Delhi Sultanate, 95
Desai, Morarji, 239, 241
Devananda Saraswati, Swami (Lakshman Dev), 226–228, 230
dhai-gharey (two-and-a-half), 93
Dilli Gate, 187–188
Direct Action, 29
Displaced Persons (Claims) Act, 1950, 170
Displaced Persons (Compensation and Rehabilitation) Act, 1954, 170

East India Company, 111
East Punjab, 6, 32, 50, 54, 57, 60, 74, 77, 108, 110–112, 128–130, 133–134, 146, 157–160, 171–172
concentration of evacuees in, 161
East Punjab Legislative Assembly, 157
Emergency period, 1977, 241
exodus of Hindus, Muslims and Sikhs, 78–91, 128–130
aircrafts, 133–134
as an organised evacuation operation, 131–132
escort by military personnel, 131
evacuating Muslims, 132, 159, 166
food and medicine for refugees, 134–135
identifying non-Muslims, 132

main camps, 132
monsoon problems, 133
provision of transport, 131–132
train journeys, 125, 133

Faridabad, 169
Fateh Chand College for Women, 218
Fazl-i-Hussain, 24
federalism, 16
Frontier Mail, 81

Gandhi, Mahatma, 3, 65, 81, 108, 130, 167
Gandhi-Jinnah appeal, 47
Ghazni, Muhammad of, xxi –xxii
Ghori, Muhammad, xxii–xxiii
Gobind (G.L. Batra), 119, 122–124, 139, 143, 145, 175, 177, 183, 198, 207–208, 211, 218–220, 226, 230, 243, 246, 250–252, 256
Government of India Act, 1935, 14–16, 21, 26, 31
Grand Trunk (GT) Road, 135
greatest migration. *see also* exodus of Hindus, Muslims and Sikhs
Gupta, Deshbandhu, 233–234
Gurukul Aryanagar, 229–230
gurukuls, 228–229

Halwai, Krishan Lal, 152
Haridwar, 243
Haryana, formation of, 231–233, 242
caste composition, 239–241
Master Tara Singh's demand, 234
origin of name, 236
political developments, 236–239
political division of Jat *versus* non-Jat, 241
region of Punjab, 233, 235
Sir Chhotu Ram's proposal, 233–234
Haryana Agricultural University, 225
Haryana Prant Front, 234
Hindu Mahasabha, 20–22, 163, 232
Hindu–Muslim relations, 6, 23–24, 36, 85, 134
Hindus, xxiii, 1, 4, 6–9, 12, 16, 18–19, 24, 26–28, 31–32, 34, 36–37, 53, 55–58, 63, 66, 69, 76, 79, 81, 84–85, 87, 102, 108, 110–114, 118, 121, 123, 128–131, 147, 153, 157–159, 166, 169, 214, 229, 232–233, 256
adoption of Sikhism, 8
Hindu Succession Act, 1956, 222
Hisar, 29, 173–176, 178, 191
agricultural productivity, 225
Babur invasion, 181
benefits of Bhakra-Nangal Project, 224, 243
under British rule, 182
children's education, 205–206
climate, 203
Haryana Agricultural University in, 225
Hindus of, 214
history, 179–183
impact of great famine of 1783, 184–185

- indigenous schools, 206
- literacy rate, 206
- livestock farm in, 200–201
- major crops and cropping pattern, 225
- market, 199
- pre-Harappan and Harappan cultures, 179
- rural water supply scheme, 225–226
- soil condition, 204
- temples in, 214
- Timur invasion, 180
- topography of, 184
- tracks of land, 204
- transformed life and agriculture in, 224–225
- transportation from Kurri to, 208
- water-collection structures, 205

Huq, Fazlul, 21

Independent States, 15
India
- accession of Jammu and Kashmir, 166–167
- Independence Day, 107–108
- Indian independence, 2–3, 70
- Indian nationalism, 20
- as member of British Commonwealth, 51

Indian Independence Act, 70
Indian Muslims, 14, 19–20, 26, 32
Indian Statutory Reforms Committee, 1930, 233
Instrument of Accession, 167
Iqbal, 16, 25
Islamic educational curriculum, 22

Jalalabad, xxi
Jallianwala Bagh tragedy, 159
Jambhaji, 240–241
Jana Sangh, 238
Janata Party, 238–239
Jat Mahasabha, 233
Jats, xxviii, 231, 233–234, 236–239
Jenkins, Evan Meredith, 55
Jhang, xxiii, 9–12, 35, 58, 69, 82, 138–139, 152, 174, 199, 214, 244–245, 256
- agriculture and irrigation in, xxvii–xxviii
- annual fair, 138–139
- geographical attributes, xxv–xxvi
- role of Khatris in development and prosperity, 100
- rural landscape, 8
- sailab lands, xxvii
- Sial tribes of, xxiv–xxv
- tehsils, xxv

Jhangis, 60, 254, xxi
Jhangi women, 1–2
Jhelum river, xxii, xxiv–xxv, xxvii
Jinnah, Muhammad Ali, 7, 14–15, 18, 23–24, 32, 46, 49–54, 57, 64–65, 105, 107, 129

kafilas, 114–118, 121–124, 141, 148
- in abandoned village, 140
- attacks against, 119
- Batra family, 40–41, 77–91, 101–105, 108, 112–115, 117–119, 121, 124–127, 138–140, 144–145, 149

brutal killings during, 119–120
crossing of Wagah border, 155
dealing with starvation, 121
escorts to, 131, 147
food arrangement, 121, 137, 140–142
funeral rituals, 127, 154
Hindu–Muslim unity and protection, 101–104, 108, 111–114, 145–147
luggage, 117–118
main camps, 132
mode of transport, 114, 116–117
monsoon problems, 138
safety during, 101–105, 112, 115–116, 125–126, 143
Kalanor, 10–11, 35, 60, 62, 109, 117, 124, 155, 162, 165, 174–176, 183–184, 191, 196, 200, 255
Kashmir, 16, 166–167
Khalsa, 95
emblems of, 95
Khan, Genghis, xxiii
Khan, Ghazi, xxiv
Khan, Ibrahim, 191–192, 200, 214
Khan, Majid, 112–113
army of staff, 104
house of, 103–104
influence in army and police, 104
Khan, Sikandar Hayat, 25, 31
Khatri Arora families, 8
Khatris, xxviii, 1, 7, 19, 24, 36–37, 92, 136, 231, 236, 238
administrative and military roles, 98
as agents and bankers to Delhi Sultanate nobility, 95
Bedi sub-caste of, 92
as chief moneylenders and capitalists of Punjab province, 96
community in Multan, 95
as a contraction of Kshatriya, 92–93
food preferences, 200
landholding, 98–99
lineage, 92
from Multan, 173
as nambardar or lambardar, 99
notable administrators in Sultanate and Mughal period, 97
participation in freedom struggle, 99
poets, writers, and historians, 99
public service, 100
as qanungos, 99
religious thinkers, 99
role in expansion of India's soft power, 97
seth and sarrafs, 96
Sodhi clan of, 94
sub-castes of, 93–94
Khattar, Manohar Lal, xviii, 242, 260
Khilafat movement, 23
Kripalani, J.B., 51–52
Krishak Praja Party, 21
Kshatriyas, 92
Kurri, 174–175, 189, 192, 214, 255
as Aryanagar, 226, 240

Bhakra-Nangal Project, 224–225
carpenters and potters, 201–202
dress sense of villagers, 201
economic prosperity, 226
Ibrahim Khan's house, 192–196

Kurukshetra, 185

Kurukshetra refugee camp, 162–165

Lahore, 3–4, 6
curfew, 5

Lahore Resolution, 16, 18, 20–23, 25, 27–28, 37

Lal, Bansi, 239

Lal, Bhajan, 221, 239–242

Lal, Chaudhary Devi, 235, 239–242

Lal, Nand, 10, 40–41, 84, 89, 102, 126, 138, 160, 172–174, 176, 196, 199, 203, 214, 219

Lal, Ram, 3, 5–7, 9, 12, 32, 34, 40–41, 66–67, 69, 78–81, 83–84, 87, 101, 113, 116, 139, 152, 154

Lok Dal, 239–40, 2442

Maghiana tehsil, xxv

Mahabharata, 27

Mahajan, Justice Mehar Chand, 57

Maken, Bhai Khan, xxiii

Mal, Dewan Sawan, 97

Mal, Suraj, 236

Mamdot, Nawab Iftikhar Hussain, 31

Mandi Hydroelectric Scheme, 76

Meham, 180, 184

Menon, V.P., 51, 167

Military Evacuation Organization (MEO), 130–132, 135, 147, 154, 159

Motilal Nehru Committee, 17

Mountbatten, Lord Louis, 31–32, 46, 57, 70–71, 76, 105–106
address to Indian and Pakistan Assembly, 106–107
Partition plan, 50, 52, 54

Mudie, Sir Robert Francis, 110–111

Mukhtyar, 9–10, 37–38, 66–69, 78–79, 82, 84, 89, 101, 110, 113–114, 124, 144–145, 153–154

Multani merchants, 96–97

Multanis, 96, 172

Multan massacre, 6

Musalmans/Muslims, 1, 3–4, 6–10, 12, 14–29, 31–32, 34, 36–37, 47, 49–51, 53–54, 56–58, 63, 65, 76, 79, 81–82, 85, 104, 106, 108, 112, 118, 121, 123–124, 128–133, 147, 157–158, 166, 169–173, 176, 191–192, 233, 239, 255–256
inter-community relations amongst, 23
in matter of marriage, 27–28
Muslim rights, 22
Muslims law, 28
social life of, 27

Muslim landlords, 24

Muslim League, 3–4, 16, 22–23, 25, 29–31, 37, 52, 54, 64, 71, 106, 129, 233
protection of minorities, 55

Nagori Gate, 180, 188

nambardar or lambardar, 63
Nanak, Guru, 9, 93
Nayyar Khatris, 98–99
Nehru, Jawaharlal, 7, 46, 48–49, 53, 57, 70, 105–107, 130
Nirmala, 3, 87
North-West Frontier Province (NWFP), 16–17, 23–24, 28, 36–37, 50, 55, 80, 93, 157, 182

Pakistan, 20, 26, 54, 65, 105, 107, 112, 221
  flag of, 129
  invasion of Kashmir, 167
  as member of British Commonwealth, 51
  Rahmat Ali's scheme, 17
Pakistan Day, 23
Pakistan Declaration, 17
Pakistan idea, 22
Panj Pyare, 95
Parmanand, Bhai, 21
Partition Committee, 53
Partition Council, 53–54, 56, 58
Partition of India, 65, 257
  Congress plan, 71
  exchange of population, 54, 128–130, 157, 167
  exodus of Hindus and Sikhs, 78–91, 128–130
  Hindu–Muslim unity and protection, 101–104, 108, 111–114
  Iqbal's proposal, 17
  Mountbatten plan, 50, 52, 54
  problems following, 66–67
  of Punjab, 5, 7, 14, 232, 235
  Rahmat Ali's scheme, 17
Passi, Prof. S.P., 222
Passi, Veena, 222
Passi family, 222
Patel, Sardar Vallabhbhai, 56, 166–167
Patiala and East Punjab States Union (PEPSU), 172, 232
Punjab Boundary Force, 58, 130
Punjab Evacuee Ordinance IV of 1947, 169
Punjabi Khatris, 1, 19, 36, 93, 173, 200, 231, 236, 238, 241–243, 253, 255. *see also* Khatris
Punjabi personality, 254
Punjabis, nature of, 150, 159
Punjab Legislative Assembly, 56
Punjab Reorganisation Act, 235
Punjab Security of Land Tenures Act, 1953, 221
Purana Quila, Delhi, 187

Qadir, Abdul, 78–80, 82–84, 86, 102–103, 109, 111, 114, 124, 145, 212–213
Qasim, Muhammad Bin, xxii
Quran, 27
Qureshis, xxviii, 10, 37, 51

Radcliffe, Sir Cyril, 57, 71, 74–76, 81, 105, 131, 155
Rahman, Pir Abdul, xxviii
Ram, Daya, 94, 175–177, 183, 186, 208–209, 218
Ram, Dhania, 88–89, 125, 160, 185, 190, 195, 197, 199, 244
Ram, Sir Chhotu, 20, 24, 233–234

Ram Rajya, idea of, 18–19
Rani, Raj, 10–12, 35, 39–40, 44, 59, 62–63, 82, 84–85, 101, 103–104, 112, 123, 126, 138, 140, 176
Rao, Apa Khande, 181–182

Rashtriya Swayamsevak Sangh (RSS), 3
Ravi river, xxii, xxvii
Rawalpindi massacre, 5, 7, 10
rehabilitation of victimised and displaced persons, 168
  allotment of land, 171–176
  assistance to allottees, 173
  compensation, 170
  makeshift shelters and sanitation issues, 176–177
  problem of rural, 170–171
  problems with rehabilitation process, 173–174
  resettlement, 169–170
Resettlement of the Displaced Persons (Land Acquisition) Ordinance, 1948, 169
Rodu Sultan, 2–4, 7–9, 11–12, 32, 35, 37–38, 41, 45–46, 51, 58, 61–62, 68–69, 79–80, 84, 89, 102–105, 109, 113, 121, 152, 160, 166, 195–197, 202, 209, 212–213, 215, 223, 244–245
  Rodo Sultan shrine, 9
Rors, 237, 239

Sagal of Buddhism, xxi
Sandal Bar, xxvi
Sanglawala Tibba, xxi
Santosh, 3
Sarai Siddhu tehsil, xxv
Saran, Ram, 34, 89, 112, 119, 139, 143, 145, 154, 175–178, 183, 186, 205–208, 217, 220, 243, 248–249, 256
Secondary Education Bill, 1940, 22
Second World War, 20–21, 26
secular nationalism, 25
self-determination, 3
Shah, Nadir, xxiii, 181
Shakeela, 103, 108, 112–113, 121, 124
Shakuntala, 160, 183, 195, 214
Sharma, Bhagwat Dayal, 236–239
Sharnarthi, xvi, xviii, 260
Shiromani Akali Dal, 7, 20, 57, 232
Shorkot, xxii, xxv, xxviii, 39, 58
Shyam, Radhe, 68, 152–154
Sials (Panwar Rajputs), 45, xxiii, xxv
Sial tribes, xxiv
Sikh gurudwaras, 57
Sikhs, xxiv, 4, 6–8, 12–13, 16, 20, 24, 29, 31–32, 36, 48, 51, 53–58, 66, 76, 79, 81, 93, 110–112, 114, 116, 120, 123, 128, 130, 149, 158–159, 166, 169, 233, 235, 239
  July 8 strike, 57
Sindh, 16, 37
Singh, Baldev, 46, 49, 51–54, 57
Singh, Guru Gobind, 93–95
Singh, Kartar, 9–10, 20, 66, 68
Singh, Lehri, 236
Singh, Maharaja Hari, 167
Singh, Master Tara, 4, 20, 31, 54, 57, 232
Singh, Padam, 143–147

Singh, Ranjit, xxv
Singh, Rao Birender, 238–240
Singh, Rao Virendra, 239
Singh, Toba Tek, 82, 84, 86, 101, 105
Singh, V.P., 240
Sobhani, Maulana Azad, 18
  speech, 18–19
Sodhi clan of Khatris, 94
Sohag, xxiii
States Reorganisation Commission, 234
Sudarshan (Bebe), 8, 86, 102, 138
Sumitra, 34, 175, 177, 183, 198, 208–209, 218, 249
Sutlej river, 57, 74–75, 186

Talaqi Gate, 180, 188
Thal, xxvi
Thomas, George (Jahazi Sahib), 181–182
Tihun Khatri, 94
Tiwana, Khizar Hayat, 4, 29
township development, 169–170
Traitors' Day, 29
Trans-Chenab, xxvii
Tughlaq, Firoz Shah, 179–180
two Muslim states, 16
two-nation theory, 15–16, 18, 32

Unionist Party, 24, 28–29, 36

violence after partition, 111–114, 118–119
  in Amritsar, 111
  attack on refugees, 111
  brutal killings, 119–120
  deaths, 86
  destruction of religious institutions, 110–111
  Hindus–Muslim conflict, 111–112
  Lahore's Anarkali bazar incident, 110
  lootings, 108
  mass murders and arson, 108, 110–111, 124–125, 158
  in Old Delhi and Paharganj, 166
  polluting village ponds, 121
  riots in Delhi, 166
  in West Punjab, 108
Vira, Dharma, 236
Vishal Haryana Party, 238

Wadhawan Khatris, 98
Wagah border, 155
West Pakistan, 172, 176
West Punjab, 32, 50, 54, 57–58, 63, 65, 70–72, 74–75, 85, 108, 111, 128, 130–133, 157–159, 162, 166, 169–171, 174, 257
World War II, 159

Zakria, Makhdun Baha-ud-din, xxviii

Acknowledgements

The literature on India's Partition and the greatest migration that accompanied it is a timeless caravan – a haunting procession of voices from victims, witnesses, and historians. To this eternal chorus, I humbly add the voices of my grandparents and father – voices that remained muted and buried under layers of unbearable memory. To pull them from the shadows of the past and verbalise them were an act of both love and trauma. I could scarcely fathom the horrors they endured, the wounds they carried. The weight of their heartrending stories often left me emotionally torn and my eyes blurred with tears.

It takes courage to retell the tales of those – the men, women, and children who survived Partition's horrors, its hatred, its rivers of blood. My grandparents and father, like millions other, lived through the unspeakable catastrophic times. It took me years to gather the resolve to write this book. Writing their memoir also came with responsibility. After all, I was taking up the task of giving words to feelings I had not experienced myself, only heard, read and seen on screen in many documentaries and feature films. It was certainly tough to step into minds of so many characters and interpret their feelings. I hope this book does justice to the extraordinary lives of my grandparents and parents, and millions uprooted during Partition. How I wish they could hold it in their hands. How fiercely I miss them!

This book is the culmination of years of research, of nights spent wrestling with history and memory. I stand indebted to the countless writers, scholars, poets, and thinkers whose works illuminated my path, shaping my understanding of Partition even as I wove it with my family's own journey. Though I have acknowledged them in the bibliography, I seek forgiveness for any omissions – for every name left unsaid, every voice uncredited.

Kafila: A Jhangi Family's Partition Memoir has been more than a book; it has been a pilgrimage. It is born from the love and resilience of my family – stories whispered by grandparents, recounted by parents, uncles and aunts. Some memories were preserved like fragile heirlooms; others slipped through the cracks of time. My brother and I spent hours piecing together fragments, while cousins – Shashi Didi, Charu Didi, Sunil, Tejinder, and my aunt Daya Bua (daughter of Veera) through her son Rinkal – generously shared what they remembered, filling the silences with their own echoes of the past. This book, in many ways, is theirs too. Creative liberties taken in the book are, however, mine. My second cousins, Jyoti Didi (Daya Bua's daughter) in Hisar and Dr Sandeep Miglani (grandson of Chando), made many calls to get me the names of my grandfather Lala-ji's sisters and other interesting facts.

Jyoti Didi connected me with her mother's elder brother Thakur Dass-ji, the oldest of the surviving children of one of Lala-ji's sisters. I had many conversations with the ninety-three-year-old Thakur Dass-ji. He shared details which filled many information gaps. Every time he spoke, his voice shaking with age and emotional surge, he revealed heart-wrenching details from those darkest years in the history of our nation. He lives in Chindwara. He may not be able to travel for the launch of the book, but I will certainly make a trip to lay a copy of the book at his feet and seek his blessings.

Many photographs in the book were provided by Sushma,

Tejinder's wife. She pulled them out of old albums tucked away out of reach for years.

To Om Books International – thank you for believing in *Kafila*, for making it the third book in our journey together (and soon, the fourth!). Shantanu, my relentless editor, you have become the silent architect of my words. This is our fourth book together, and already, the fifth beckons, and two others in discussion. Your keen eye transforms my raw thoughts into something luminous. For that, I am forever grateful. I was truly humbled when after editing the manuscript you texted, 'This is your best book thus far.' It means a lot. To me each book is dear and one better than the other though some become bestsellers.

To my friend Sakshi Chanana, my deepest gratitude for reading the early draft and helping with the copyediting.

Five books in two years, each one carved from stolen hours, from moments I should have spent with my family – my wife Asha, boy Dev, and girl Siya – you are my anchors. Your love is the reason I can write at all. Every book I craft belongs as much to you as it does to me.

And to you, dear reader – thank you for walking this path with me. A book is nothing but ink and paper until it is held, until its words breathe in your hands. I am honoured that you have chosen *Kafila* to be part of your story. May it stir something in you – a recognition, a question, or simply the quiet solace of shared humanity.

Finally, though this book is the work of many, its flaws – if any – are mine alone.